St Leonard's Forest, West Sussex

A Landscape History

Worthing Road. Horsham. West Sussex. RH12 1TD

Copyright Notice

Every effort has been made to identify copyright and gain proper permission. If any have been missed, please accept my apologies and note I would be happy to rectify.

Foreword

Sussex is blessed with a wealth of different environments for the traveller to discover. Some, like the South Downs and the coast, are well known and therefore more intensively visited. But there are others, and in this book Dr Maggie Weir-Wilson invites us to join her in the less well known St Leonard's Forest. St Leonard's is but one of several Sussex 'forests', such as Worth Forest or Ashdown Forest. Exactly why the 'forest' terminology was applied to them all remains something of a mystery. As Dr Weir-Wilson explains, certainly they were not all wooded, and neither were they technically 'forests' in the sense of a medieval hunting forest, reserved for the use of the sovereign or other elites. Woodland certainly, and hunting also, but not necessarily as a royal pastime. However, the names have stuck and continue to lend a certain enchantment to the places as we explore them.

We tend to consider environments such as this as being relatively unchanging, but this is certainly far from the case with St Leonard's. And so we are fortunate to have, in what follows, a supremely well qualified guide to take us on an historical journey through St Leonard's Forest. Having undertaken undergraduate and postgraduate studies in landscape history at Sussex University, initially as 'relaxation' from her all-consuming post in the probation service, Maggie's scholarly work has now paid off in a handsome way, as readers of this book will quickly recognise. Covering a long time scale we are taken through the Forest's landscape development in a thematic treatment, each illuminated by her own knowledge and her own artistic flair.

This is a book to inform, to enjoy, to guide. And as this foreword is being written during the misery of 'lockdown' during the Covid-19 pandemic, we surely cannot wait to explore and more thoroughly appreciate such wonderful surroundings as are set out here.

Brian Short
Emeritus Professor of Historical Geography
University of Sussex

Acknowledgements

Firstly, I would like to give my sincere thanks to Emeritus Professor Brian Short of University of Sussex who has encouraged my efforts in writing this book. His support has extended from being my supervisor and guiding me towards my DPhil thesis in 2014, through to writing the foreword for this book, thank you Brian.

Heartfelt thanks go to my friends Tom and Ros Aldridge for their unfailing encouragement. Most particularly to Tom who read through the drafts, advised and commented. I am most grateful for this time-consuming effort which has undoubtedly improved my book.

I would also like to thank Jeremy Knight, Museum and Heritage Officer of Horsham Museum, who spent time reading through the draft and offered detailed feedback.

Also, I would like to acknowledge the excellent guidance and encouragement I received from Botanic Artist and tutor, Leigh Ann Gale, whose workshops I have really enjoyed.

I also appreciate all the encouragement and support from my good friend Liz Crathorne and her introduction to Steve Morris who assisted in map definition. I would also like to thank all my friends in Horsham. Friends from the Olive Leaves Book Club, Quaker friends, fellow authors from Horsham Writers Circle. Finally, to Author's Pen: Mathew Bridle for designing my cover and my website, for typesetting and laying out my book and correcting the proofs, to Lesley Hart for proof-editing the final version and for detailing its illustrations and glossary, and to both Lesley and Mathew for helping me to publish. Thank you to you all.

Contents

Chapter 6: Society and Community

Chapter 7: A Final Word

Appendix – St Leonard's Forest Timeline

Bibliography

List of Illustrations

Glossary

Index

The Ancient Sentinel

I stood by the massive bulk of the oak,
saw barbed wire threatening its great girth.
This sentry pollard, time's silent watcher,
bark grooved, worn, trunk hollow and squirreled,
patient survivor of eight hundred years.
Generations have ridden past, storms come
and gone, still it grows, grounded, guardian.
The Sun Oak stands, ancient forest sentinel.

In early days the forest was larger
than today, the Sun Oak near its centre.
Men came to dam the ghylls and dig the mines.
First, they built the bloomeries, then the blast
furnaces pouring out the molten iron,
casting cannon, guns and pig iron mouldings.
The forest was alive with flame and smoke
as if St Leonard's dragon had awoke.

The Sun Oak stands on old Hammerpond Road
marking the drive up to St Leonard's House.
Along its road the smuggling gangs had ridden
to reach a safe house, food and fresh horses,
stashing brandy under trees and hedges.
Ghosts of headless horsemen haunted the footpaths,
while the mythic dragon, all scales and slime
slithered here, venomous and serpentine.

The forest is quiet now, the Sun Oak
stands alone without companion oaks,
felled for house beams and ships timbers.
Dog owners amble the forest footpaths, while
joggers and mountain bikers race through,
catching sight of skittish Fallow deer or Roe,
and Lily of the Valley, white and pink emerging.
The Sun Oak stands, the ancient forest sentinel.

The Sun Oak on Hammerpond Road.

Chapter 1

Introduction

St Leonard's Forest is a strange place – a gloomy forest in which it is too easy to lose one's way by taking a wrong path. Its history seems to hang heavily amongst the heathland and trees and yet locally little is really known about it apart from myth and legend. One is reminded of Kipling's poem 'A Way through the Woods' which conjures up a ghostly atmosphere which chimes well with St Leonard's Forest:

> Yet, if you enter the woods
> Of a summer evening late …
> You will hear the beat of a horse's feet,
> And the swish of a skirt in the dew
> Steadily cantering through
> The misty solitudes,
> As though they perfectly knew
> The old lost road through the woods …
> But there is no road through the woods.

I came to live near this Forest on the edge of Horsham 20 years ago and was intrigued to know more about it, and so began my journey of discovery amongst internet searches, dusty records and maps.

Little has been written about St Leonard's Forest and so I am hopeful that this book will go some way towards filling that gap in local historical knowledge. It is important for the community that their unique forest heritage is not lost or undervalued. Also, as interest and necessity grow in creating resilient communities with sustainable futures, the knowledge of how things were done in the past through using the local environment and its resources is valuable knowledge that should not be lost for lack of interest or research. This can also have an impact on planning and conservation, which is particularly important in the context of those local forests which are under continuing threat of being mismanaged or sold. For example, with regard to St Leonard's Forest, new knowledge of the archaeological remains of pillow mounds which are associated with rabbit husbandry should impact on the management by Forestry England (formerly the Forestry Commission) in their areas.

Where is St Leonard's Forest

Today St Leonard's Forest (hereafter referred to as either St Leonard's Forest or the Forest) covers an area of about 12 square miles on the eastern edge of Horsham town, and south west of Crawley, West Sussex, see illustration 1: right. It is approximately 20 miles north of Brighton on the south coast and 40 miles south of London. There are two main villages in the Forest, Colgate in the north on Forest Road (B2195) and Lower Beeding to the south of Plummers Plain on Sandygate Lane (B2110). Today much of the Forest is in varied private ownership such as private estates, schools, farms, gardens and golf clubs and is closed to general public access. However, a portion is retained by three public bodies: West Sussex County Council, Horsham District Council and Forestry England (formerly the Forestry Commission).

1. Map showing approximate position of St Leonard's Forest in UK and Sussex. By kind permission of Dr Steve Morris.

West Sussex County Council in the north of the Forest owns 69 ha (170 acres)[1] of Buchan Country Park, and to the south Horsham District Council owns areas called Leechpool, Owlbeech, Severals Bottom and Forest Walk, which add up to about 45 ha (110 acres), all of which are managed by their Countryside Services Unit. The middle section of the Forest, which includes Sheepwash Gill, Mick's Cross and the Lily Beds, a total area amounting to 289 ha (712 acres), is owned by Forestry England (formerly the Forestry Commission) and is under the management of Natural England. All these areas are still open to the public, with access through car parks to footpaths and rights of way. Two long distance walking trails cut through the forest: The High Weald Landscape Trail runs east beginning at Horsham railway station for 94 miles to Rye, and the Sussex Ouse Valley Way begins just south of Lower Beeding and runs 42 miles to Seaford Bay on the coast.

---

1. Hectares will be used when modern measurements are given, otherwise with reference to archives before a metric system of measurement was adopted in 1971, acres will be adhered to. Conversion is 1 acre = 0.414 ha.

Forest Geology, Topography and Archaeology

To understand any historical changes in the landscape it is important to know the underlying geology of the area on which these changes occur. This is because geology has a crucial impact on the agriculture, industry and activities that are economically and socially viable in a forest area. Horsham lies on the western edge of the High Weald and so the Forest falls completely within this region. The natural regions describe the underlying geology and in the High Weald these are the Hastings Beds, see illustration 2: below. The Hastings Beds consist of three main subdivisions, Ashdown Beds, Wadhurst Clay and Tunbridge Wells Sand. The Forest lies on the Upper Tunbridge Wells sand, an area of high ground running from Felbridge in Surrey, south east of Guildford, to Horsham in a five-kilometre-wide band with a gentle north-north westerly dip. Outcrops of this sandstone are estimated to be of a thickness of up to 75 metres in St Leonard's Forest.

Wooldridge and Goldring in their book *The Weald* describe the High Weald as a country of ridges rather than valleys. They suggest that roads and settlements were confined to the forest ridges due to steep ghylls cutting though the sandstone and forming wet wooded valley floors which were difficult to navigate or settle. In St Leonard's Forest there are also areas of flat ground or plains of sandstone, for example the extensive Shelley Plain to the south east, and smaller areas around Stonelodge Plain, Colgate and Forest Grange. It was these areas that were more suited to agricultural purposes, the higher ridges being heathland and poorer soil.[2]

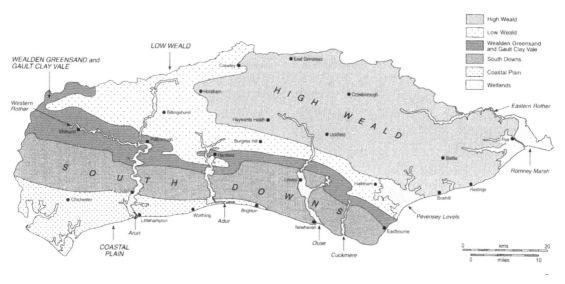

2. Natural Regions of Sussex showing Horsham on the western edge of the High Weald, with kind permission from B. Short and K. Leslie (eds.1999) An Historical Atlas of Sussex, p.7.

2.Wooldridge, S.W. and Goldring, F. (1960) *The Weald*, London: Collins, p. 88-89.

To the north of the Forest the sandstone ridges are dissected by the rivers Arun and Mole, and similar sandstone outcrops can be found at Roffey, Colgate and Shelley Plain, with a contrast between the light sandy soil and a silty mudstone. To the south of the Forest, and west of Mick Mills Race, clay-ironstone can be found amid greater dips and faulting of the underlying rock. The Forest is a watershed not only for the Arun and the Mole to the north, but for the headwaters of the Adur and Ouse to the south. The sands and clays give rise to a very distinctive forest landscape of high flat forest ridges with heathland and sparse woodland, cut through by these headwaters which form deep wooded ravines or 'ghylls' in which mosses and liverworts continue to thrive.

Further features of St Leonard's Forest landscape are the mine pits, mainly to the west and south of Mick Mills Race, where ironstone was dug from clay outcrops. Amateur Reigate researcher and bookbinder, Ernest Straker, did an enormous amount of research in the 1920s and early 1930s into the Wealden Iron Industry. He identified and photographed a large number of mine pits in the area now owned by Forestry England (formerly the Forestry Commission), which showed large craters up to 9 metres across and 2.5 metres deep, where horizontal beds of ore had been dug. Just over 50 years later these mine pit positions were confirmed by Cleere and Crossley in their study entitled *The Iron Industry of the Weald*.[3] Today these pits are difficult to spot amid the conifer plantations. However, in 2011 a Lidar survey, which uses a remote pulsed laser to record surface features, was able to penetrate the woodland canopy with very useful results. In addition to the mine pits, it revealed remains of rabbit warrens in the form of pillow mounds and boundary banks, adding to the important historical landscape features that had not been fully appreciated before this survey was undertaken.[4]

It should be noted that little archaeological work has been conducted on the Forest despite some interesting early finds. In the 19th century, local historian Dorothea Hurst mentioned in her book *Horsham: its History and Antiquities* that workmen draining fields in 1864 at Willis Farm on Plummers Plain found six fragments of bronze celts (axe heads). Thomas Honywood, Horsham property owner, photographic pioneer and amateur archaeologist explored the Forest and reported that five bronze celts, one broken, were found at Hammer Farm in the 1870s. He also reported numerous findings of flint implements and flakes, although he mistakenly thought the mine pits were evidence of occupation.[5] However, a later examination of his collection revealed a very unique working of the flint into microliths. These microliths were made by hollowing out the base of each pointed flint and this represented a very distinct way of working. It demonstrated a particular archaeological culture which has become known as the Horsham

3. Straker, E. (1931, 1969) *Wealden Iron: A Monograph on the Former Ironworks in the Counties of Sussex, Surrey and Kent:* Newton Abbot: David and Charles Ltd., pp. 106-7, 434, and Cleere, H. and Crossley, D. (2nd edn) (1995) *The Iron Industry of the Weald,* Cardiff: Merton Priory Press, pp. 16-17.

4. Butler, C., Blandford, V., Locke, A. (2011) *A Lidar-Enhanced Archaeological Survey of St Leonard's Forest, West Sussex,* Chris Butler Archaeological Services for Forest Enterprise and Weald Forest Ridge Historic Environment Awareness Project (hereafter Lidar 2011). Unpublished, Accessible through: www.highweald.org/look-after/our-projects/weald-forest-ridge.

5. Hurst, D. (1868) *Horsham: its History and Antiquities,* London: William Macintosh, pp. 159-160, and Honywood, T. (1877) Discovery of Flint implements near Horsham, in St Leonard's Forest. *Sussex Archaeological Collections,* XXVII, Lewes: The Sussex Archaeological Society pp. 177-183.

culture, dating from the Mesolithic period about 6,000-5,000 BC. As, geologically, flint does not occur in the Horsham area it is likely to have been brought from the South Downs to have been worked, perhaps in camps, in the Forest.

The 1961 archaeological excavation of Money Mound, a burial mound just to the east of Willis Farm, on Plummers Plain near Lower Beeding, suggested that the movement of people through the central Weald would have been easy along the forest ridges, and that there were numbers of flint sites in the area ranging from the Mesolithic to early Bronze Age, c.5,000-800 BC. In his archaeological report of this excavation, Beckensall noted a number of finds which included flint flakes and arrow heads. He also reported to have found Roman coins and pottery which indicated that the site had been used for some considerable time. A later report published in the 1970s states that further barrows, or burial sites, were identified at Shephersfield and Black Hill, both near Colgate.[6]

3. On the left, early bronze axe head, possibly deliberately broken in ritual, found near Colgate, and on the right flint arrowheads, on display at Horsham Museum and Art Gallery (Horsham District Council).

6. Beckensall, S.G. (1967) *The Excavation of Money Mound, Sussex Archaeological Collections*, 105, pp. 13-30.

Forest Ecology and Environment

The ecology and environment of St Leonard's Forest has undergone many changes in the preceding centuries, but in the 20th and 21st centuries this has been due to the ownership of part of the Forest by Forestry England (formerly the Forestry Commission) with its original policy of planting pines for timber, so today the landscape differs from that of earlier centuries. Currently the Forest lies within the High Weald Area of Outstanding Natural Beauty (AONB) and features three main Sites of Special Scientific Interest (SSSI).

1.   St Leonard's Forest SSSI is made up of three units of broadleaved, mixed and yew lowland woodland covering 70 ha (172 acres) and one unit of standing open water (Hawkins Pond) covering 5 ha (12 acres).

2.   The second SSSI area is St Leonard's Park Ponds, situated in the grounds of St Leonard's Lodge and consisting of two units of standing open water (Golden Folly Pond and Dry Pond) together covering 3 ha (7 acres), illustration 4: below.

3.   The third SSSI area is again ponds, this time to the north of the Forest in Buchan Country Park known as Buchan Hill Ponds, three ponds covering 19 ha (46 acres).

4. Dry Pond, one of St Leonard's Park Ponds.

These SSSIs were all designated in 1954 for a variety of reasons. The main St Leonard's Forest SSSI remains a remnant of more extensive deciduous forest with varied vegetation. In the woodland can be found bracken, bramble, honeysuckle, bluebell, primrose, and common violet, while at the Lily Beds site is a colony of wild lily-of-the-valley, although sadly depleted following the use of Forestry England (formerly the Forestry Commission) heavy machinery. On the upper sandy ridges there is heathland vegetation: ling, cross-leaved heath and ivy-leaved bellflower; however, the heathland is much reduced from its 18th and 19th century extent.

The SSSI woodland in the central part of the Forest is mainly pedunculate oak, beech, and the two common birches, with an understory of holly, hazel, hawthorn, blackthorn and guelder rose. Included in this site are the plantations of Scots pine and Corsican pine, particularly to the east, which has created an unfavourable habitat for native broad-leaved woodland plants and creatures, although with careful management this is improving. Relict flora such as mosses and liverworts from the warm wet 'Atlantic' climate period, c.8,000-4,500 BC, survive in the microclimate of Sheepwash Gill, see illustration 6: below, and indicate continuous woodland since this time. At the time of designation there was a population of the purple emperor butterfly, and the supporting habitat is still regarded as favourable for this species. A diversity of woodland birds including nightjar, redstart, wood warbler and three types of woodpecker were originally identified, and it is assessed by Natural England that restoring the pine plantations to broadleaf woodlands would assist their continued habitat.

6. Sheepwash Gill

5. Ling and bramble in the Forest.

St Leonard's Park Ponds were originally designated by Natural England as an SSSI due to the species-rich nature of the wooded ponds which supported the variable and ruddy darter damselfly, and the downy emerald and brilliant emerald dragonflies. However, when it was reassessed in 2009 the conditions were regarded as unsuitable for supporting a good dragonfly population due to the margins being overshadowed by willow scrub, large rhododendron bushes and two stands of bamboo. One of the ponds is heavily stocked with carp and is used by a fishing club.

Buchan Hill Ponds were designated because these three ponds were 'The best example in West Sussex of Wealden hammer ponds on acid Tunbridge Wells sands', plus they had unusual wet woodland and 17 different species of dragonfly, which were identified as a nationally significant population. This area was last inspected in November 2009 and the habitat found to be unfavourable as a result of invasive plants, but recovering following work to control the rhododendron and other conservation management tasks.[7]

7. Postcard of silver birches in St Leonard's Forest. Early 20th century.

7. Natural England website, accessible through: www.sssi.naturalengland.org.uk

A Forest Story

In this book I am going to explore the landscape changes to the Forest: changes both in perception and reality, from a devalued heath and sparse woodland area, suitable only for rabbits, to one of natural scenic beauty sought after by wealthy merchants and business men escaping the great metropolis of London in the 19th and early 20th centuries. This will be the main focus of the book although I will of necessity touch on the landscape before and after this time frame.

The Forest lies to the east of the market town of Horsham, and until the enclosures of 1812, only the heathland area of the Common lay between it and the town. Worth Forest and Copthorne Common, which are further to the east in the Rape[8] of Lewes, have similarities with both St Leonard's Forest and Horsham Common. There are similarities in geology and topography, but the activities and communications in a market town like Horsham are different, thus there are unique social, economic and environmental influences that structure the particular landscape and character of St Leonard's Forest as opposed to other forests on the Wealden Forest ridge.

It is worth stating at the beginning of this story that in common speech a forest is understood to be woodland, or a plantation of trees. However, the concept of a forest in the legal sense was introduced in the early medieval period by William I who brought the practice over from Normandy. At this time in England the land was held by landowners such as gentry or the Church, not necessarily by the Crown, and often with commoners' rights to graze animals and take timber. The new forest legal system was established to protect the deer of the forest for the sport of the monarch so that he or she could keep, hunt and kill the deer. The King's deer were usually introduced to an area and stayed, without necessarily the need for the hedge and ditch, fence and pale of a park, but with pollarding and grazing forming a woodland pasture landscape. However, with this new system there could be conflicts with the existing residents of an area because of their customary rights to graze animals and collect wood. Resentment was caused where the welfare of the deer and boar appeared to override that of the local population.

Myths have grown up telling of the cruelty and injustice, the depopulation and enclosure imposed on the Anglo-Saxon people by the oppressive Norman monarchy. It has been suggested that in their writings, medieval clerics such as the 11th century monk Oderic and the Archdeacon of Oxford, Walter Map, perpetuated the myth that whole villages and parishes were swept away to create the New Forest as a private hunting reserve for William I. The legend of Robin Hood is linked to this myth of sylvan liberties where all was well and just in the English greenwood before Norman tyranny.[9]

The nature of royal forests differed in that they could be situated in many types of landscape, wooded, moorland or heathland, depending on the underlying geology and

---

8. Rape is the name for a Sussex administrative area, probably Saxon although could be earlier, similar to the Kentish Lathe, and in Sussex they ran from the coastal strip up into the Weald.

9. Schama, S. (1995, 2004) *Landscape and Memory,* Hammersmith: HarperCollins Publishers, p 140.

topography, but most were situated near royal estates. Royal forests were governed by a forest law, the extent of which could stretch beyond the physical forest. The purpose of forest law was to establish the right to keep deer for the Monarch, appoint forest officials, hold courts in order to bring to trial any offenders against the forest law, and fine them. Thus, it often cut across common practices of having the right to use forest resources for gathering wood and grazing. Although this did vary according to the forest, the Monarch owned the deer in his forest but not necessarily the land so it could be owned by an individual and there could be commoners' rights. If the Monarch granted a forest to a subject then it became a chase, and the forest law did not apply. Parks were set up for specific purposes within forests and chases and hence were bounded by a pale, or fence. St Leonard's Forest was not a royal forest but a chase, held after 1066 by the Lords of Bramber, the de Braose family. Unfortunately, the existence of an outer pale around St Leonard's Forest cannot be identified through current archival or archaeological evidence.[10]

All five forests of the Sussex Wealden Forest Ridge have their own unique histories. Worth Forest, which included Tilgate Forest, was contiguous with St Leonard's Forest and although the geology was similar, aspects of the social and economic development were different, such as the early establishment of Worth Priory in the Forest, near the Surrey border and village of Crawley. Ashdown Forest is geologically and topographically different in that it is on sand and silt and is the highest part of the weald, with higher rainfall and poorer drainage than the other ridge forests. Unlike St Leonard's Forest it was a royal hunting forest and then a free chase, with around its fringes tenants of the Manors of Duddleswell and Maresfield with commoners' rights, rights which have been well defended over the centuries. It is therefore important to research specific forests and woods in order to draw out their unique historical aspects.

10. Rackham, O. (2006) *Woodlands,* London: Harper Collins, pp. 141-3, and James, N.D.G. (1981) *A History of English Forestry,* Oxford: Basil Blackwell, pp. 1-17.

Beech leaves with nut cupule, *Fagus sylvatica* by Dr Maggie Weir-Wilson.

Chapter 2

Landscape of the Forest

Early Shape of the Forest

The six administrative and defensive rapes of Sussex each included a forest, a port, and a castle. The rapes were named after the castle, for example Bramber Castle was in Bramber Rape. St Leonard's Forest was in the north of Bramber Rape, to the east of Horsham town and extended south to the village of Cowfold. It has been suggested that the Sussex forests were remnants of the great Andredeswald, an area of ancient woodland from which the forests of Waterdown, Ashdown, St Leonard's and Worth were more than likely to have been contiguous or semi-contiguous woodland. James's 1981 outline map of medieval forests and chases in southern England identifies a swathe of five forests, see illustration 8: below. The most westerly of the five is St Leonard's Forest, with Worth Forest and Tilgate to the east of it, then the Ashdown Forest, all following the forest ridge.[1]

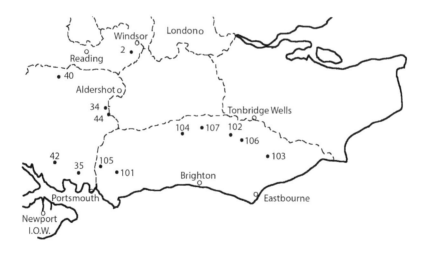

8. The Sussex forest ridge showing positions of individual forests, section from Map 1. Key indicates 104 St Leonard's Forest, 107 Worth Forest, 102 Ashdown Forest, 106 Waterdown Forest, 103 Dallington Forest.

---

1. James, N.D.G. (1981) *A History of English Forestry*, Oxford: Basil Blackwell. p. 79.

A more recent map of forests produced by the High Weald AONB Unit in their study area of the forest ridge gives an indication of forest pales in around 1610, and shows a large St Leonard's Forest stretching from Crawley to some way south of Horsham. This would have included in it the parks of Knepp and Sedgwick, Chesworth, Shelley and Beaubush, all disparked around this date. Tilgate Forest is shown as a much smaller area but it would have been an integral part of the original Worth Forest which James suggests stretched from the Surrey borders to Cuckfield, although – like St Leonard's Forest - there are no records of the boundary.

Although the Domesday survey of 1086 was a most comprehensive document of land use, the boundaries of forests were not always clearly defined, and not all forests and woodlands were mentioned. For example, there is no mention in Domesday of St Leonard's Forest or the park of that name which William de Braiose formed in Bramber Rape.[2] The earliest mention of St Leonard's Forest, as a named forest, therefore appears to be in 1207 in the accounts of the Bishopric of Winchester when timber from St Leonard's Forest was taken to Dorking, Kingston and Southwark. [3]

It is also suggested that the earliest mention of the Forest was later in a report to the King in Counsel, the Placita Coronae et de Assisis 7 Edward 1 (r.1272-1307) when Stephen de Dee and Walter de Buckley complained that William de Braose[4] took from them 200 acres in St Leonard's Forest belonging to their freehold in Slaugham. William denied their claim and they lost. [5] The Forest may, of course, be far older as a managed forest than these fleeting mentions, perhaps Anglo Saxon or Roman, given the network of interests in the Forest across the rape of Bramber.

In the last decade or so Jack Langton and Graham Jones of Oxford University have been using available archive material to map British forests, and thus the map of St Leonard's Forest that I have taken from their data, see illustration 9: page 25, is probably the most definitive to date. It is interesting that in defining the likely outer boundary, the position of the annual November fair, when still in the Forest, and chapel at the south west edge of the core forest, becomes central. The core referred to is the area coloured dark green on illustration 9: page 25. Jones suggests that the fair probably predated the chapel and the arrival of the St Leonard cult circa 1100. He wrote that 'Given the proximity of the Sussex-Surrey border, the chapel, fair and park may have lain close to an important early territorial, perhaps tribal, boundary.' There is of course no evidence for this, but he compared this arrangement to Wychwood Forest in Oxfordshire where buildings and ditches pointed to substantial Roman occupation and a possible shrine, and noted other links of forests and fairs with possible religious sites.[6]

2. Darby, H.C. & Campbell, E.M.J., (eds) (1962) *The Domesday Geography of South-East England*, Cambridge University Press. p. 473.

3. Legge, W.H. (1907,1973) Page, W. (Ed) *The Victoria History of the Counties of England: A History of Sussex, II,* London: The Institute of Historical Research by University of London.

4. The spelling of Braose varies, earlier versions having an added i as in Braiose. Brandon (1998, 1999) stated that the family took their name from the town of Briouze in Calvados, Normandy.

5. Cartwright, E. (1830) *The Parochial Topography in the Western Division of the County of Sussex,* Vol. II, London: J.B. Nichols & Son, p. 364.

6. Jones. G. (Langton, J. and Jones. G. eds) (2010) A 'Common of Hunting,' *Forests and Chases of Medieval England and Wales c 1000 to 1500*, University of Oxford, St. John's College Research Centre, p. 61.

With regard to size and boundary, Jack in her 1997 article for Sussex Archaeological Collections wrote that in the 16th century the Forest crossed two parishes, Beeding and Nuthurst, and was thought to be of 25-30 miles in circumference with a paling fence to keep deer in, and was divided into five walks.[7] However, Legge in *The Victoria History of the Counties of England: A History of Sussex, Vol II* (usually abbreviated to VCH) wrote that in 1553 the Forest lay in Crawley, Cowfold, Horsham and Beeding parishes, while Christopher Saxton's map of 1579 shows a large St Leonard's Forest seeming to impinge on four parishes, paled and pear-shaped stretching from Ifield in the north to Cowfold in the south, Nuthurst and Horsham to the west outside the Forest, and Slaugham on the east, outside the Forest. Due to the lack of any definitive boundaries or further evidence it is impossible to know the relative extent and character of woodland and heathland in the Forest at this time, or indeed in the 18th and 19th centuries. One is left with inference from maps and other surviving documentation such as journals and recorded oral reports.

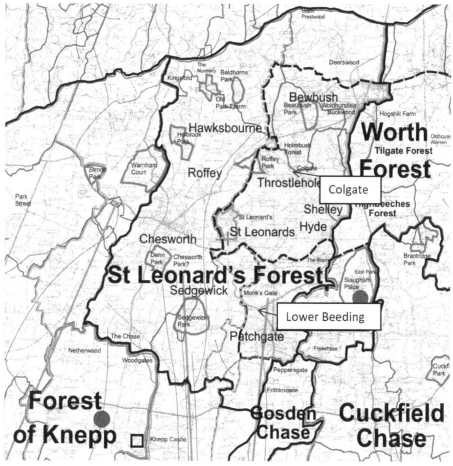

9. Map created from information given by Dr John Langton and Dr Graham Jones of Oxford University www.sjc.ox.ac.uk to indicate boundary of likely greatest historic extent of the Forest in lighter green and the core of the Forest covered in this book in dark green, with assistance from Dr Steve Morris.

---

7. Jack, S.M. (1997) Ecological destruction in the 16th century, the case of St Leonard's Forest. *Sussex Archaeological Collections* 135 pp. 241-7 (hereafter Jack, 1997).

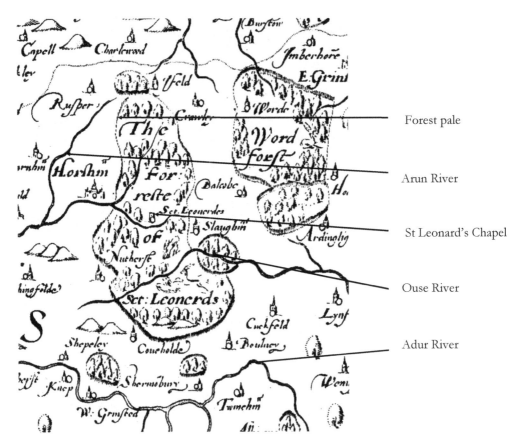

Forest pale

Arun River

St Leonard's Chapel

Ouse River

Adur River

10. Detail showing paled area of St Leonard's Forest from Christopher Saxton's map of 1575. Original scale 2.5" to 10 miles. (Margary, 1970, plate 3a) By kind permission of Harry Margary, editor, at www.harrymargary.com

In the centre of the forest on Saxton's map is a building or village marked as St. Leonard's. This could be the chapel to St. Leonard but the annotation of a circle and tower is unclear. It is likely that the forest took its name from this chapel dedicated to a French hermit, St. Leonard, a saint favoured by the Benedictine monks who had early control both of Sele Priory, in the modern-day Parish of Upper Beeding, and St. Leonard's Forest through William de Braiose. On John Norden's later map of 1595 he shows this chapel feature as a circle with a flag to the left, which in the key denotes a castle; however, circles with a flag to the right denote chapels, and since both Bramber and Arundel, known castles, are shown on the map to have a flag to the right, it appears that the key is wrong and a flag to the left does in fact denote a chapel: St. Leonard's chapel.

There is documentary evidence of a chapel in the forest, as one of the named witnesses to the confirmation of the Priory of Sele by Reginald de Braiose is a man named Robert, identified as the chaplain of St. Leonard, which indicates that there was in the early medieval period a chapel in the forest. It is recorded that it was founded in 1208 as a free chapel, or chantry, and the chaplaincy remained in the gift of the Lords of Bramber until the

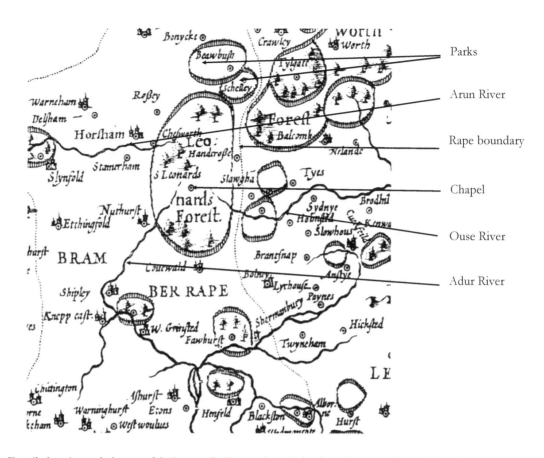

Parks

Arun River

Rape boundary

Chapel

Ouse River

Adur River

11. Detail showing paled area of St Leonard's Forest from John Speed's map of 1610, based on that of John Norden of 1595. Original scale 1" to 4 miles. (Margary, 1970, plate 4a). By kind permission of Harry Margary, editor, at www.harrymargary.com

chapel was dissolved by the Duke of Norfolk in, or just before, 1547 following the Chantries Acts of 1545 and 1547 which allowed patrons to reclaim property and endowments. [8]

John Speed's map of 1610, see illustration 11: above, based on John Norden's work clearly shows a long oval of St Leonard's Forest, surrounded by a pale with the Chesworth Estate in the north just outside this pale, and the Chapel of St Leonard in the middle of the Forest denoted this time just by a circle and dot. Separate parks of Bewbush and Shelley are shown reaching almost into Ifield, and in the south the extent of the Forest stretching just short of Cowfold village. To the east in Lewes Rape, the dotted line showing the division of the Rapes, and almost abutting St Leonard's Forest, are Tilgate and Worth forests. Three rivers are also shown on the map to have a source in the Forest and flow east, west and south; these are respectively the Ouse, Arun and Adur, demonstrating that the Forest was, and still is, an important watershed for the rivers of Sussex.

---

8. VCH Vol. VI.3, p. 26, and Thirsk, J. (1984) *The Rural Economy of England: collected essays*. London: The Hambledon Press, p.20.

Numerous parks either bordered on, or were situated within, St Leonard's Forest in the 13th century. For example, Knepp and Sedgwick to the south of the Forest, Chesworth, Shelley and Beaubush to the north. Chesworth was the smallest at around 233 acres, Shelley contained 600 acres and was thought to be part of a wooded district called Shepherds Field Forest, and Beaubush was the largest enclosure with 757 acres. Both Shelley and Beaubush were in the possession of Sir John de Ifield in the 13th century, and Burchall suggests that a church and rectory was established on Shelley plain at this time. However, following imparking and population loss in the 15th century, they appear to have been absorbed into Crawley parish in the 16th century. Local historian Burchall records that both Cartwright and Lower wrote of Chapel Fields in the location of Shelley Park and a possible Chantry chapel to Our Lady of Shelley.[9]

A record made in the reign of Edward II (1307-1327) estimated that Knepp Park amounted to 1,000 acres while St Leonard's Forest itself was thought to cover 7,000 acres. [10] By the late 15th century there were divisions within the Forest into seventeen bailiwicks which can be identified as Roffey, Bewbush and Alkynburne in the north, Hyde and Shelley in the east, Gosden and Patchgate in the south, Horningbrook in the west and Whitebarrow, Horestock, New Park, Rickfield, Sedgwick and Chesworth in the south west with Knepp further out to the south west. The centre of the Forest is thought to consist of the unidentified bailiwicks of Thrustlehole and Heron.[11]

It was quite usual for any forest of a good size to be divided for administrative purposes into sections which were known as bailiwicks, walks or wards, and not uncommon in the 16th century for them to change name from bailiwicks to walks, as with the forest of Essex. This clearly occurred in St Leonard's Forest as the bailiwicks, some of which have the same name as the park divisions, came to be called 'walks'. The writer Legge, in the *Victoria County History,* notes that in the accounts for the year 1441 of Thomas AnKnapp, there were identified four walks in the south of the Forest and six in the north, amongst them Throstlehill, Thornyngbroke, Beaubush, Shelley, Forterslond, Whiteberewe and Hyde. Legge suggests that the accounts are more than likely a misspelling of those of Thomas Att Knepp, the Chief Ranger of St Leonard's Forest. [12]

In 1720, William Pawlett of Holborn, who was the nephew of Mary Calfe and joint inheritor of her late husband, Peter Calfe, with Lucius Henry and Lord Viscount Faulkland, raised a mortgage of £4,200 on parcels of land in St Leonard's Forest. The document names the divisions of the Forest with acreage adding up to some 5,224 acres, although not all the parcels of land are given acreage. Also, where the document cites 'wall' it is suggested that this may well have been 'walk' and was misread in copying. The parcels of land are as follows:

9. VCH Vol. II, p. 307 and Burchall, M. (2010) A Lost Parish, Sussex Family Historian Vol. 19 No 4 December 2010, pp. 190-195.
10. VCH Vol. II, p. 307
11. VCH Vol. VI.3, p. 13
12. VCH Vol. II, p. 308.

- Middle Wall or Rangers Lodge 1,005 acres with a Lodge House and including Cyndar Croft or Coal place, one acre, Russels Close, four acres, and Runt Field at four acres.
- Carters Wall 600 acres with Lodge House occupied by Henry Shepherd.
- Dawkers Lodge Walk with Lodge House, cottage and two pieces of land called Hassells Laines and Steeres amounting to 700 acres.
- Hammer Pond House, lands called Russels with cottage formerly occupied by Elizabeth Nurton and all the benefit of a Fair kept on these premises and occupied by Edward Greenfield.
- New Lodge Walk and Coolehurst, 600 acres occupied by Michael Mills (who appears to have given his name to the straight track called Mick Mills Race in the centre of the forest).
- Stone Lodge, North End Walk with the Lodge House 839 acres.
- Monks Lodge Walk, 400 acres, with all houses in occupation of Thomas Naylord.
- Unnamed 200 acres in occupation of Emanuel Burges.
- South End Walk of 800 acres in occupation by Lynoll Calford
- Forest and Crab Tree Farm of 80 acres.
- And all the game, breeding of rabbits and coneys on the above premises, (until the later 18th century adult rabbits were referred to as coneys and the young as rabbits). [13]

Some of these names are familiar on later maps as the names of buildings, such as Stone Lodge, and Carters Lodge which give some clue as to where these walks were, however the exact locations are unknown, as are their relationship to the original bailiwicks. Place names of gates also give further clues as to where the various walks, or internal boundaries were. One could consider that Monks Gate was north west in the Forest on the A281, Parkgate and Peppersgate were in the south of the Forest, below Crabtree, again on the A281, and Faygate and Colgate were where the villages of those names now are in the north of the Forest, and they could all have been internal passages. It is interesting that even today a farm on Forest Road, east of Colgate, has the name Shepherdsfield Farm thus echoing the 13th century Shepherds Field Forest which was part of the Shelley Park enclosure.

Early Control of the Forest

The Domesday Survey of 1086, made it clear that landholding after the Norman Conquest was a complicated affair. Sussex had been divided into five baronies, or rapes, the last one was the rape of Bramber in 1073. The major landholder in the rape of Bramber, which included the Manor of Beeding and St Leonard's Forest, was the Norman lord, William de

---

13. West Sussex Record Office (WSRO) ADD MS 32,961. Where the original historic landholding is in acres it is recorded it as such, and not converted to hectares.

Braose. He established himself by building a castle at a strategic crossing point of the Adur river and the village of Bramber grew around the castle. In 1075 he founded Sele Priory in Bramber as a daughter house to the Benedictine Monastery of St. Florent of Saumur, France. The monks were housed in the church of St Nicholas by the castle and later in the enlarged St Peter's church in Beeding which became known as Sele Priory church. The priory was endowed with rights over the resources of St Leonard's Forest, which was about 15 miles to the north of the priory and village of Bramber. The rights given were for the monks to allow their pigs to forage for beechmast, acorns, and leafy greens known as pannage, graze their cattle, and raise tithes from others doing the same, plus cut wood and underwood, clear the woodland for agriculture, known as to assart, and take foals. The rights endowed to Sele Priory were continued by the de Braose family successors, but as the sixth William de Braose (1255-1326), had no immediate male descendant part of the inheritance passed through his daughter, Aline, via her marriage to John de Mowbray, to the house of Mowbray and the Earls of Nottingham who were at the time given Royal recognition of the succession to the Bramber barony, or rape, and the forest, i.e. 'free chase of St Leonard's Forest'. A male grandson, Thomas, inherited other de Braose lands which included Chesworth Manor, but this male line died out with a later Thomas in 1395, whose tomb is in St Mary's Church, Horsham.

Sele priory was small, housing no more than about 16 monks, the Prior, six monks, two priests, a deacon and others not regarded as clerics. Links with the monastery in France were severed in 1396 by Richard II for political reasons, so although it was now independent it lost finances and support so was poor and declining. In 1459, the Priory was finally suppressed and John, 1st Duke of Norfolk, a descendant of the Mowbrays, gave permission for the property to be transferred to the Bishop of Winchester and his newly founded college at Oxford, Magdalen College. Tithes from the Forest were now paid to Magdalen College, whilst they took on the responsibility of upkeep, appointment and wages of the parish vicars. Shortly after taking over the priory property, Magdalen College rented the buildings to the Carmelite Monks of New Shoreham who had been flooded out of their own priory by the River Arun, thus reinstating monastic services at Bramber. [14]

Land ownership of the rape of Bramber remained with the Dukes of Norfolk until the accession of Henry VII, first Tudor monarch in 1485. Due to the Howard's family support of the Yorkist side in the Wars of the Roses the King forfeited their property and gave the Lordship and Rape of Bramber, including the Forest, to Thomas West, 8th Baron De la Warr, who later sold it back to the Howards. However, Thomas, 3rd Duke of Norfolk became the subject of a Bill of Attainder in 1547 [15] cancelling all his rights to property, and so the Rape, Manors and the Forest reverted to the Crown and was granted to Thomas Seymour, Baron Seymour of Sudeley, Lord High Admiral. Seymour was a political rival of Thomas Howard with whom Howard had been keen to form an alliance by offering him his daughter in marriage, an offer that was refused.

---

14. Church leaflet (1999) *The Parish and Priory Church of St Peter (Sele Priory) in the Parish of Beeding and Bramber with Botolphs*. Published by the Parish and available from St. Peters, Upper Beeding.

15. Being attained in English medieval criminal law meant being arrested for a serious crime like treason, punishable by losing one's life, property and any hereditary titles.

Thomas Seymour, was a man of prodigious ambitions. The family seat was Wolf Hall in Wiltshire, readers will no doubt be familiar with the title of *Wolf Hall* (2009) Hilary Mantel's first book in her historical trilogy about Thomas Cromwell. Jane Seymour, Henry VIII's third wife, was one of Seymour's four sisters, and his elder brother, Edward, became Duke of Somerset, Lord Protector and Governor of the young King Edward VI. Although a prosperous landowner and aristocrat, Thomas Seymour wanted more. He married Henry VIII's widow, Katherine Parr, and schemed to usurp his own brother by kidnapping the young King Edward and the King's stepsisters Mary and Elizabeth. It was said he made inappropriate advances to the young Princess Elizabeth, hoping to procure marriage with her after Katherine's death in childbirth. However, his plotting and schemes were uncovered, and he was attained, examined and executed for treason on 20th March, 1549. It was reported that on hearing this news Elizabeth said 'This day died a man with much wit, and very little judgement'.

An interesting postscript to Seymour's control of the Forest was that a memorandum attached to Sele Priory records, and endorsed by Magdalen College, noted that tithes were due from Thomas, Lord Seymour of Sudeley to the college out of the lands held by him in Bramber, Horsham, Knepp and St Leonard's Forest but instead of receiving the tithes due, they had received a letter informing them that:

> 'the lorde admirall aforesaide will buylde a towne within the foreste of St Leonarde, wher increase of p'vie tythes may grow to the college, or els a compostion betwene the said lorde and the college for th tythes; wheras now we have but 3s. for the herbage of the forest' (sic, 1547).

The Rev. Turner, writing in 1858 for Sussex Archaeological Collection Vol. X, suggested that Seymour had in fact gone far enough with his plans of building a new town to identify a site in the Forest, and produce a plan, but only a mention of this survives, not the plan itself or the location. However, this interpretation is queried by Victoria County History (VCH) and it is suggested that Seymour changed his mind over a nucleated village in the Forest and instead divided part of the Forest into small farms and dwellings, although again the location of these was not identified. [16]

Following Seymour's execution, when the land ownership reverted to the Crown, the Forest was then granted in 1553 to Sir Thomas Wrothe, although by 1561 it was back with Thomas, 4th Duke of Norfolk. However, as he was in debt to the Crown he offered to pay the Crown mortgages for the manors of Sedgwick, Chesworth, Beaubush and Shelley, with St Leonard's Forest and the ironworks. This was accepted, but 11 years later in 1572 the 4th Duke himself was attained and executed, the mortgages annulled and the manors and Forest came back into the full possession of the Crown. After all the changes in control one would have thought more stability would be good for St Leonard's Forest but sadly the opposite was the case.

---

16 Centre for Kentish Studies, Maidstone, CKS/U269/E276/1 transcribed by Janet Pennington.

In July, 1631 there was a brief survey of the Manors including the forest of St Leonard's which confirmed that Sir John Caryll had 30 years of his lease yet to run on the Forest, iron mills and forges, with the right to dig stone and ore, take 250 loads of charcoal and 30 cords of wood a year, plus rights over the ponds. There were seven copyholds in fee [17] noted over 173 acres, all paying rent, with the three largest areas held by Richard Wood with 50 acres, Sir Walter Covert with 45 and William Barstow with 40 acres. [18]

However, it appears that in the same year of 1631 Charles I granted the reversion of the Forest in trust to Sir William Russell, Bt., who three years later conveyed his interest to Sir Richard Weston and his sons John and George. Sir Richard Weston was an advocate of agricultural improvement, bringing back to England techniques he had seen on the Continent. This family were still in control of the Forest in 1659. In the north and east of the Forest the Middleton family were in possession of Shelley and Bewbush, having had a lease granted from Sir Thomas Sherley of Wiston. During the Commonwealth (1649-1660) Thomas Middleton was MP for Horsham but was suspected of being involved in the Royalist uprising at Horsham in 1648 and so his estates were sequestered, or confiscated, along with all other iron workings belonging to the crown and royalists. The St Leonard's Forest iron forges were destroyed by Parliamentary forces under Sir William Waller, presumably fearing they could supply the Royalists with iron for weapons. With the restoration of the monarchy in 1660, Middleton's estates were granted to Edward Montagu, 1st Earl of Sandwich, while Charles II conferred the forest of St Leonard itself on his physician, Sir Edward Greaves, who died in 1680. Following his death, the Forest descended via his daughter, Mary Calfe, [19] to her nephew, Captain William Powlett and hence to his cousin John Aldridge of St. Martins in the Field, London, and then to his brother, Abel Aldridge in 1746.

Game Management, Wood and Charcoal

Management of forests for resources of food, wood for fuel, repair and other uses, gave the Forest a particular shape within the landscape, as areas were divided, fenced and gated. The purpose of the divisions of a forest into parks or walks was mainly for the preservation of deer and game. Fallow deer were introduced into England by the Normans as a smaller, easier to manage species than the native Red deer, as Fallow deer could be contained by an oak fence, or pale. Due to the proximity of Chesworth, Sedgwick and Knepp, Edward I and Edward II would undoubtedly have hunted over St Leonard's Forest with staghounds.

Rabbits were introduced into England by the Romans. This was evidenced by a rabbit bone fragment which was found in Fishbourne Roman Villa, near Chichester, being recently identified as such. However, adult rabbits took a while to establish in this cli-

---

17. As opposed to Freehold or Leasehold, Copyhold was land held as part of manorial tenure, and entered in Manorial Court rolls. The Lord of the Manor was due a fee simple, or payment, when the land changed hands.

18. Centre for Kentish Studies, Maidstone, CKS/U269/E276/1 transcribed by Janet Pennington.

19. The name Calf is variously spelt with and without a final 'e'. As it mostly appears with an 'e' this spelling has been used throughout.

mate. The fact that the Lord of Bramber claimed 'free warren' over the Forest meant that the Crown had granted him the right to any animal that could be taken by a large hawk, which would be mainly the hare, rabbit, pheasant and partridge, and he could prosecute anyone hunting and taking these animals, which was what he did. According to the *Victoria County History* (VCH) [20] a claim of free warren was brought to the Horsham Assizes in 1278 by the Lord of Bramber, William de Braose. This showed that on Shrove Tuesday any knights, or free tenants of the barony, could hunt and carry off a wild beast. Furthermore, Sir Roger de Covert, a tenant, claimed this privilege and the right to 'cut bludgeons in the woods to throw at the hares', clearly rather a strange local sport, but it does indicate a variety of game available in the Forest.

Edward III granted to Sir John de Ifield rights over Schullegh (Shelley) Beaubusson (Beaubush) and Knepp to pasture his horses, cattle and sheep, and pannage his swine in these parks. [21] Rights of pannage, which was the right to allow ones pigs to forage in the forest for acorns and beech mast, were also granted and confirmed in 1235 by John de Braose, 'to the Church of St. Peter of Sele and the brethren living under rule there, belonging to the monastery of St. Forent of Salmur (sic) ... tithes of pannage and herbage of the forest of St Leonard and of Crochurst as they have peacefully received them hitherto'. Later, in 1247, a dispute between Hugh, Chaplain of the Chapel of St Leonard in the forest, and the monks over these Rights, demonstrates that the Forest was producing calves, foals and cheese which were all called the 'tithes of herbage.'[22]

The division of a forest into parks or walks enabled not only better management of the areas for venison and game, but for wood and charcoal as well. Sections of forest could be used for coppicing and the animals excluded while the undergrowth and young tree shoots recovered, Rackham called this a 'compartmented' park.[23] Making charcoal involves the slow burning of coppiced wood, which was essential for the smelting of iron in bloomeries or later blast furnaces. It is perhaps an indication of charcoal production in the north of the Forest that the village of Colgate on Forest Road, between Horsham and Pease Pottage, had connections in 1279 with a family called Godelene de la Collegate which Glover, in her book *Sussex Place-Names*, noted as meaning 'dweller at the (char)coal gate'. This, of course, suggests that an early iron-smelting works were nearby. [24] From the Roman period iron and charcoal were being produced in St Leonard's Forest on a sustainable scale through the use of basic iron furnaces known as bloomeries, but production increased with the introduction by French iron workers of blast furnaces so that by the early 16th century iron masters were making good profits.

The Chapel of St Leonard was still operating in 1535 and there is archival evidence that the incumbent, Alan Coke, received money for rents, oblations and profits from wood sales and other casual revenues. Shortly after this date there is more evidence of

20. VCH Vol. II, p. 307.

21. VCH Vol. II, p. 307.

22. Salzman, L.F. (ed.) (1923) *The Chartulary of Sele Priory.* Cambridge: W. Heffer and Sons, pp. 32-33.

23. Rackham, O. (1986) *The History of the Countryside,* London:. J.M. Dent and Sons, pp. 125-6.

24. Glover, J. (1997) *Sussex Place-Names, their Origins and Meanings,* Newbury: Countryside Books, p. 55, also referenced in Mawer, A. and Stenton F.M. with Glover, J.E.B. (1969) *The Place-Names of Sussex, Part I The Rapes of Chichester, Arundel and Bramber,* Cambridge University Press, p. 203.

the productivity of the Forest following the attainder, or arrest, in 1549 of Thomas Seymour, Lord High Admiral, as mentioned earlier in this chapter, when an inventory of all his possessions was undertaken at Chesworth. In Knepp Park there were 100 oxen, 53 sheep and one cow, plus 13 young gelding horses. In Sedgwick there were ten pigs and 100 deer, while at the 'Litill Park in the forest', possibly the area of the later St Leonard's Estate, there were 80 deer. In addition to this were the payments to underkeepers of animals, at Beaubush and Shelley Parks, John Berde received money plus nine cattle and 20 horses, while John Myles at the Litill Park received 60s a year and 'serteyn catall'. Mention is also made of a water bailiff with oversight of ponds and fisheries so fish as well as meat were being produced. [25]

Prof Brian Short wrote in *The English Rural Landscape* that medieval forest administration declined during the later Tudor period due in part to a lack of enthusiasm of the royals for hunting, particularly as Queen Elizabeth I grew older and subsequently died in 1603. The result was the encroachment of pasturing into forests, and although Charles I attempted to reverse this trend and enforce forest laws, this was unpopular and the policy died with him. The new Commonwealth (1649-1660) was more interested in disafforestation [26] and land improvement, with the consequent increase in the value of the land and profits for the land owners, rather than the preservation of woodland for game. This new drive continued with the restoration of the Monarchy, so that generally a focus of forest production became timber, glass and iron if improvement of the land for agriculture was not successful.

Folklore and Myth

At the beginning of the 17th century there was a story that came out of St Leonard's Forest, which in many ways harked back to early medieval fears of wild and dangerous forests. The story was published as a pamphlet in London in August 1614 that described a serpent, or dragon, living in the Forest 'in a vast and unfrequented place, heathie, vaultie, full of unwholesome shades, and over-growne hollowes'. The serpent was reported to have a territory of three or four miles and had been seen near Faygate, to the north of the Forest, and within only half a mile of Horsham town. There was a very detailed description attributed to John Steel, Christopher Holder and a widow woman living near Faygate. The serpent, or dragon, was reported to be nine feet or more in length, and as thick as a cart axle, thicker in the middle, and left a noxious slimy trail. It was further described as having had a white circle of scales around its neck, black scales along its back and a red stomach. It could raise its head and neck and look about. It had large feet, and perhaps more worryingly, two big bunches on either side of its body which, it was supposed, would develop into wings. It could spit venom a distance of four rods, or 20 metres, and by doing so had killed a man, a woman and two large dogs, although it had not eaten

---

25. Ellis, H. (1861) Inventories of Goods etc., in the Manor of Chesworth, Sedgwick, and other Parks, the Manor Place of Sheffield, and in the forest of Worth, with the Iron-works belonging to the Lord Admiral Seymour, at the time of his attainder, taken 1549. *Sussex Archaeological Collections* XIII, pp. 118-131, (hereafter Ellis, 1861).

26. The legal change of status of a forest to ordinary land, and the felling of trees.

these bodies as it was thought it fed on a rabbit warren which had been found to be 'much impaired'. There was apparently a further pamphlet which told of the killing of the dragon, but sadly this has not survived. [27]

In 1861 M. A. Lower wrote a paper in *Sussex Archaeological Collections* about Sussex folk-lore and expressed the thought that superstition could have converted a misshapen log into a dragon, and the disappearance of rabbits could be attributed to poachers. He further dismissed a suggestion that it was a lampoon of a petty tyrant, unnamed, of the district. It could of course have been a hoax, although Lower does consider it might have been encouraged, if not instigated, by smugglers and gamekeepers to keep people away from the Forest. [28] However, Djabri points out that smuggling activity was not prevalent in the Forest until at least a century later. In researching the likely truth of the story, Djabri examined the Horsham Parish register for the period to identify the names of the people involved, and found some likely candidates. She also suggested that the rabbit warren in question could have been that situated on the Bewbush estate, north east of Colgate, the Sibball's Field Warren. There is certainly a ring of truth in such a detailed description of the serpent which Djabri thought could have been an African Black Cobra which may have arrived through ports on the south coast, and then been carried via the busy transport of iron and timber into the forest.[29]

12. Image of a winged serpent from Edward Topsell's *Historie of Serpents* 1608.
© private collection.

---

27. Dudley, H (1836, 1973) *The History and Antiquities of Horsham,* Horsham: J. Cramp Ltd. p. 46-51, (hereafter Dudley, 1836) and Knight J. & Semens J. (2007) *Horsham's Dragon,* Horsham, Horsham Museum Society.

28. Lower, M. A. (1861) Old Speech and Manners in Sussex. *Sussex Archaeological Collections,* XIII, pp. 209-223 (hereafter Lower, 1861).

29. Djabri, S. C. (2006) The 'Dragon' of St Leonard's Forest. *Horsham Heritage,* Issue No. 14, Spring, Horsham Museum Society, pp. 3-16.

A further consideration of the story of the dragon is by Andrew Hadfield in his article *News of the Sussex Dragon*. He suggested that the story could be viewed two ways. One as an eye witness account of a dragon that actually existed, and the other as an early popular and sensational publishing story. With regards to this latter possibility it seems that the publisher of the pamphlet, John Trundle, had form for producing far-fetched text, or fake news, and understood only too well the public desire for entertainment, through his contact with the theatre. The author of the pamphlet, an enigmatic 'A. R.', perhaps Trundle himself, appeared well educated with access to books such as Edward Topsell's *History of Serpents,* so the pamphlet appears more sophisticated than others of that vintage.[30]

It does appear that stories of dragons, wyverns and worms were common in Britain in the 17th century. Essex had a story of a serpent appearing on the Blackwater marshes, also disseminated by a pamphlet dated 1669. Sarah Perry based her 2016 historical fiction story *The Essex Serpent* on this pamphlet. Even as late as 1707 in America there were stories of 'dragons' and 'fiery flying serpents' in New England's primeval forests. [31] The image of a winged serpent appeared in Edward Topsell's *'Historie of Serpents'* in 1608, only six years before the Horsham story was published, and this image is remarkably similar to description of the St Leonard's Forest serpent, see illustration 12: page 35. A description by Pliny the elder in his *'Natural History'* also has very similar characteristics. Perhaps this is not surprising given Jones' argument in his book *An Instinct for Dragons* that a deep-seated human fear of a composite predator, made up of the characteristics of snakes, birds and big cats haunt all humans, and follow us in myth through history and cultures. With regard to the dragon of St Leonard's Forest, anyone wanting to make up a story of dragons would be likely to use these characteristics, but as to why they should create a story about a dragon and scare people away from the Forest is open to conjecture.[32]

Stories of dragons in folklore tend to get mixed up with knights or saints who slay them, and this is the case with the St Leonard's dragon. A.C. Crookshank wrote of St Leonard as a brave Saxon man living in Worth and battling Normans, wolves and hard winters, building the Church at Worth with his own hands, and finally settling as a much-respected hermit in St Leonard's Forest. Here he asked the angels to stop nightingales from singing as they were disturbing his prayers. He talked to the dragon and then shot it with a bow and arrow, which seemed a bit unfair. Finally, on his death, his hermit cell disappeared to be replaced by a carpet of Lily of the Valley.[33] Crookshank did not reference his sources and it is likely he had made much of it up to improve his story, Symonds agrees and suggested it was a somewhat misconceived book, half myth and half historical novel. [34] Dudley wrote that St Leonard prayed 'The adders never stynge, Nor ye nyghtyngales synge' [35] and Lower repeated this with a slight twist in writing that the saint was asked what reward he would like for his services and he replied that he would like the eternal silence of the nightingale, which was granted within the Forest. Simpson tells of an old

---

30. Hadfield, A. (2012) News of the Sussex Dragon, *Reformation,* 17.1, pp. 99-113.

31. Tuan, Y-F. (1979, 2013) *Landscapes of Fear,* Minneapolis, MN (USA): University of Minnesota Press, p. 81.

32. Jones, E.J. (2000) *An Instinct for Dragons,* London, Routledge, pp. 138-147.

33. Crookshank, A.C. (1928) *Saint Leonard of Sussex* London: Arthur H. Stockwell.

34. Symonds, R. (2012) The Story of St Leonard, *Horsham Heritage,* Issue No. 21, Autumn, Horsham Museum Society, pp. 3-12.

35. Dudley, 1836, p. 46.

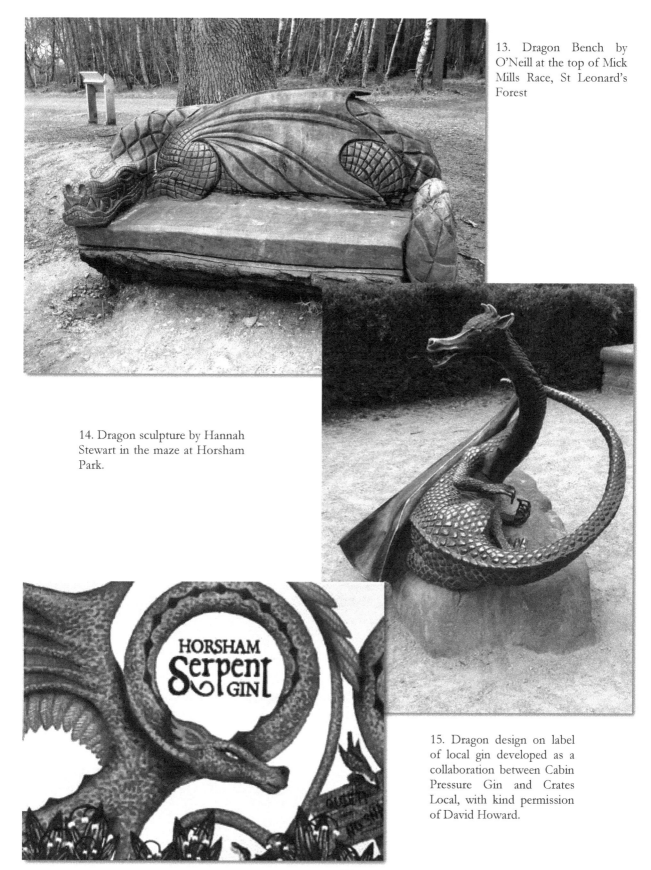

13. Dragon Bench by O'Neill at the top of Mick Mills Race, St Leonard's Forest

14. Dragon sculpture by Hannah Stewart in the maze at Horsham Park.

HORSHAM
Serpent
GIN

15. Dragon design on label of local gin developed as a collaboration between Cabin Pressure Gin and Crates Local, with kind permission of David Howard.

legend of St Leonard, a French hermit, living in the Forest and undertaking a long and ferocious battle with the dragon, which he killed, and that lily-of-the-valley sprang up where his blood was spilt. [36] Even today people repeat the myth that the flowers of the lily -of-the-valley in the forest are tinged pink due to the blood of the Saint. However, a variation suggests that the blood spilt on the lilies was that of the dragon, given that most parts of the lilies are highly toxic.

One could consider such often repeated myths from a psychological perspective. Chalquist is an American environmental psychologist who developed the concept of terrapsychology, which explores the relationship between people and places, or the human soul and the soul of locality. He suggests that myths are important in this regard as they indicate links between inner and outer, people and places, known and unknown. Or as Chalquist wrote, they rise from a 'kind of unconscious, a psychic layering of the world'. Place motifs such as the St Leonard's Forest dragon continue to recur; the dragon turns up in stories, names of public houses, sculptures and carved benches in the forest. However, the meanings of such a motif would need further study.[37]

A chilling legend, possibly invented by smugglers, is that of the headless horseman. Dudley describes it well when he wrote that it was 'woe to the luckless wight', who should cross St Leonard's Forest alone on horseback during the night, for no sooner had he entered 'its darksome precincts, than a horrible decapitated spectre' of Squire Paulett jumps up on his horse, sits on the saddle behind him, and no amount of prayers or menaces can dislodge him until out of the Forest. Although Captain William Powlett of the Horse Grenadiers in the reign of George I inherited the Forest and lived at New Lodge, he died in 1746 complete with his head, and it is not clear how or why this myth came to be. [38] Tuan suggested that ghosts are the last of the supernatural beings to lose their grip on the landscapes of Europe, fading slowly from the imagination and only kept alive by storytelling. This story of the headless horseman would certainly have kept respectable people indoors at night allowing the smugglers to go about their illegal trade without hindrance.[39]

Another such legend, told by Hurst, was of Mike Mills,[40] a smuggler who lived in the Forest. The Devil was determined to carry off his soul and had had a few abortive attempts to do so. One dark night he confronted Mike with his contraband, Mike put down his tubs and challenged the Devil to a race, and if he won then the Devil was to leave him alone. The Devil agreed and Mike raced away down the mile and a quarter pine-tree-lined avenue of Race Hill in the forest, and outran the Devil by a quarter of a mile. The 1720 mortgage, itemised earlier in this chapter under Shape of the forest, names Michael Mills as occupying 600 acres of the forest including New Lodge and Coolhurst. Was he a smug-

36. Simpson, J. (2009) *Folklore of Sussex*, Stroud: The History Press, pp. 31-33.

37. Chalquist, C. (2007) *Terrapsychology, Reengaging the Soul of Place*, New Orleans, USA: Spring Journal Books, pp. 11, 60-83.

38. Dudley, 1836, p. 45-6 and Lower, 1861, p 222-3

39. Tuan, 1979, pp. 126-8.

40. Hurst refers to Mike Mills, the name however is more commonly known as Mick Mills as in Mick's Cross at the bottom of Race Hill on OS map TQ217302.

gler? This would have been before the occupation of the Aldridges, but maybe they carried on the business thus giving credence to Albery's reporting of James Lindfield's reminiscences of contraband in the forest.[41]

Winslow writes that before 1740 there had been a Sussex custom amongst the wealthy, landowners and farmers of smuggling wool to avoid export tax, with the poor of Sussex considering it a legitimate part of the local economy. Only later, with the illegal import of tea and brandy of a much higher value, did the business turn particularly violent and was met by the full force of the militia and revenue officers. A two-year campaign instigated by the Duke of Richmond in 1748 followed the brutal murder of Galley and Chater, a customs officer and an informant, respectively. This resulted in 35 people hung after five trials, although as Winslow points out, many benefitted from smuggling but only the poor went to the gallows.[42]

16. Post card of Mick Mills Race, 1904.

A Changing Landscape

It is clear from the surveys of the 17th century that St Leonard's Forest was becoming less of a valuable and sustainable ancient timber forest and more of a devalued woodland of secondary growth and heathland. Jack's whole premise in her 1997 article in *Sussex Archaeological Collection,* Vol. 135, was that St Leonard's Forest was an example of late medieval ecological destruction, and it is hard not to agree with her. There were repeated warnings throughout the 16th and 17th centuries that the mismanagement of the forest would end up destroying it. These warnings came from those who knew about forest management, the surveyors of the woodlands, the rangers and some landowners, but sadly the rising price of wood and the promise of individual profits won over the future sustainability of the Forest ecology – a struggle that still has resonances today in increasingly fragile environments around the world, such as the Amazon.

41. Albery, 1947, pp. 474-501, and Hurst, 1868, pp. 162-8 and West Sussex Records Office (WSRO) ADD MS 32,961.

42. Winslow, C. (1975) *Sussex Smugglers*, Hay, D., Linebaugh, P., Thompson, E. P. (eds) *Albion's Fatal Tree, Crime and Society in Eighteenth-Century England,* New York: Pantheon Books, pp. 119-166.

Arable improvement of perceived wasteland had been on the agenda since the Commonwealth,1648-1660, driven by the search for improved rents and profitability. The Westons, Sir Richard and his sons John and George, who leased the Forest from the Crown initially in 1634 and then during the Commonwealth, made attempts to improve the land in the Forest, mainly by experimenting with different manuring techniques on a sandy soil. However, they had little success as what was needed in addition was effective drainage, and this did not develop until the following century. Occupation in the Forest was begun by Sir Thomas Seymour in the 16th century and by the beginning of the 17th century Peter Brandon estimated that some 2,500 acres of St Leonard's Forest had been let as farmland with about 40 small holdings set up as farms and cottages, mostly for part time iron workers. Sir Edward Greaves, the next incumbent of the Forest, followed a policy of establishing larger rabbit warrens to enhance his profits, rather than agricultural improvement, which had largely failed.[43]

The last iron forges had closed during the Commonwealth and with them the economic imperative for coppiced wood, so new growth of woodland was not protected against the grazing of sheep, cattle and rabbits, and thus the heathland expanded. It is clear there were rabbit warrens at the beginning of the 17th century although they are not noted on early maps. On the Bewbush estate to the north east of the Forest was Sibballs Field Warren, identified first in 1608 and said by 1650 to be of 834 acres and well stocked. It appeared that there were more warrens set up in the centre of the forest with names such as Great Warren being a good indication of size and importance.[44]

In depositions taken in 1684 by the Exchequer for the Crown with regard to mismanagement of the Forest under lease, a witness said that the Forest 'hath been a warren for near 40 years past' while another said 'that there is not now or hath been for several years last past soe many coneys by half in the said forest as there were about 20 years ago'. Sir Edward Greaves, who died in 1680, passed his estate on to his daughter Mary, who was married to a Peter Calfe, and it was this couple who were the defendants in the case. Many of the witnesses talked of great waste and destruction in the Forest, and that this was due to the sale of timber such as 200 loads of beech timber. They also mentioned the mismanagement of new growth by not fencing the coppices or underwood after felling, keeping cattle and sheep in the Forest, and burning the heath to produce better feed for the rabbits.

Others said that Peter Calfe was not to blame, Edward Garston of Nuthatch who had been his Wood Reeve said in the two years he had worked for him he had not cut more than 100 cords of wood and the underwood was well protected, but one detects some personal motive in not condemning himself as well as his employer, Peter Calfe. John Stone of Beeding said that the coppices of the wood were utterly destroyed by Captain Stollman under the 'Usurper' i.e. Oliver Cromwell, for want of fencing and preservation. Although some warreners said they did not set fire to the heath, Nicholas Michell, warrener of Beeding, said that he and other warreners usually burnt the heath in the plain part of the Forest. This was to make feed for the rabbits and sheep, but they never set fire

43. Brandon, P (2003) *The Kent & Sussex Weald,* Chichester: Phillimore and Co. Ltd., p.123.
44. VCH Vol. VI.3, p. 15.

to the heath amongst the birches and coppices. Several times it had caught fire by accident, but he did not think it did either any damage or any good. However, there may well have been too many 'accidents' which would have prevented the regeneration of woodland, leaving the areas of heathland particularly suitable for rabbit warrens.[45]

Perhaps the last word in the destruction of the medieval St Leonard's Forest should go to Michael Drayton, 17th century topographical poet, who wrote of the destruction of all the forests on the Sussex ridge in his poem Poly-Olbion, an epic comment on the landscape changes in each county of England, published in 1612 and 1622. He imagines the distressed spirits of the trees and lays the blame at the door of the iron foundries and changing agricultural practice. The social ecologist Heller might see this poem as the romanticising of nature and forest as women, in need of rescuing, or in need of a hero to slay the dragon of new industrial technology. This is perhaps a romanticised version of green concerns that still echo today, and thus a distraction from the real ills of disenfranchisement of the poor from economic and political democracy. However, Dasgupta suggests that Drayton's poem is a radical departure from previous landscape writing. Whilst acknowledging his poignant awareness of landscape change and destruction, she sees a real and modern concern with the environment and its interface with the economic, political and social changes of the day, and the ethical dilemmas these inevitably cause.[46]

The Daughters of the Weald

(That in their heavy breasts had long their griefs concealed),
Foreseeing their decay each hour so fast come on,
Under the axe's stroke, fetched many a grievous groan.
When the anvil's weight, and hammer's dreadful sound,
Even rent the hollow woods and shook the queachy ground;
So that trembling nymphs, oppressed through ghastly fear,
Ran madding to the downs, with loose dishevelled hair

'Jove's oak, the warlike ash, veined elm, the softer beech,
Short hazel, maple plain, light asp, the bending wych,
Tough holly, and smooth birch, must altogether burn;
What should the builder serve, supplies the forger's turn,
When under public good, base private gain takes hold,
And we, poor woeful woods, to ruin lastly sold'.[47]

---

45. The National Archives (TNA) E134/36Chas2/East22

46. Heller, C. (1999) *Ecology of Everyday Life, Rethinking the Desire for Nature,* London: Black Rose Books, pp.13-39, and Dasgupta, S. (2010) Drayton's 'Silent Spring': Poly-Olbion and the Politics of Landscape. *The Cambridge Quarterly* 39(2) pp. 152-171.

47. As quoted in Lucas, E.V. (1904) *Highways and Byways in Sussex,* London: Macmillan and Co. Ltd., p. 125.

Hawthorn, with blossom and berries, *Crataegus monogyna* by Dr Maggie Weir-Wilson.

Chapter 3

Industry and Agriculture

Iron Production

The production of iron and timber continued to be an important economic activity for St Leonard's Forest into the 16th century and impacted the landscape of the forest profoundly. There is no evidence to suggest that St Leonard's Forest was connected with glass production, unlike the wooded areas around Kirdford to the north-west of Horsham, however, the production of iron in the Forest through the use of blast furnaces spread rapidly in the 16th century, and by the 1570s there were a dozen forges and furnaces within a ten mile radius of the Forest as well as within it.

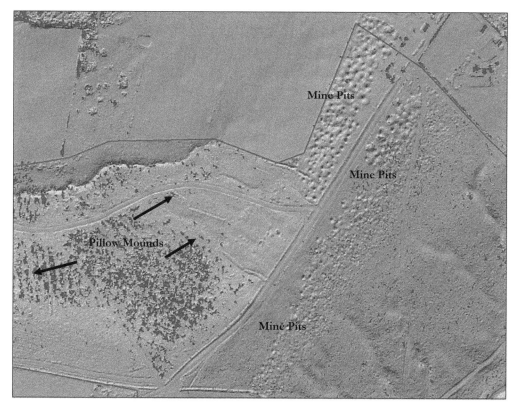

17. Mine pits and pillow mounds, from Lidar- enhanced Archaeological Survey of St Leonard's Forest, West Sussex, June 2011. Figure 17 p 51. With kind permission of Chris Butler Archaeological Services Ltd.

There is archival evidence from the 13th and 14th centuries for bloomery furnaces at Roffey in the north of the forest. Bloomeries were pits with chimneys and bellows for heating charcoal and iron ore to produce a workable bloom or mix of iron and slag. Archaeological excavation confirms that near Roffey was a large, established site making arrows - both heads and shafts - and horseshoes.

Cleere and Crossley in *The Iron Industry of the Weald* wrote that in the western Weald iron ore was dug out of mine pits by digging a shaft of about 1.8-2.4 metres diameter down from the ground surface into the iron bearing rock, up to a depth of 12 metres, and then widening out along the seam of ore. This must have been a dangerous business with the likelihood of dug out shafts collapsing, but a series of pits were dug, with the new pit filled with the spoil from the previous one. Horsham Parish burials for July 10th 1613 notes that a William Atkins, mine digger, was killed in a mine pit, which gives credence to the danger of this work. The local name for iron ore was 'mine' and so these workings are known as mine pits. A Lidar survey [1] in 2011 identified considerable mine pit activity the forest, identifying 28 sites that were particularly dense in the Colgate area. Mine pits can be identified as small deep pits with rounded spoil heaps in a horseshoe shape around the edge. From observation of the Lidar results they are packed surprisingly close together.[2]

18. Photograph of mine pits, from Lidar- enhanced Archaeological Survey of St Leonard's Forest, West Sussex, June 2011. Photo 2, p.18. With kind permission of Chris Butler Archaeological Services Ltd.

1. Lidar was originally developed in the 1960s and 70s for submarine detection. The name stands for Light Detection and Ranging, also known as airborne laser scanning. It measures the height of the ground and can identify hard to see features in a large landscape through using a pulsed laser beam.
2. Butler, C., Blandford, V., Locke, A. (2011) *A Lidar-enhanced Archaeological Survey of St Leonard's Forest, West Sussex,* Chris Butler Archaeological Services for Forest Enterprise and Weald Forest Ridge Historic Environment Awareness Project (Hereafter Lidar survey 2011).

The landscape of the Forest was ideal for the next development of blast furnaces, given that the blast of air could be delivered by water-powered bellows, and the long narrow ghylls could be dammed to create a pond, with the dam or 'bay' forming a causeway. Furnaces were built near the bank on the side of the valley so that charcoal and iron ore could easily be loaded into the top of the chimney or flue via a charging platform. The higher temperatures of the blast furnaces compared to the bloomeries meant that the iron absorbed some carbon from the charcoal and so was brittle when cold. It therefore had to undergo another treatment, that of fining. This required the slabs of raw cast iron, called pigs or sows, to be melted and hammered thus reducing the amount of carbon in the iron. The wrought iron was then transferred to another hearth, a chafery, where it was hammered using a heavy water-powered hammer into a bar for sale.

Two large iron works were developed in the south of the Forest around 1562 by John Broadbridge. Upper Forge was on Hammer Pond and had a forge, whilst Lower Forge, on Hawkins Pond and to the west of Upper Forge, had both forge and furnace. Hodgkinson, in his 2008 book *The Wealden Iron Industry*, wrote that many French migrants were being recruited in the first half of the 16th century from the Pays de Bray in north-eastern Normandy, south of Dieppe, where they had learned valuable iron-working skills, but lack of investment and the rising price of wood had closed the French furnaces. Migration reached its peak in the 1520s, although by that time many families had come over and settled, with their descendants often remaining in the iron trade. There is little doubt that this immigration had helped to develop the skills needed to manufacture ordnance, and a good export trade in guns and canon was established before the Spanish Armada sailed up the English Channel in 1588. However, after this event the Government began to control the trade centrally through the issue of licenses for fear of supplying weapons to the enemy.

That the French were in St Leonard's Forest is confirmed by the burial on 21st January 1556 of 'Peter, a Frenche man, a colier that was cruelly murderyd in the forest of Seynt Leonerde'.[3] According to David Hey in his *Oxford Companion to Local and Family History*, before the 19th century colliers were not exclusively coalminers but wood colliers or charcoal burners, so presumably Peter the Frenchman had been working in the Forest in the iron industry, either digging iron ore or making charcoal, before he was murdered. This murder may highlight the tensions that were beginning to develop between contested forest resources, or perhaps just individual jealousy and xenophobia. The iron forges needed plentiful supplies of wood, iron ore and water power, but this latter was limited and neighbouring ironmasters encroached on each other's catchment areas to the detriment of all.

At this time, in the mid-16th century, control and use of the Forest becomes much more complex as the Crown issued leases that were sublet, and disputes arose. In 1573 the Crown issued 21-year leases to John Blennerhasset and William Dix, retainers in the Duke of Norfolk's household, for the iron mills and forges in the forest of St Leonard along with the stone, ore and all necessities for producing iron. The underlease was held by Roger Gratwick who died in 1570 and left the lease to his son, another Roger Gratwick who held the two forges. However, there were disputes between Gratwick the younger and

3· Garraway Rice, R. (ed.) 1915, The Parish Register of Horsham in the town of Sussex, 1514-1635, Burials, Sussex Record Society, Vol. XXI, p. 310.

Walter Covert of Slaugham Place over various payments and this appeared to escalate. Gratwick also seems to have upset Edward Caryll of Shipley who had the Gosden furnace which was south of the Forest in the Adur valley, and Covert sided with Caryll against Gratwick. These three men were all wealthy iron masters and the grievances were mainly over shared diminishing resources in the Forest. Dispute followed dispute; one argument was over fishing in the hammer ponds, the next was about rent being paid to the Crown. Gratwick complained that Covert, Caryll and others conspired to deprive him of his title and term in the ironworks and take by force all his wealth and substance. Fighting did break out amongst their retainers, and Straker in his book *Wealden Iron* describes how 20 or more of Caryll's men, the most dissolute, disordered, quarrelsome and riotous persons, set upon Gratwick's men in a warlike manner with swords, daggers, staves and other weapons, wounding and beating them.

In another incident, a leading Caryll man went to the mine pits, struck a Gratwick man with a mattock, threw him in the pit and threatened to follow up with stone, seemingly not to care if he killed him or not. These disputes even carried into Horsham town with daggers being drawn and victims chased. It seems that Gratwick did in fact lose out, and in 1601 Sir John Caryll of Warnham, nephew of Edward, was granted a 60-year lease on the greater part of the manors of Sedgwick, Chesworth and the Forest; however, part of Sedgwick and Chesworth were further sublet to Sir William Ford who then sublet it in 1642 to a John Gratwick, presumably the same family as Roger Gratwick. Chesworth by this time had been disparked, or removed from private hunting park ownership, and divided into ten small farms while Sedgwick also had been disparked and split into 11 farms plus the 372 acres that was Sedgwick Lodge and grounds.

Most damaging for the survival of St Leonard's Forest as a woodland landscape with valuable timber was the ownership of the Forest passing from the 4th Duke of Norfolk to the Crown. In 1561 the Duke offered the forest and parks to the Crown in exchange for his debts and stated that there were 'plenty of woods for fortifications or ships'. Once the Crown had full control it was then leased and sublet, Sir John Caryll obtaining the greater part including Sedgwick and Chesworth, and then sublet further, although Caryll retained his right to hawk, hunt, fish and obtain deer. Sir William Ford was a lessee who reserved for himself the 'great timber' but sublet further to John Gratwick. The effect of this on the Forest was the over-exploitation of resources through total lack of regulation. Legge gives an example of the enormous destruction of the Forest by stating the fact that in 1578 one lessee, Sir Thomas Sherley of Wiston, obtained a warrant to take 2,000 cords of Beech, Birch and Oak a year, but by 1597 he had taken 75,016 and a half cords, or 180,000 tons of wood (a cord being 128 cubic feet or 2.4 tons), this being twice the amount he was authorised to take. Another lessee, Edward Caryll had taken 8,580 cords over this time making the total loss from these two lessees of over ten million cubic feet of wood, or over two million tons in this period alone.[4]

---

4. VCH Vol. II, p. 309. Legge does in fact say a loss of over a million cubic feet of wood but the figures he provides gives a total of over ten million rather than a million.

Jack suggests that after the Duke of Norfolk's demise there is no clear evidence of the forest courts meeting in order to oversee the granting of warrants and prosecution of transgressors. It therefore appears that Royal Court warrants were issued without any reference to the resources available or good management of the forest environment. Protests were raised by the keepers and rangers, particularly with regard to the effect this deforestation was having on game and their ability to preserve it. The Deputy Surveyor of Wood, Roger Taverner, surveyed St Leonard's Forest sometime between 1566 and 1572, around the time of the Duke's attainder, or arrest, as noted in the previous chapter. Jack quotes Taverner as assessing the Forest to be well supplied with desirable timber, oak and beech of great age. However, he warned against the taking of timber from the 'plumps' or clumps of trees, which grew on the exposed slopes, as this would allow the wind to blow through and thus damage the trees and create erosion of the soil. He also warned against the taking of the undergrowth and said that this should also be properly managed. He proposed sensible changes to preserve the Forest and its timber so that a supply of wood to the Navy could be sustained.

Taverner's good advice was not heeded for long; warrants continued to be granted to such as Sir Thomas Sherley and the large timber trees were felled, wood continued to be taken for the charcoal burners and the iron forges, and wood was also taken for dwellings and raw materials by people who settled in and near the Forest. Zell quotes from an Admiralty report dated 1578 which stated that there were about 100 furnaces and iron mills in Sussex, Surrey and Kent, most of which were in Sussex, and which had greatly added to the 'spoil and overthrow of woods and principal timber'.[5]

As the Forest landscape deteriorated, disputes arose over rights to the diminishing resources, so that Taverner stepped in to prosecute Roger Gratwick, ironmaster, for taking 1,000 trees for buildings, these trees being selected by George Hall, a self-styled deputy surveyor, mainly for his own convenience in felling and working rather than good forestry. Another case was against Thomas Sherley of Wiston and John Middleton, ironmaster, so that a Commission of Inquiry at the end of the 16th century asked whether there was any wood standing after Sir Thomas Sherley's ravages. They found that there were only 696 cords of wood worth anything, and that the destruction was irreparable. Straker noted that Arthur and John Middleton of Horsham and Stephen French of Chiddingly, ironmasters who had been granted a lease on the eastern part of St Leonard's Forest around 1574, including Bewbush furnace, took advantage of their right to take timber and between 1589 and 1596 cut 56,000 cords of wood worth £4,200. In addition, they took 80 dead, stub and pollard trees for the repair of their houses. At the time of Thomas Middleton's sequestration, i.e. the seizure of his goods and property, in 1649 it was noted that 'Mr Thos. Middleton and his predecessors have so destroyed the woods and timber with more abounding upon the several parks of Shelley and Bewbush and neglected to follow the said furnace, that it has stood emptie for about seven yeares last past'.[6]

---

5 Jack, 1997, pp. 241-7 and Zell, M. (1994, 2004) *Industry in the Countryside, Wealden Society in the Sixteenth Century*, Cambridge: Cambridge University Press, pp. 126-7.

6 Jack, 1997, p. 245.

In the 1630s, Sir Henry Compton had brought the matter of the Forest's mismanagement to the Exchequer Court. He complained of the decay of the park palings, deer and cattle coming onto his land and the burning of heath in 'new and unusual places'. Jack noted that Sir John Caryll had allowed the grazing of larger quantities of sheep and cattle in the Forest, and also sublet to farmers with permission to plough and improve the forest land. So that by Charles I's reign (1625-1649) a survey found no great trees or valuable timber save one old tree worth £1 and other young timber worth £30.

A Parliamentary survey of St Leonard's Forest conducted during the Commonwealth in 1655 itemised two Iron forges in the forest. The Upper Forge had two fires, two great bellows, one hammer, a warehouse, tenement with six rooms, a little barn, watercourses, an orchard and garden, all in one acre. [7] The Lower Forge had three fires, three bellows, one hammer, a little warehouse with yard and a little barn, watercourses and all again in one acre. Along with these forges, the surveyors noted the lessees' right to dig Horsham stone and iron ore from the Forest, to produce annually 250 loads of charcoal for the forges and 30 cords of wood. It is clear at the time of this survey there was a dispute over lease ownership of the forges and the Forest itself. Elizabeth I had granted the lease of the majority of the western part of the Forest to Sir John Carill, [8] however Charles I had given leases to William Collins and Edward Fenn, except for the iron forges which were retained by Sir John Carill and his heirs.

The surveyors must have been surprised when they found the Lower Forge in the possession of Walter Pawley, who said he had purchased it from John Carill, heir of the original Sir John Carill, although there appeared to be a dispute about the boundary, since he owned adjoining land, and one wonders whether it was a case of encroachment. William Pawley presented a number of 'ancient inhabitants' to back his claim, but the surveyors were not impressed and wanted proper documentation. They noted that one forge which used to be by Lower Forge had been destroyed through neglect and concluded their report with the remark that there had been a 'very great destruction of the woods within the afforested Forest since the said grants (of leases) but there is sufficient coppice wood yet remaining to make good the said coals and woods if well preserved'.[9] There was still some worth in the Forest in the mid-17th century, but this was yet another warning that proper forest management was necessary for the preservation of what wood was left. Both the forges were out of use by 1664 and derelict by 1667. As the iron industry moved north, the controlled coppicing ceased and, as Rackham noted, this was the time when the woodlands were at their most vulnerable to destruction, when industry had moved on and care was no longer taken of the woodland.[10]

7. Hughes, A.F. (2005) St Leonard's Forest, *Horsham Heritage*, Issue No. 12, Spring, Horsham Museum Society, pp. 21-29. Dr Annabelle F. Hughes, a specialist in timber built houses, noted that this tenement with its six rooms probably still survives.

8. Spelling of the Carill name differs from Carill to Carrill and Caryll and there are at least two generations of John Carill, and an Edward Caryll involved in taking leases.

9. Daniel-Tyssen J.R. (1872) Parliamentary Surveys of the County of Sussex 1649-1653. *Sussex Archaeological Collections* XXIV, pp. 238-241—I have normalised the English in the quote.

10. Rackham, O. (2006) *Woodlands*, London: Harper Collins, p. 124-133.

For centuries the iron industry had used managed quantities of wood in the furnaces, and dug ore from the Forest, but resources were finite and had begun to run out. Thus, the industry moved on to exploit the larger deposits of coal and iron ore in the Midlands. However, it was not the iron industry but the felling of large timber trees for wood sales that caused damage to the existing woodland cover and the opportunities this provided for over-grazing. It was this that effectively changed the landscape of the Forest from the late 17th century.

Quarries, Mines and Bricks

Diggings for stone, clay, sand and marl changes the profile of the landscape and leaves evidence that can be seen today. The Horsham area was, and still is, well known for the production of large grey flat Horsham Stone, which could be split and was therefore mainly used in roof tiling and paths. This had never been quarried in the Forest, but nearby, to the south and west of St Leonard's Forest. The main outcrop was a low ridge that ran from Monks Gate through Nuthurst and west towards Sedgwick and Denne Hill. The area around Sedgwick was particularly abundant, as is evident in the buildings and gardens of Sedgwick Place, while the Denne estate had numerous productive quarries which produced a useful annual income.[11] However, it is clear that ordinary sandstone good enough for building could be obtained in St Leonard's Forest, as Horsfield, Cartwright and Burke all mention that Thomas Broadwood's mansion at Holmbush was built with stone quarried on the estate.[12]

The 2011 Lidar survey identified four quarries in their survey area of the central forest; two were close to Forest Road, the Horsham-Pease Pottage road, and it is suggested in the survey that these were used for quarrying stone for road building. It is however, also possible that they could have been used to provide building stone for the few early 19th century stone houses erected at Colgate nearby and perhaps Lower Beeding. It is interesting to note that in 1848 it was reported by Lewis in his *A Topographical Dictionary of England* in reference to the Forest that 'Ironstone is found, and building stone of excellent quality is plentiful and extensively quarried'.[13] Leases such as the head lease of 1801 between John Aldridge and Railton and Hull details all quarries mines and pits together with other assets within the St Leonard's Forest estate; however, John Aldridge specifically kept for his own use and those to whom the lease would revert, the right to 'dig and carry away any quantity of stone from the quarry on Barnsnap Hill for their own use and not for sale'. This quarry, also known as Great Ground, was situated south of Colgate near Springfield farm, one of the few 18th century farms established in the centre of the Forest on Aldridge land. It must have been a real and sustainable asset to have building stone on an estate for new build or repair.[14]

---

11. Birch, R. (2006) *Sussex Stones, the Story of Horsham Stone and Sussex Marble*, Birch, pp 33-7, and Djabri, S. C. (2008) The Eversfields of Denne House, Part 1, *Horsham Heritage*, Issue No. 17, Autumn, pp. 11-33.

12. Horsfield,1835, p. 222, Cartwright, 1830, p. 365 and Burke, 1852, p24.

13. Lewis, S. (ed.) (1848) *A Topographical Dictionary of England*, pp. 194-9. Accessible through: http://www.british-history.ac.uk/report.aspx?compid=50789

14. HM, MS 1200.

The Forest does appear to have been pitted by a variety of diggings from the 19th century. An OS map from 1879 gives good detail of old gravel pits, quarries and sand pits. As they are specifically marked as 'old' one could assume they were out of use by the late 19th century. An example of an old clay pit can be seen identified to the west of the Windmill Burrow, and east of Colgate, see illustration 24: page 57. There are three old gravel pits identified, one at Leonardslee, one across the road at South Lodge, and one in Holmbush - all three estates had large gardens in which the gravel would have been of great use. One sand pit can be identified south of New Lodge in the parkland and another in the Forest itself. There is an old quarry marked to the east of Carters Lodge and another east of French Bridge and Hawkins Pond, and another south of Hammer Pond, all near the road from Horsham to Cowfold, and so they could have been used for road stone or building stone.

Iron bearing ore had been dug from the Forest in the 16th and 17th centuries to fuel the local iron manufacture, and so the remains of these mine pits would have been clearly visible in the 19th century Forest landscape. The 2011 Lidar survey picked these up well and identified 28 sites of mine pits, which were particularly dense around the Colgate area. Mine pits can be identified as small deep pits with rounded spoil heaps in a horseshoe shape around the edge, and the Lidar results indicate that they were dug surprisingly close together.

Clay outcrops also occurred in the Forest, and so brickmaking was another Forest resource which impacted on the landscape. As early as 1584 a clamp of bricks was burnt in St Leonard's Forest and used both for building Gosden Furnace and for building the house of its ironmaster, Roger Gratwick. There is however no evidence as to where exactly this clay was dug from in the forest or where the bricks were burnt. There was a brickyard at Plummers Plain on the edge of the Leonardslee estate in 1803 which lasted about 80 years, and another at Crabtree, further south, in 1816. By the later 19th century a brickyard had been established in the centre of Lower Beeding village, but the most well-known brickyard was on the Holmbush estate. It seems likely that although the clay was a local natural resource, it was not until the growing pressure of population, the subsequent need for houses and the fashion for brick-built houses that these brickyards developed.[15]

Rabbits and Wastes

In 1813, the Rev. Arthur Young published his report on agriculture in Sussex for the Board of Agriculture for the purpose of improving agricultural yields. It is useful to see how he described the landscape of St Leonard's Forest at the turn of the 19th century, although it must be remembered that he was an agriculturalist and saw no value in forest and heath. A fold out sketch of the soil of Sussex shows the Wealden Forest Ridge as sand and waste, and within that a large oval east of Horsham where St Leonard's Forest is situated labelled 'waste'. Indeed, writing about this area he estimated that St Leonard's Forest had 10,000 acres of 'poorest barren sand'. He noted that the depth of the sand on

15. Beswick, M. (1993,2001) *Brickmaking in Sussex, A History and Gazetteer*, Midhurst: Middleton Press, pp 181-2.

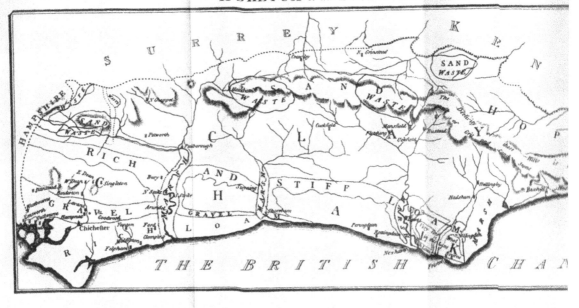

19. A Sketch of the Soil of Sussex showing 'waste' to the east of Horsham, reproduced from frontispiece of Young, A (1813,1970) *General View of the Agriculture of the County of Sussex*, Newton Abbot: David & Charles Reprints. By kind permission of David & Charles.

the rabbit warrens varied from 12 inches in many places to several feet in depth around Handcross, south-east of the Forest. However, he did also record that birch, hazel and beech, and other undergrowth, provided some profit.[16]

In his chapter on 'Wastes', Young did wonder why such immense tracts of land, intersected by turnpike roads and only 35 to 45 miles from London, were left unimproved. He recommended paring and burning and cited the Petworth estate as an example, in which 'an entire forest scene … of no kind of use' was improved to produce 'extraordinary fine crops of wheat and oats'. He gave another example of improvement nearer to St Leonard's Forest in Tilgate Forest where six acres of land which had been a rabbit warren, were turned over to more profitable potatoes. Young was certainly not an advocate of rabbits; he wrote that they were a nuisance to the county and flourished in proportion to the size of the wastes. He added that from Horsham Forest and Ashdown Forest considerable quantities of rabbits were sent to London. This confirmed that at the beginning of the 19th century the landscape of the forest was still unimproved barren heathland, used mainly as rabbit warrens.[17]

16. Young, A. (1813, 1970) *General View of the Agriculture of the County of Sussex*, Devon, David & Charles Reprints, pp 8-9 (hereafter Young, 1813).

17. Young, 1813, pp. 187-190, 391.

20. Pillow mound forming part of boundary bank, cover photograph from Lidar- enhanced Archaeological Survey of St Leonard's Forest, West Sussex, June 2011. With kind permission of Chris Butler Archaeological Services Ltd.

In the summer of 1823, William Cobbett rode south from Crawley town and then west towards Horsham on his rural rides. He memorably wrote that he had just ridden 'over six of the worst miles in England, which miles terminate but a few hundred yards before you enter Horsham'. He then described the ride, which went through the Buchan Hill and Holmbush estate, through the northern part of St Leonard's Forest and across the remains of Horsham Common, which had been enclosed ten years previously. Cobbett noted positively that the land was elevated, which meant he could see the North Downs, Blackdown and the South Downs, and which also indicated that the forest must have been reasonably clear of trees, despite Lord Erskine's tree planting projects in the previous decade.

Brought up on a Surrey farm, William Cobbett moved from soldier to political journalist to radical commentator with much to say about the agrarian changes to the landscape that he saw in his rural rides through the southern counties of England. It is worth quoting Cobbett at length, as his descriptions are very valuable as a first-hand report of what the landscape of St Leonard's Forest was like in the first two decades of the 19th century.

'The first two of these miserable miles go through the estate of Lord Erskine. It was bare heath with here and there, in the better parts of it, some scrubby birch. It has been, in part, planted with fir-trees, which are as ugly as the heath was; and, in short, it is a most villainous tract. After quitting it, you enter a forest; but a most miserable one; and this is followed by a large common, now enclosed, cut up, disfigured, spoiled, and the labourers all driven from its skirts. I have seldom travelled over eight miles so well calculated to fill the mind with painful reflections.'[18]

One is left in little doubt that this was not desirable land; it was bare, scrubby and above all 'miserable'. It was poor arable land but rabbits had been a profitable resource in this Forest heathland and a passing comment from Cobbett while he was visiting Romney Marsh provided an indication of another useful product of the Forest, that of young cattle. While on the Marsh he was impressed with the sight of red, loose-limbed Sussex cat-

18. Cobbett, W. (1830,1979) *Rural Rides*, Harmondsworth: Penguin Books Ltd., p. 113.

tle, and marvelled that from Ashdown Forest and 'Saint Leonard's Forest, to which latter Lord Erskine's estate belongs, these wretched tracts and the not much less wretched farms' breed the cattle that fatten on the Marsh'. He described how the cattle calve in the spring, are weaned on grass then put on stubble and fallow land, spend the winter in the yard on rough hay, pea husks and barley straw, and then graze the next two or

21. Picture of a rabbit as illustrated in Memoirs of British Quadrupeds, by William Bingley, 1809, p 426.

three summers in the Forest, before going to Romney Marsh or other places with better pasture to be fattened up for slaughter. Such grazing in the forest would have maintained the open heathland and been operated by the farms on the edge of St Leonard's Forest, and presumably in conjunction with some of the remaining warrens.[19]

An indication of the presence of rabbit warrens in the Forest was given by the 1614 story of the dragon, or worm, in the forest eating rabbits from a nearby warren. Place names on old maps such as at Windmill Burrow near Colgate on Forest Road is also a clear indication of a warren. However, there is solid archival evidence of the presence of warrens in the Deputation of Gamekeepers records of the 1780s. Evidence also comes from leases and legal documents where property is described. For example, the 1801 Head Lease from John Aldridge to George Railton and William Hulls mentions the Great Warren and Plummers Plain Warren, with rights to kill rabbits and conies. As noted previously, the 1799 advertisement in the *Oracle and Daily Advertiser* for this same land itemised warren houses and three extensive warrens in a 30-acre enclosure which produced 1,200 dozen conies a year. To the north of the Forest in the sales particulars of 1787 it was noted that part of Little Bewbush and Hopper Farms was a rabbit warren of 1,597 acres with warren houses. In 1819 Lord Erskine sold part of Holmbush and Shelley, 1,460 acres in total, to William Sadler with sitting tenants. Amongst these sitting tenants were Charles Bartloy in Shelley Farm with a warren, and Richard Tester in a lodge house, with lands, grounds and a warren; he was also in occupation of Sibbalds Field Farm and warren.[20]

The Lidar-enhanced archaeological survey of St Leonard's Forest confirms that there is substantial evidence of the Great Warren in the central part of the Forest. Despite past and more recent destruction by heavy forestry machinery, 15 pillow mounds and associated warren enclosures were identified. Although it is difficult to imagine today, this does

19. Cobbett, p 190, and Webb, N. (1986) *Heathlands*, London, Collins, pp. 46-8 (hereafter Webb, 1986).

20. BL, MS 5685, and HM, MS 3142 and WSRO Add MS 22,961, and *Oracle and Daily Advertiser* (London) Saturday, June 29 1799, Issue 22023.

confirm the archival evidence that in the late 17th and 18th centuries the central part of St Leonard's Forest was open heathland managed for rabbit production in warren enclosures by skilled warreners. New agricultural techniques and crops were being introduced to raise productivity, and rabbit farming could be considered a viable option on poor soils. However, by the late 18th century warrens were being taken out of use due to several factors: lower prices for rabbit meat and fur, due to the increased availability of wild rabbits and cheap imported fur, and improved agricultural and forestry practices which allowed more marginal land to become economically viable.[21]

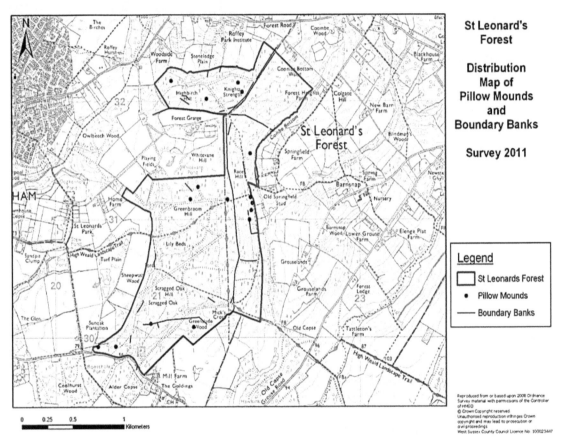

22. Distribution map of pillow mounds and boundaries from Lidar- enhanced Archaeological Survey of St Leonard's Forest, West Sussex, June 2011. Figure 15 p 49. With kind permission of Chris Butler Archaeological Services Ltd.

Rabbits were initially a high maintenance stock, coming as they did with the Romans from a Mediterranean climate. They were susceptible to damp and cold, the quality of the meat and fur being dependent on dry weather, with rabbits responding surprisingly quickly to spells of good weather. Warreners dug ditches and erected banks and walls in order

21. Williamson, T. (2007) *Rabbits, Warrens & Archaeology*, Stroud: Tempus Publishing Ltd., pp. 18-9. (Hereafter Williamson, 2007) and Sheail, J. (1971) *Rabbits and their history*, London: David & Charles Ltd., pp. 74-100 (Hereafter Sheail, 1971) and Sheail, J. (1978) Rabbits and agriculture in post-medieval England, *Journal of Historical Geography*, 4, pp. 343-55.
22. Sheail, 1971, pp 17-71.

to deflect water, encourage drainage, and keep the rabbits as dry as possible. These earthworks also protected the rabbits by keeping them within the warren and deterring their many natural predators, such as foxes, stoats, cats, hawks and rats. Rabbits took time to settle into a warren and so warreners assisted them through the construction of pillow mounds within the warren, which were low mounds of soft earth. These were mostly post-medieval and some had specific uses such as maternity units, but mostly they encouraged the rabbits in their initial burrowing while protecting the animals from wind and rain. They also made it easier to harvest the rabbits, as deep burrows could be a problem for warrener and ferret or dog, and 'purse' nets could easily be put over the burrow entrance, or long nets put the whole length of the pillow mound, between the mound and the warren wall.[22]

23. Photograph of remains of a pillow mound, from Lidar- enhanced Archaeological Survey of St Leonard's Forest, West Sussex, June 2011, Photo 6, p. 21. With kind permission of Chris Butler Archaeological Services Ltd.

Pillow mounds were more common in the south and west of Britain, and were usually constructed on sloping ground and at right angles to the contours. They could be single or in groups, conjoined or not, some being rectangles, and some having flat tops. There were local variations, and Sussex appears to have had some very long pillow mounds - Williamson states that these were mostly more than 50 metres in length and in some cases over 200 metres. Tebbutt, in observing earthworks which he identified as pillow mounds on Ashdown Forest, wrote that a typical example was long and straight, or slightly curved, a bank thrown up between two ditches, about two foot in height and 22 feet in depth and

23. Williamson, 2007, p. 94 and Tebbutt, C.F. (1968) Rabbit Warrens on Ashdown Forest, *Sussex Notes and Queries*, Vol

up to 150 yards long (137 metres). Tebbutt also suggested that the shape was due to the method of taking the rabbits and thought the long banks were associated with the traditional long rabbit nets which were set up at night between the rabbit feeding grounds and the burrows. An interesting feature on an early OS map of 1875 clearly shows pillow mounds to the east of Colgate, just north of the Horsham to Pease Pottage road, and identified as Windmill Burrow. Four mounds radiate out from a central point, and the whole measures approximately 100 metres by 75. [23]

Until this century there was limited archaeological identification of pillow mounds within St Leonard's Forest despite archival evidence of warrens from the 17th century. The nearest identified ones appear to be at Windmill Burrow near Colgate, see illustration 24: page 57, and at Oldhouse Warren in Tilgate Forest, to the east of St Leonard's Forest, according to OS Explorer map 134, Crawley and Horsham, at TQ 295343. However, with the Lidar-enhanced archaeological survey completed in June 2011 pillow mounds were identified within the modern boundaries of St Leonard's Forest. Much of the area surveyed covered the central part of the Great Warren, between Hammerpond Road to the south and Forest Road to the north. Unusually, boundary banks or walls that defined and divided the warren were identified, as well as the pillow mounds, although survival of earthworks regarded as warren boundaries of the Great Warren were noted in the VCH by referral to 1981 OS map and grid references given.[24]

Interestingly, a unique circular pillow mound was identified, of 148 metres in circumference with a pronounced bank of the uphill side of about one and a half metres high, and a ditch one metre wide. This was an isolated pillow mound in the south east of the area at OS reference TQ213300, and one wonders whether this could be a maternity unit, away from bucks which could kill the young, and protective of the valuable does from predators and where the nets for culling would not apply. Another pillow mound was found built into a boundary bank with rounded top, approximately 26 metres long with ditches one metre wide. Four pillow mounds were found together on very steeply sloping land which dropped away to the eastern boundary of the survey area, running down to Combe Bottom, which could hardly have been used for anything else. These were found to be 34 to 45 metres long and up to one and a half metres high and between three and four metres wide with flat tops, and nearby were enclosing warren walls which the researchers regarded as unusual to find in south east England.[25]

The landscape of the forest was certainly altered by the husbandry of rabbit production in the throwing up of banks, ditches and pillow mounds, and the building of warren lodges and the establishment of place names associated with warrens.

Lodges were tall remote buildings standing at the highest point of the warren to allow the warrener good oversight of his charges. Inside were kept nets, traps and guns, racks for drying rabbit skins and food for the rabbits in winter. Shakespeare uses the simile 'as

17, pp 52-4.

24. Hudson T.P. (ed.) (1987) Forest, *The Victoria History of the County of Sussex* Vol VI Pt 3., The Institute of Historical Research by Oxford University Press, p 15 (hereafter VCH Vol VI.3).

25. Lidar survey 2011.

26. Shakespeare 'Much Ado about Nothing' Act 2 Scene 1.

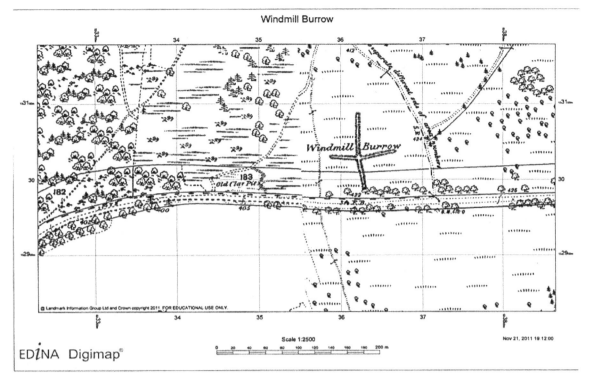

EDINA Digimap©

24. Windmill Burrow, Colgate, OS County Series 1:2500 1st Edition, 1875, reproduced by kind permission of Edina Historic Digimap.

melancholy as a lodge in a warren' although he may have had in mind the lonely isolated lodges of Breckland in Norfolk rather than Sussex lodges, but those in St Leonard's Forest would have stood alone.[26] The Gardner and Gream map of 1795, see illustration 29: page 72, shows two Lodge Houses in the Forest, one to the south east, the other to the north west, and these may well have been the old warren lodge houses. The one in the south east appears to be Carter's Lodge in the later maps. Edward Carter, husband of Elizabeth Aldridge, built a new brick house at this site probably around the time of the Gardner and Gream map, and this survives to the present day. The one in the north was renamed Rangers Lodge at some point, although this lodge disappeared in the 19th century.

The landscape of St Leonard's Forest has accumulated some place names that are resonant of rabbit husbandry. Generally, these names can vary from the straight forward 'warren', which is the post-medieval name for a place of rabbit farming, to the older 'coneygarth', and variations of this such as 'coneygres', 'coneygar' or 'cunygre'. For example, Coneycroft Wood in Warnham, previously Conyefelde', and Coneyburrow Shaw in Mayfield, were clearly places of rabbit farming. Pillow mounds were commonly called 'berries', 'buries' or 'burrows' by the 16th Century and so these names too could be applied to certain areas used for rabbit farming, such as Windmill Burrow near Colgate, although such place names often refer to nearby earthworks which are not necessarily pillow mounds. Gelling, in her books on place names, suggests the derivation of the Old English

27. Glover, J. (1997) *Sussex Place-Names*, Newbury, Countryside Books, p 57 and Gelling, M. (1984) *Place-Names in the Landscape*, London, J.M. Dent & Sons., pp 127-8.

28. VCH VI.3, p 15.

'beorg', or the Anglian 'berg', means hill or mound, and warns of the similarity to other words of different meaning. Apart from Windmill Burrow which has now disappeared from 20th and 21st Century maps, St Leonard's Forest has two other place names suggesting rabbit husbandry. One is Warren Wood to the south of the current Forest and originally central, unsurprisingly adjacent to Carter's Lodge,[27] and the other one is Hole Warren which was the known name of a field near Lower Beeding in 1838.[28]

The impact of rabbits on the Forest landscape could also be seen in the presence of certain herbs and plants. Rabbits avoid plants that are woody, hairy, spiky, stinging or poisonous, and they enjoy young plants, seedlings and the bark of young saplings. They will intensively graze clover and trefoil to extinction, and to the benefit of bracken, nettles and other tough plants. A sufficiency of the right food was therefore a problem for the warreners, particularly in winter, as rabbits could easily die in a hard winter, thus reducing their profits and pride in their husbandry. One way of increasing the quality and quantity of grass was to pare the turf from the ground and burn it in heaps, the ash then being spread on the earth. Crops could be grown for a short rotation, and then grass put down again. This method could double the number of rabbits in an area and there is some evidence that burning of turf was normal practice in St Leonard's Forest in the 17th century, with fires sometimes getting out of control.[29]

Rabbits were normally killed at the end of the year when their fur was thickest, the silver-grey being the most prized and interbreeding discouraged while the price of this fur was high. Silver-greys were bred mainly in Lincolnshire. Black rabbits were also bred for their fashionable fur, although the common grey fur was popular as it was cheap and could be treated by taking off the skin and napping. Sheail wrote that in Sussex rabbits were killed in August, before their fur could develop a thick coat, because there was usually not enough food to keep them until their fur was ready. They were thus called flesh warrens as the rabbits could only be sold for meat. Rabbits often went hungry in winter and spring and could make a nuisance of themselves on nearby agricultural land, although it was only from the late 18th century that they began to be viewed as a pest.[30]

A newspaper report from January 1814 commented on the extremely severe weather and wrote that a Member of Parliament travelling though Sussex from London had stated that 'The wild rabbits in St Leonard's Forest in great numbers were standing more like sheep, eating hay near the road', one can assume that the rabbits from the warrens were now wild and having to fend for themselves in harsh winters.[31]

The devaluing of the rabbit warrens occurred partly due to rabbits becoming better adapted to the climate and countryside and establishing wild warrens, and partly due to foreign cheap imports of fur. Rackham wrote that the price of a rabbit had fallen from

29. The National Archives (TNA) E134/36Chas2/East22.

30. Sheail, 1971, pp 74-103.

31. *The Morning Post*, Wednesday 19 January 1814, Issue 13415.

32. Rackham, O. (1986) *The History of the Countryside*, London, Dent & Sons Ltd., pp 47-8, and Sheail, 1971, pp 78-81.

33. HM MSS 1200, 1200A, 3119.

34 HM MSS 3142, 3143.1, 3143.2.

seven pence in 1600, half a daily wage, to five pence, about one fifth of the daily wage, by 1760, and that in the 19th century they became even cheaper, as tariff reforms allowed the import of cheap rabbits from Belgium. Sheail quoted from the 1872-3 House of Commons Select Committee which reported 'both high and low now use rabbits; it is quite an everyday dish in every house'. Landowners therefore began to consider other ways of using their land, and trees for timber were becoming a viable alternative. It is difficult to know exactly when and how the warrens in St Leonard's Forest were abandoned or broken down, but it is likely to have happened by the turn of the 19th century.[32]

Archival evidence shows that at the start of the 19th century parts of the Great Warren were being parcelled up and leased out with permission given to kill and destroy all the conies and rabbits on the premises. In 1807 John Watling of Lambeth sublet to Lawrence Coddington Worthy of Middlesex 480 acres of Great Warren known as the Rangers House. Permission was given for a road to be laid and it is clear some further division of the Forest had taken place, as the lease mentioned land divided by rail and post from that in the occupation of a Charles Bartlett, and from a plantation of fir trees belonging to Stone Lodge, and from other pieces of land that were occupied by a Mr Wilcoke, John Watling and Mrs Aldridge. These sections of land were all fenced off from one another, and the requirement of a 'good and sufficient hedge' was recommended to be established between them.[33]

In 1811 there was an assignment of the original lease of 3,000 acres in the centre of the Forest to eight London merchants. All of these were corn merchants, apart from one timber merchant, Baker, and Peter Barlow from the City. After some of these merchants went bankrupt, further agreement was made for the assignment of the whole lease to this Peter Barlow, and it was subsequently inherited by his three daughters, Abigail, Elizabeth and Sarah in 1837. It is interesting that London corn and timber merchants were involved in dividing up parts of the Forest. This was either purely financial business or they were interested in profiting from the small amount of existing timber, as it seems unlikely that there would be any prospect of arable crops being grown in any quantity or quality. More likely was the growing attraction for small farms and estates as prospects for a home within easy reach of London. By the mid-19th century the Forest was beginning to be considered as a quiet secluded attractive place to live.[34]

Fir plantations were beginning to be established by the first decade of the 19th century. Dorothea Hurst wrote in the 1860s that 'many years ago there was an avenue of firs called Mike (or Mick) Mills Race about three quarters of a mile in length. It stood on high ground, and was a remarkable feature in the country'. She described how it was nearly destroyed by a violent hurricane on 29th November 1836. She also quoted from an 'older publication' called *The Mirror*, no date given, which reported a 'beautiful avenue a mile and a quarter long, containing 15,000 full grown trees'.[35] Ellis, in referencing *Murray's A Hand Book for Travellers in Kent and Sussex* wrote that the principal avenue in the Forest was Mick Mills Race and the 15,000 trees were 80 years old, the older avenue having been entirely destroyed. Ellis also repeated the myth of racing the mile, but with a different twist to that

---

35. Hurst, D. (1868) *Horsham: it's History and Antiquities*, William Macintosh, pp. 160-2.

noted in Chapter 2, which was that Mike Mills ran for a wager and dropped dead at the end of the race. This has slightly more credibility than racing the devil and winning. There is the suggestion that the avenue was in fact planted by Michael Mills who was recorded in that area of the Forest in 1720. This seems likely, but no reason for the planting was given, so perhaps there is a grain of truth in racing for wagers.[36] Burstow recounts in his diaries of witnessing horse racing in the Forest, but at a much later date and situated to the west of New Lodge. However, other races or sports were possibly the origin of such a feature, such as those held at Robert Aldridge's coming of age celebrations at New Lodge.[37]

William Cobbett noted in 1823 after riding over Lord Erskine's estate of Bewbush and Holmbush in the north of the Forest that 'It has been, in part, planted with fir-trees, which are as ugly as the heath was' which indicates that by that time some planting of fir had been completed. When 3,033 acres of Holmbush was bought by Thomas Broadwood after Erskine's death in 1822, he began the creation of a new house, gardens and pleasure grounds. Horsfield noted in 1835 that firs grew pretty well on the land, and that the landscape scenery has been greatly improved. By the 1850s when Burke made his 'visitations' to this estate, he wrote that 'the owner has at different periods planted more than a million trees – larch, fir, oak, sweet chestnut, and other varieties'. So, there was considerable planting of trees in the northern part of the Forest in the first decades of the 19th century.[38]

At this time there were still old pollards of oak and beech left in the centre of the Forest, specifically around the south end of Mick Mills Race. Hurst notes that at the time of her writing in the 1860s there were some 'magnificent beech trees and fine oaks' still remaining, and she singles out the 'splendid tree called the 'Sun Oak' by the lodge' which was at the southern entrance to the Aldridge estate. It is still standing today, with a girth of 8.9 metres and therefore an approximate age of 835 years (see frontispiece).[39] Richard Mabey in his book *Flora Britannica* mentions cycling past the Sun Oak on his way to Collyer's School in Horsham, and noting how amazing it was in the summer. He had read in the West Sussex County Times that it got its name from its enormous rounded crown.[40]

36. Knight, J. (2006) *Horsham's History, Volume 1 Prehistory to 1790AD*, Horsham: Horsham District Council, p. 65 and Ellis, Parks and Forests, footnote 111.

37. Albery, W. (ed.)(1975) *Reminiscences of Horsham being Recollections of Henry Burstow*, Norwood, USA: Norwood Editions, pp. 30-3.

38. Horsfield, 1835, p 222-3 and Burke, B. (1852) *A Visitation of the Seats and Arms of the Noblemen and Gentlemen of Great Britain and Ireland*, Vol 1, London, Colburn, p 24, and HM MS 3119.

39. Woodland Trust Ancient Tree inventory and ready reckoner for aging UK Oak species, and email exchange with Dr. Sarah MacKenzie, University of Sussex, 4.11.2011.

40. Mabey, R. (1998) *Flora Britannica, The Concise Edition*, London, Chatto & Windus, p. 87.

English Oak with acorns, *Quercus robur* by Dr Maggie Weir-Wilson.

Chapter 4

Routeways and Trade

Routeways

Routeways, the footpaths and lanes through the Forest, were always an important means of communication for trade and commerce. Thus, they impacted on the development of the market town of Horsham on the Forest's western edge, which in turn contributed to the traffic though the Forest and the value placed on Forest land and resources. Chatwin and Gardiner suggested that patterns of communication such as routeways were also indicative of the differing patterns of woodland development and exploitation. It is therefore useful to consider what roads and footpaths crossed and came near to the Forest as part of the development of the Forest and its hinterland. It is clear that the underlying geology and topography of the forest ridge was crucial in finding passable routes through the Forest. However, drove roads from the south were stopping short of the Forest, which indicates the lack of a medieval manor and traditional outlier (woodland pasture) system which drove animals from lower to higher pasture and woodland. Cattle were becoming an important aspect of the Horsham markets, but arrived by hoof to the north-west of Horsham from Wales. For a period of time they were an economically important trade for the area.[1]

The existence of gates indicates passages, footpaths and tracks through the Forest linking, or passing through, the walks or enclosed bailiwicks. These would have developed for both economic and social purposes. Perhaps the oldest route through the Forest was identified by Margary as Track VI: Ashdown Forest –Turners Hill – Pease Pottage – Horsham Ridgeway. Margary identified it as a Roman track and probably a pre-Roman hard greenway track along the forest Ridgeway which had been used for centuries and improved by the Romans. It branched at Turners Hill to run past Worth Priory and through St Leonard's Forest, east to west from Pease Pottage to Colgate and Horsham, and possibly on to Denne Park. Margary suggested that these types of tracks were thoroughfares, linked to a network of tracks, and used to gain access to the forest iron ore.[2] Peter Brandon in his book *The Sussex Landscape* wrote of drove roads coming up from Washington to the Crockhurst swine pastures south of Horsham, and his map of old droving roads shows the linking of Upper Beeding through Henfield and Cowfold to its outlier at Lower Beeding. It is thought these routes were used for pannage, the fattening of pigs on acorn and beech mast in the Forest and wood pasture, and for driving livestock to markets.[3]

---

1. Chatwin, D. and Gardiner, M. (2005) Rethinking the early medieval settlement of woodlands: evidence from the western Sussex Weald. *Landscape History, Journal of the Society for Landscape Studies.* Vol 27, pp. 31-49. (hereafter Chatwin and Gardiner, 2005).

2. Margary, I.D. (1965) *Roman Ways in the Weald.* London: Phoenix House, p. 258 (hereafter Margary, 1965).

3. Brandon, P. (1974) *The Sussex Landscape.* London: Hodder and Stoughton, pp. 72-75.

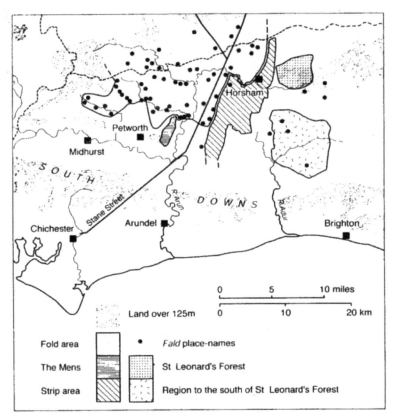

25. Map reproduced from Chatwin & Gardiner article in Landscape History, Vol 27, page 45, 2005, 'Rethinking the early medieval settlement of woodlands' Fig 9 Areas of settlement in the western Sussex Weald. With kind permission of Dr Mark Gardiner. Note 'The Mens' is an ancient woodland in the Low Weald. Fald or Fold place names identified such as Slinfold, Cowfold, Alfold, Kingsfold.

However, Chatwin and Gardiner suggest that there is not a one-size-fits-all theory of woodland development and it is not necessarily the case that woodland was developed as part of the outlier, or outpost, of a manor, and thus subject to grazing by cattle and pigs from that distant manor. They suggest that the pattern of drove roads from the coast to Horsham was influenced by the fact that St Leonard's Forest was high open heathland with poor soil and thus undesirable as an outpost for grazing, hence the drove roads stopped in the more fertile region at the southern outer boundary of the forest. Chatwin and Gardiner's map of areas of settlement and woodland development in the western Sussex Weald, see illustration 25: above, shows a 'strip' area running north-easterly up to Horsham, which would have been a typical linear field system of arable strips and lanes. The 'fold' areas were less planned than the manorial open field system and formed by an older settled landscape of common grazing, fields, wooded areas and roads. The area to the south of St Leonard's Forest was characterised by the north-south drove roads leading to the edge of the forest and fields generally aligned north-south.[4]

4. Chatwin and Gardiner, 2005.

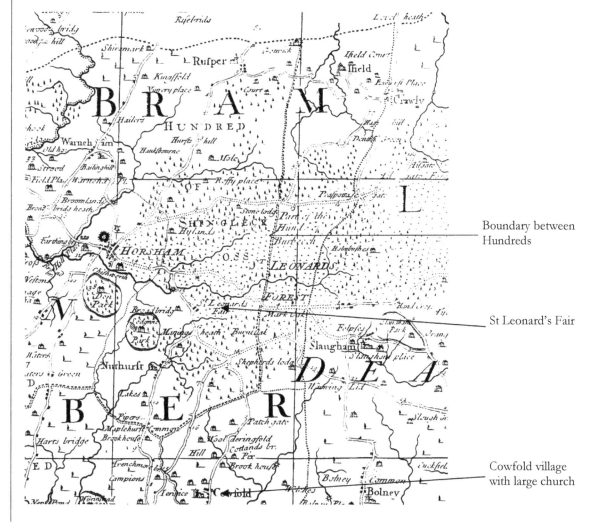

Boundary between
Hundreds

St Leonard's Fair

Cowfold village
with large church

26. Detail showing position of St Leonard's Fair on the southern edge of St Leonard's Forest, from Richard Budgen's map of 1724. Original scale: 1" to 1 mile. (Margary, 1970, plate 6). By kind permission of Harry Margary, editor, at www.harrymargary.com

The routes through the Forest and up from the coast would have been used for all sorts of trade. Horsham town was growing in importance as a market town in the medieval period, and there is archive evidence, again from the accounts of Thomas Att Knepp, that as a Ranger he received tolls and dues from a fair held on the feast day of the saint in St Leonard's Forest itself. The fair was originally held on St Leonard's Day, 6th November, in 1438 and 1441, according to records, and it was thought that this was mainly for the sale of horses.

It seems that the time of year and site of the fair changed over time, with cattle superseding horses in importance. Richard Budgen's map, produced in 1724, clearly shows that the site of the fair in the early 18th century was at the south-west edge of the Forest. This accords with the Pawlett mortgage document of 1720 referred to earlier, which places the fair on land called Russels near Hammer Pond House, in all probability next to the Hammer Pond in the south of the Forest. The village further south of the Forest called Cowfold perhaps gave credence to the movement and importance of cattle to be marketed in this area. Knight suggests that the size of the church in Cowfold underlined the economic importance of cattle and noted that they came from as far away as Wales to the yearly fair.[5]

Brandon described no drove roads travelling from the west to the east which clearly there would have been to drive cattle from Wales to the Weald. However, Roland Harris' map produced for the High Weald AONB organisation in his research document '*The Making of the High Weald*' does show a limited number of old track ways crossing both east -west and north-south over the Weald, see illustration 27: below.

Paul Hindle in his slim volume *Medieval Roads and Tracks* identified distinctive drove roads across Britain, which show on aerial photography as sinuous wide roads and multiple track ways. He based his speculative maps on Roman roads, contemporary maps and market towns. However, Chatwin and Gardiner are not convinced by the supposed alignment of Roman and drove roads with prehistoric tracks. They note a more significant relationship between Roman roads and drove roads but suggest the exact relationship remains uncertain. [6] Witney, in his study of the Kent Jutish Forest, suggested that prehistor-

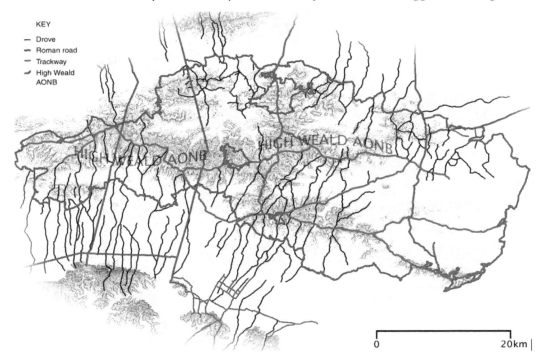

KEY
— Drove
— Roman road
— Trackway
— High Weald AONB

27. Map of early routes in the High Weald Fig 7., p. 22, reproduced from Harris, R.B., Nov 2003 version 2.2 '*The Making of the High Weald*'. Accessible through www.highweald.org

5 Knight, J. (2006) *Horsham's History Vol I Prehistory to 1790 AD*. Horsham District Council, p. 62.

6. Hindle, P. (2002) *Medieval Roads and Tracks*, Princes Risborough: Shire Publications, pp. 14-16, 35, and Chatwin and Gardiner, 2005, p. 38.

28. Driving Welsh Black Cattle. With kind permission of the Welsh Black Cattle Society.

ic tracks could be surmised from parish or hundred boundaries due to the fact that settlement in the Weald came later than the Forest droves. However, he noted that most radiated from centres of population, and few were east-west as there was little use for these, apart from those on drier ridges which would have been well used.[7]

It seems likely that the driving of cattle from the Welsh borders to Sussex has had a long history perhaps due to the fact that William de Braose, due to his military prowess, was granted lands both in the Welsh marches and Sussex by William I after 1066. There would therefore have been traffic of various types between both these areas which were controlled by the same Lord.

It has been pointed out by Moore-Colyer how very difficult it is to identify the movements of Welsh drovers through England, but there are local clues in the wide grass verges, local tales concerning drovers and the numerous 'Welsh' place and field names identifying the original purpose of a droving route.[8] Witney has no mention of Welsh cattle going so far as the Kentish Weald, whether across Sussex or not, before the 14th century.[9] However, Skeel has later evidence of Welsh cattle being sold in Maidstone market in 1686.[10] Rather more sobering evidence, which confirms that the Welsh drovers were indeed in Horsham, is from a burial notice of November 18th 1609 of Roger Lewis, 'a Welchman, a drover of cattle'. The reason of death is not given but a sad event so far from home.[11]

William Cobbett, travelling between Cricklade and Cirencester on his rural rides between 1821 and 1832, reported seeing 'in separate droves, about two thousand Welsh Cattle on their way from Pembrokeshire to the fairs in Sussex, the greater parts of them were heifers in calf.[12] This would indicate a fairly continuous traditional trade. Skeel quotes a fascinating oral history from a Mr Edward Browne of Albury Heath, south-east of Guild-

7. Witney, 1976 Witney, K.P. (1976) *The Jutish Forest, A Study of the Weald of Kent from 450 to 1380 AD*. London: The Athlone Press, pp. 29,30. (hereafter).

8. Moore-Colyer, R (1974) *Welsh Cattle Drovers in the Nineteenth Century – 2*. National Library of Wales Journal, Summer 1974, Vol. XVIII/3. No page numbers. Extracted onto pages of GENUKI by Gareth Hicks April 2003. Accessible through: www.genuki.org.uk. (hereafter Moore-Colyer, 1972).

9 Witney,1976 pp. 29,30.

10. Skeel, C. (1926) *The Cattle Trade between Wales and England from the Fifteenth to the Nineteenth Centuries*. Transactions of the Royal Historical Society. Fourth Series, *Vol. 9*, pp. 135-158. (hereafter Skeel, 1926).

11. Garraway Rice, R. (ed.) (1915) *The Parish Register of Horsham in the County of Sussex, 1541-1635, and 1635-1753 Burials*, *Sussex Record Society, Vol. XXI* (hereafter Garraway Rice, 1915) – there are two more entries for Welshmen, a John Williams and Hugh Bowen in April and November, 1586, although neither are identified as drovers.

12. Cobbett, W. (1893) *Rural Rides During the Years 1821 to 1832: with economical and political observations. A new edition with notes*. London: Reeves & Turner. Accessible through: www.archive.org.

ford, whose father and grandfather remembered the droves in which 500 or 600 small black Welsh cattle came over from the direction of the Hogs Back, now the A31, and travelled eastward till all were sold. It was suggested that from Albury Heath the drove would go east to Dorking or south to Horsham.

In considering the route that could have been taken, a place name clue can be seen on OS 145 Explorer map 2007 at TQ 095437: a Radnor Road, Radnorshire now being part of Powys, bordering England. At Ewhurst there are the remains of a Roman road, a branch road off Stane Street which links to the north of Horsham. Margary says there were several ancient trackways around this branch road, one going northward from Farley Heath to Albury and Newlands Corner.[13] Moore-Colyer was able to identify, from 19th century drovers' account books, the drove routes taken by a David Johnathon of Dihewyd. This Welshman sold cattle at the fairs of Romford, Brentwood, East Grinstead, Horsham and Kingston, coming down from Reading through Blackwater to Albury, Ewhurst and Horsham.[14] Clearly, a well-used route.

In time the venue for the November St Leonard's cattle and horse fair in the south of the Forest, held from about the 15th century, became a less popular place for a cattle market. This was probably because the cattle would have been driven past, or through, Horsham town, with all the disruption that would cause as the town became busier. The fair and cattle market was first moved to the Common on the south-east side of the town and then when the common was enclosed in the early 19th century the cattle fair moved to the Bishopric, on the Guildford Road and the western edge of the town, nearer the drove roads.

The drovers may have been Welsh speakers, although the language had been suppressed and many English speakers had moved into the Welsh marches diluting it further. However, from Skeel's oral history source comes a wonderful quote which brings alive the drama and noise of the drove, which must have been well known for years to the people of Horsham in the run-up to the fairs and cattle markets:

'The noise consisted of the shouting of the drovers combined, I suppose, with a certain amount of noise from the cattle. But it was the men's voices that chiefly attracted attention. It was something entirely out of the common, neither shouting, calling, crying, singing, halloing or anything else, but a noise in itself, apparently made to carry, and capable of arresting the country-side.'[15]

A glimpse of routeways around Horsham and St Leonard's Forest in the year 1751 comes from the diaries of a Dr John Burton, written by him in Greek and translated by W.H. Blaauw in the mid-19th century. Dr Burton was a tutor in Greek at Oxford University and thereafter a Fellow of Eton College, vicar of Mapledurham, Oxfordshire, and Rector of Worplesham, Surrey. He had reason to travel to Sussex from Oxford in the

13. Margary, 1965, p.86.
14. Moore-Colyer, 1972.
15. Skeel, 1926, pp. 135-158

summer of 1751 as he wished to visit his mother who had remarried to a Dr John Bear, the Rector of Shermanbury, a village situated to the south of the Forest and Cowfold. He travelled by horseback via Henley, Windsor, Hampton Court, and Epsom where he wrote that he stayed with the hospitable Beauclerk family, who were later associated with St Leonard's Forest through their purchase of the southern part of the Aldridge estate. From Box Hill and Leith Hill on the North Downs he came down into Sussex and found roads which were 'most abominable'. Dr Burton described how their horses had difficulty negotiating the muddy tracks, 'sliding and tumbling on their way, and almost on their haunches, with all their haste got on but slowly'.

He and his companion arrived in Horsham which he described, somewhat surprisingly, as 'the metropolis of all in the Weald of Anderida, ancient and populous'. He noted the presence of the County Gaol, Assize Courts and the weekly market where he saw London salesmen buying, with ready cash, many thousand chickens. He also commented on the 'famous' Horsham stone, split and used for house tiles, and the thriving trout in the river Arun. He gives a picture of a prosperous small market town, somewhat cut off by its poor roads from the outside world, but nonetheless attracting wealthy London traders. Dr Burton moved on south from Horsham town and travelled through St Leonard's Forest which he described as 'extensive and easily travelled through', presumably due to its sandy soil, heathland and treeless ridges, after which he found the roads particularly impassable causing 'tumbles and much muddiness'.[16]

Morris noted in the introduction to Celia Fiennes' journals, written during the reign of William and Mary, that the 'worst horror was the liquid mud of Sussex where the Horsham Assizes were held once a year at Midsummer'.[17] The Spring, or Lent Assizes, were originally held in March at either Horsham or East Grinstead, but due to the continuing difficulty of access they were switched in 1735 to be always held at East Grinstead with the summer Assizes being held in alternate years at Horsham and Lewes.[18] In 1752 Horace Walpole had a dreadful experience travelling through Sussex at the height of summer and so wrote that if one loved good roads, conveniences, good inns, plenty of postilions and horses, then never go into Sussex, adding that 'Sussex is a great damper of curiosity'.[19]

Daniel Defoe, living during the same period as Celia Fiennes, added his comments on the state of the roads noting that once he saw a large tree being pulled by 22 oxen and which he suggested would take two or three years to complete its journey through the Weald to the port at Chatham.[20] The Rev. Arthur Young wrote that before 1756 the London to Horsham road was so 'execrably bad that whoever went on wheels, were forced to go round by Canterbury, which is one of the most extraordinary circumstances that the history of non-communication in this kingdom can furnish'.[21] This does seem somewhat

16. Blaauw, W.H. (1856) *Extracts from the 'Iter Sussexiense'* of Dr John Burton, Sussex Archaeological Collections, VIII, pp. 250-265 (hereafter Blaauw, 1856).

17. Morris, C. (ed.) (1947) *The Journeys of Celia Fiennes*, London: The Cresset Press, p. xxxi.

18. Albery, W. (1947) *A Millennium of Facts in the History of Horsham and Sussex 947-1947*, Brighton: Southern Publishing, p. 217 (hereafter Albery, 1947).

19. Brandon, P. (2003) *The Kent and Sussex Weald*. Chichester: Phillimore, p. 178 (hereafter Brandon, 2003)

20. Defoe, D. (1731, 1962) *Tour thro' the whole Island of Great Britain: Divided into Circuits or Journeys* Vol. 1, London: J.M. Dent, pp 128-9

of an exaggeration but the point is thoroughly made that the roads were bad and needed improvement. Brandon suggested that it was the primitive roads that isolated Sussex and made it a self-supporting, rural county with deep roots in Roman and Saxon tradition that lingered to manifest itself in aspects of culture in the late 19th century.[22]

Communications, particularly with the expanding capital of London, were crucial to the economic, social and cultural development of the area. It is clear from these 18th century diary accounts that roads linking Horsham to the outside world would hold back this development if something was not done. It is useful to know from Dr Burton's diary that tracks through the Forest remained dry and manageable in the 1750s due to the underlying geology and topography. The main routes through the Forest commonly used were indicated by Ivan Margary, who, in examining Richard Budgen's map of 1724, noticed small numbers appearing on the map. He doubted that these were milestone indicators and thought that they linked routes, thus he understood them to be recommended routes. Such a recommended route was that from north Horsham to Crawley through the edge of St Leonard's Forest, past Buchan Hill, which was privately turnpiked in 1795. Another recommended route went to East Grinstead from Horsham through Colgate in the Forest and Pease Pottage out through Worth and Crawley Down. This was turnpiked in 1771. A southerly route went from Horsham into the Forest and over the embankments of Hawkins and Hammer ponds, skirting Plummers Plain, and on to Slaugham to link with the London to Brighton road. Parts of this route were turnpiked in 1792.[23]

Gardner and Gream's map of 1795, and the Ordnance Survey Old Series one inch map published in 1813, show that there were in addition to the main routes described above, numerous other pathways or routes through the Forest.[24] The Gardner and Gream map of 1795, see illustration 29: page 72, shows eight paths radiating out from New Lodge, at this time the home of John Clater Aldridge, MP from 1784 to 1790 for Queenborough, a rotten borough on the Isle of Sheppey in Kent, and then MP for Shoreham, Sussex, from 1790 to 1792, he was also the principal storekeeper to HM Ordnance, and died in 1795. The house was inherited by his son, John Aldridge the younger, Captain in the Royal Sussex Militia.

The 1795 map shows one path links to Stone Lodge on the Horsham-Colgate-Pease Pottage main route, whilst another runs across the centre of the Forest linking New Lodge to Lodge House and on to Grouts Gate.[25] Another runs to the south and then loops north to link in with Sandy Gate (spelling unclear) and runs parallel to the previous path. These three routes all end at the London to Brighton road. Most of the paths run south-west to

21. Young, Rev. A. (1813, 1970) *General View of the Agriculture of the County of Sussex*, Newton Abbot: David & Charles Reprints, p.418

22. Brandon, P. (2010) *The Discovery of Sussex*, Chichester: Phillimore & Co. Ltd., p. 9 (hereafter Brandon, 2010).

23. Margary, I.D. (1971) *Traffic Routes in Sussex, 1724, as shown by 'Milestones' on Richard Budgen's Map, Sussex Archaeological Collections*, CIX, pp. 20-3.

24 Margary, H. (ed.) and Skelton, R.A (1970) *Two Hundred and Fifty Years of Maps in the County of Sussex: a collection of reproductions of printed maps published between the years 1575 and 1825*, Kent: Lympne Castle, Maps 16 and 20.

25. Although this is Grouts on the 1795 map, it seems likely that the spelling is in fact Grouse as it is situated on what became known as Grouse Road.

north-east across the Forest, although there are exceptions, one strong diagonal path follows a forest ridge and runs from the north-east at Pease Pottage gate, through Grouts Gate, between the two ponds and ends at the southern road. This cross-Forest route is one of the few that survives into the 21st century as Grouse Road. Another exception is a path that runs north to south from Holmbush, home of William Manners in 1795, south across the Forest, the central straight run being known as Mick Mills' Race, and then running down to meet the southern road near Goldings Farm.

The 1813 Ordnance Survey map, see illustration 30: page 72, shows fewer main pathways or routes but more links between them. On this map the Aldridge mansion of New Lodge, by then the home of John Aldridge the younger's widow, Anna Maria, and his infant son, Robert, has a more formalised parkland with routes across it, and on this 1813 map Stone Lodge remains linked to it. Grouts Gate and Sandy Gate are no longer marked, but Hyde Farm and three enclosures are now shown in the south-east corner, all linked by a cross-forest path to the London-Brighton road. Plummers Plain to the south of the Horsham-Slaugham road is shown as a barren triangle of land with routes around the edge and one diagonally through the middle, below this is a more wooded area with two main routes to Crabtree and Patch Gate, one of which is the Brighton road from Horsham, through Crabtree and Henfield. There are numerous smaller routes through this southern part of the Forest which was later to become known as the Leonardslee estate. Interestingly, the earlier 1795 map shows this area as heathland with small field enclosures to the east and few footpaths, suggesting some consolidation of parcels of land had occurred between 1795 and 1813.

The first Turnpike Act for Sussex was passed in 1696, with a preamble which noted that the road to London through Steyning, Horsham and Crawley was 'very ruinous and almost impassable' and beyond the existing laws for repairing. In the High Weald, roads could be broad tracks, broadening out to find a firm surface and hence often 60 or more feet wide (18 metres). Alternatively, depending on the underlying geology, they could be sunken hollows, the surface having been worn down by heavy wheeled traffic. Repair of roads was the responsibility of the parish through the levying of rates and supply of parish labourers, but lack of skilled workers, funds and lack of suitable hard material, such as limestone and Horsham sandstone, made systematic repair difficult. Iron slag had been used by iron masters to repair roads near them in Tudor times. Burstow (1826-1914) wrote that Horsham stone was plentiful but tended not to be used for road building, presumably as it was more valuable as roof tiles and pavements. He observed that during this early period only the new turnpike roads had hard surfaces and the country lanes were just as diffi-

26. Albery, W. (ed.) (1975) *Reminiscences of Horsham being Recollections of Henry Burstow, The Celebrated Bellringer and Songsinger,* Norwood, Pa (USA): Norwood Editions, p. 19, (hereafter Albery, 1975).

29. Section of plate 16, William Gardner and Thomas Gream Sussex map, scale one inch to one mile, 1795, showing St Leonard's Forest with footpaths and forest ridges shown. Reproduced from Margary, H. & Skelton, R.A.(1970) *Two Hundred and Fifty Years of Map Making in the County of Sussex*. By kind permission of Harry Margary, editor, at www.harrymargary.com

30. Section of plate 20, Ordnance Survey, Old Series one-inch map, scale one inch to one mile, 1813, showing St Leonard's Forest with footpaths and forest ridges shown. Reproduced from Margary, H. & Skelton, R.A. (1970) *Two Hundred and Fifty Years of Map Making in the County of Sussex*. By kind permission of Harry Margary, editor, at www.harrymargary.com

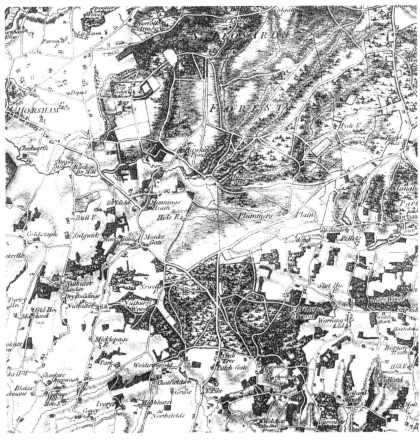

cult to negotiate. This is borne out by the fact that many of the cases coming before the Quarter Sessions in the years 1767 to 1800 concerned the repair of roads.[26]

In response to the awful state of roads came the setting up of turnpike trusts and the building of turnpike roads. This included the building, improvement and maintenance of roads and the subsequent charging of travellers for the new improved road at entrance toll booths. Pawson identified two main periods in the development of turnpikes, 40% of them were laid in the period 1750 to 1770 and the remainder after that. The last turnpikes were created in 1836, and two of these were in Sussex. Adoption of turnpikes tended to be London-centric due to the heavy traffic flow connecting the capital with provincial cities, ports and agricultural markets. However, an incentive to adopt was also due to the pressure on local parishes as internal movements increased, and the advantage of a turnpike trust was that it charged tolls in order to finance road repair, maintenance and improvement.[27]

In early 1755 a Bill was presented in Parliament by Sir Lionel Pilkington, MP for Horsham, requesting leave to improve the Horsham, Warnham, Capel, Dorking, Leatherhead, Epsom road, and which was described in the petition as having become 'ruinous' and, in many parts, very 'narrow and incommodious'. This evidence was accepted, the Bill was granted and a Turnpike Trust appointed.[28] However, there was opposition. The Rev. Arthur Young was astounded that there was opposition to this turnpike, but thought that it would soon be overcome by the rise in farm rents per acre from seven shillings to 11 shillings. A legal Market Deed was drawn up and signed by 80 residents fearing that Horsham market would be bypassed and goods, particularly meat, sold direct from the farm gate.

Ivan Margary noted that turnpikes were initially unpopular, as people were at that time almost free of taxes and restrictions so that the tolls were regarded as irksome and repressive. [29] Knight suggested that this opposition was probably an anxiety due to the lack of financial infrastructure and experience of what was effectively a mortgaged road. [30] Pawson noted that highways had a 'right of passage' for every subject of the Crown and this was a communal property right, nevertheless he found little evidence to support riot and protest against the turnpikes. Young also noted and approved the impact of better communications with London, writing that 'before the communication with London, low rents, low prices, a confined consumption, and no improvements: open the communication, and high rents, high prices, a rapid consumption, and numerous improvements.' He

27. Pawson, E. (1975) The Turnpike Trusts of the Eighteenth Century: A Study in Innovation and Diffusion, Research Paper 14, School of Geography, University of Oxford, pp. 13-35, (hereafter Pawson, 1975).

28. An Act for widening and repairing the Road leading from Horsham in the County of Sussex, through Capel, Dorking, Mickleham and Leatherhead, to the Watch-house in Ebbisham in the County of Surrey; and from Capel to Stone Street, in the Parish of Ockley in the said County of Surrey, 1755, House of Lords Journal Vol. 28, pp. 362 -381. Accessible through: ProQuest House of Commons Parliamentary Papers.

29. Margary, I. (1950) The Development of Turnpike Roads in Sussex, *Sussex Notes and Queries*. XIII, p. 49 (hereafter Margary, 1950).

30 Knight, J. (2006) *Horsham's History Vol 1 Prehistory to 1790AD*, Horsham: Horsham District Council, p. 204, (hereafter Knight, 2006a).

31. Pawson, 1975, pp. 11, 20, and Young, 1813, p 418.

was right on this important economic point with regard to the changes that were coming, not least to the Forest.[31]

The first local turnpike was soon followed by others. Margary saw a pattern in their establishment in Sussex. He identified that the first links were from London to the Assize Towns, such as Horsham. Next were the ones heading to the coastal towns and in particular Brighton. Finally, a network of cross links and, after 1800, schemes became bolder and included new straight lengths and improvement to routes. Pawson wrote that a nationwide turnpike network was recognisable by 1750 and extensive by 1770. Locally, in 1764 the road running from Horsham south of the Forest to Shipley, and on through West Grinstead, Ashurst, Steyning, Bramber and Beeding was turnpiked, connecting the farming hinterland to the market at Horsham. The route through the north of the Forest from Horsham, Colgate and Cuckfield was then turnpiked in 1771, followed by the Brighton road in 1792 which connected Horsham through Crabtree and Henfield to the newly fashionable resort in Brighton. Thereafter the road to Worthing through West Grinstead was turnpiked in 1802 and to Guildford in 1809.[32]

These developments offered opportunities for new residents to settle nearby and so some of the costs of road building were borne by them in order to make their properties more accessible. For example, seven miles of the Horsham to Crawley turnpike, which superseded the 1771 Horsham-Colgate-Cuckfield road, was fully paid for by Thomas Broadwood in 1823. The building of this turnpike was undertaken by J. L. McAdam who was promoted by Thomas Broadwood for his skill and invention in new roadmaking skills. The skill of McAdam was the innovative and economical use of successive layers of small stones to make firm, dry and well drained road beds. Thomas Broadwood subsequently built his mansion called Holmbush House, designed by Francis Edwards, in 1826 on the northern slopes of St Leonard's Forest near the site of an older house. Likewise, the two sons of Sir William Burrell, MP and antiquarian, built fashionable residences at Knepp Castle and West Grinstead Park respectively, after financing the part of the Horsham to Worthing turnpike which allowed them good access to these estates.[33]

The improved turnpike roads made coach travel easier and quicker, and in effect opened up Sussex and Horsham to travellers and commerce. Wheel width was also important as it was now possible to have narrower wheels on coaches carrying people and post much faster on the improved roads, as opposed to the wider wheeled heavier wagons carrying goods. Writing in 1868 Dorothy Hurst noted that for some years the turnpike roads had been very good, and that before the railways several stage coaches passed through Horsham on their way from London to Brighton, London to Worthing and Bognor, and from Brighton to Windsor and Oxford.[34] Indeed, Albery gives more detail: by 1775 there was an early coach from The Talbot in Southwark once a week, another from The Falcon in Southwark three times a week, and a faster earlier coach from The

32. Margary, 1950, pp. 50-1, and Pawson, 1975, p. 34.

33. Albery, 1947, pp. 604-5; Brandon, 2010, pp. 58-9, and Elwes, 1879, p. 28.

34. Hurst, D. (1868) *Horsham: its History and Antiquities*, London: William Macintosh, p. 37 (hereafter Hurst, 1868).

Spreadeagle in the City twice a week. The length of time to get to London from Horsham was about five hours and the price at this time between six and seven shillings. Mail coaches developed faster travel after the 1820s on the Macadam roads, reaching ten to 12 miles an hour while loaded with passengers and luggage.[35]

Along with turnpiking, canal building was particularly prevalent in Britain in the mid-18th century, but Horsham and the Forest did not benefit from this. The Forest itself was on high ground, so any canal building would have been focused on the Arun valley to the west of Horsham. Defoe had noted in 1727 that wheat was more expensive in Horsham than in Guildford because of the transport difficulties of moving grain in and out of Horsham, and in particular the lack of water transport.[36] Guildford was to benefit further from improvements to the Wey and Arun canal which eventually linked the south coast to the Thames by 1816, the impetus being the vulnerability of cargo on the Channel at the time of the Napoleonic wars.[37]

The Duke of Norfolk made several attempts, but failed, to gain enough subscription money to extend the river Arun from Newbridge Wharf at Wisborough Green through Slinfold to Farthing Bridge on the Guildford Road to the north west of Horsham, which would have connected Horsham to the sea at Shoreham. Later, in 1826, the navigation of the Adur river was extended to Baybridge Wharf in West Grinstead and this was as near as navigable water came to Horsham. Within 20 years the railway would in any case take over as the most efficient and economical method of transport, and would open up the Forest, through stations at Faygate and Horsham, to the modern concept of the commuter, living in the tranquil Forest and working in London.[38]

Markets and Fairs

Markets and fairs were essential to Horsham town and its hinterland, which included St Leonard's Forest. Their importance was in developing economic prosperity, particularly given its isolation on the edge of the Weald. There was potential future growth also in the town's proximity to London and Brighton, both centres of growing consumer demand and work opportunities.

According to Dorothea Hurst in her 1868 book *Horsham: Its History and Antiquities* there were five annual fairs in Horsham. As mentioned above in discussing cattle, St Leonard's Forest Fair was situated in the south of the Forest and had been held since the mid-15th century, or earlier, on Saint Leonard's day of 6th November for the sale of feral horses. The date was changed to the 17th November after the 1752 change to the Gregorian calendar and correction of 11 days. The fair moved away from the forest to the south-east of the Common near St Leonard's Road, and then when the Common was enclosed in 1813 it was moved to a site on the Brighton Road, opposite where the old Queen's Head public house was, on the edge of town, the cattle business moving to the Bishopric.

35. Albery, 1947, p. 609.

36. Brandon, 2003, pp. 177-8.

37. Short, B. (2006) *England's Landscape, The South East*, London: Harper Collins, p. 155.

38. Albery, 1947, p. 606

For many years this fair had been trading in both Welsh cattle and horses, but it seems there were other surprising items for sale. There is a report in the recollections of Henry Burstow, local boot maker and diarist, that at the November fair of 1825 a journeyman blacksmith exhibited his wife and three children for sale. The deal was done for two pounds and five shillings for the wife and one child. It is not clear what happened to the other two children but a Magistrate was contacted by concerned local people, although nothing further was done, and indeed sales of women were recorded both before and after this November fair in the July fairs.[39]

E.P. Thompson wrote in his book *Customs in Common* that there were two types of wife sale in this period, one very public in the market place with the woman delivered in a halter around her neck or waist, which was the 'ritual' type of sale, and the other a more private agreement but with a contract signed by witnesses and usually conducted in a public house or bar. Thompson suggests that the 'ritual' sale was an invented tradition in the late 17th century possibly as a response to war and the frequent breakdown of marriages as it was a quick and public method of obtaining a divorce and re-marriage. Part of the agreement, thankfully, being that the wife consented, and often was already in a relationship with the purchaser. The increased reporting of wife sales in the early 19th century reflected the rising current of disapproval fed by evangelical, rationalist and radical, or trade union sources. This, he suggested, led to the cessation of the practice and possibly drove it into more secretive places.[40] Thomas Hardy used the sale of a wife as the major construct of his novel *The Mayor of Casterbridge*, published in 1886 but set two generations earlier in the 1820s, and which explored the social and individual consequences of such an event when lightly undertaken.[41]

Albery, in writing down his *Recollections of Henry Burstow*, noted that fairs and markets were important not only economically but as a means of providing fun and entertainment for the working population. He wrote that the business of the July Fair, which was mainly sheep trading, was confined to one day, whilst the pleasure fair could last from three to nine days, dependent on what day of the week July 18th fell. Booths and stalls were set up in the Carfax and adjoining roads, and provided food, entertainment and sport. Drinking appears to have featured heavily and was available not only in the booths but in temporary drinking houses identified by boughs of greenery above the doors, and hence called bough houses.

Four annual fairs were briefly mentioned by Dudley in his early 19th century history of Horsham that confirms other accounts of a pre-Whitsun fair on April 5th for sheep and lambs, one on July 18th for cattle and pedlars, and a cherry fair on September 5th for cattle, and presumably for cherries as well. He dated the November fair as the 27th for cattle and toys and stated that there was also a monthly market for cattle on the last Tuesday of every month. He did not mention the St Leonard's fair in November, but by the early

39. Albery, 1975, pp. 73-4.

40. Thompson, E.P. (1993) *Customs in Common, Studies in Traditional Popular Culture*, New York: The New Press, pp. 404-466 (hereafter Thompson,1993).

41. Hardy, T. (1886, 2003) *The Mayor of Casterbridge*, Harmondsworth: Penguin Classics, pp. 3-15.

31. Remaining section of Common towards Dog and Bacon public house.

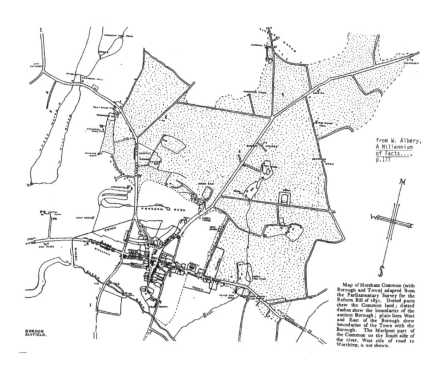

from W. Albery,
A Millennium
of Facts...,
p.177

Map of Horsham Common (with
Borough and Town) adapted from
the Parliamentary Survey for the
Reform Bill of 1831. Dotted parts
shew the Common land; dotted
dashes shew the boundaries of the
ancient Borough; plain lines West
and East of the Borough shew
boundaries of the Town with the
Borough. The Marlpot part of
the Common on the South side of
the river, West side of road to
Worthing, is not shewn.

GORDON
SLYFIELD.

32. Drawing by Gordon Slyfield of Albery's map of Horsham Common from Bowen. E.J. The Enclosure of Horsham Common, page 10. © Horsham Museum and Art Gallery (Horsham District Council)

19th century this had moved to the town, and most likely coincided with the cattle fair on the 27th.

In addition to the annual and monthly markets described, there were weekly markets. Three of these weekly markets were probably established at some point in the late medieval period, the Saturday market being the most successful and thriving due to the sale of poultry to London traders. This increased with the improved roads in the 18th century and Horsham began to take the Dorking corn trade as well as its poultry trade. By 1832 the Saturday market specialised in corn and a Monday market specialised in poultry.[42] Hurst tells us that there was also a fortnightly fat stock market on a Wednesday which sold remarkably fine animals in the run-up to Christmas. In addition to the thriving market for grain, poultry and fat stock, there is the report from Rev. Arthur Young in 1813 that from Horsham Forest and Ashdown Forest considerable quantities of rabbits were sent to London.[43]

Commerce and the Common

Thomas Charles Medwin, an attorney with a considerable private practice in Horsham, prepared a draft list in November 1784 of all the tradesmen in the town. This was on the request of William Bailey for his first nationwide trade directory. It gives a very useful insight into the commercial businesses of Horsham at that time and in fact Medwin concluded his list by noting that 'Horsham is a prime market in Sussex for grain and poultry. The only manufacturing here are leather, hats, sacks and brooms'. Indeed, the list of 19 trades noted two tanners, one tanner and currier, one sack manufacturer, one hat manufacturer amongst single drapers, grocers, mercers, cutlers, builders and maltsters. Professionals were also listed and there were in fact three Attorneys and two Surgeons. One highly skilled watch maker is also mentioned. Perhaps not surprisingly a Timber Merchant is listed, presumably sourcing at least some timber and perhaps oak bark for tanning from St Leonard's Forest.[44]

Broom manufacturers used natural materials of birch, hazel, heath and willow, which were available on the Common. Garth Groombridge, in researching his family history, noted that broom making, or broom dashing, was one of the traditional trades in Horsham. He published a description of the craft skill written by his grandfather and it is clear from the variety and quantity of brooms made that these were much in demand. It may well have been that materials were sourced from the Forest, in addition to the Common, certainly there is mention of Lord Erskine of Holmbush and Buchan Hill selling the strongest heath to a broom maker in the early 18th century.[45] Groombridge also wrote that in the early days each broom manufacturer would travel around visiting the large estates which had woodlands, these woodlands being cleared or coppiced every 15 years. A

42. Hudson, T.P. (ed.) (1986) *The Victoria History of the County of Sussex*, Vol. VI Part 2, The Institute of Historical Research by Oxford University Press, p. 172, (hereafter VCH Vol. VI.2 and Windrum, A. (1978) *Horsham, An Historical Survey*, Chichester: Phillimore & Co. Ltd., p. 118.

43. Young, 1813, p. 391.

44. Horsham Museum (HM), MS 323.

45. British Library (BL), MS 40605, Peel Papers Vol. CCCCXXV 1807-May 1825 (hereafter Peel Papers).

price was bid for so many acres, a contract made, and it would be agreed that the buyer could enter the woodland, make his own roads in, set up camps and light fires for the workers, and cut and cart away the different types of wood for his needs until the woodland was exhausted. These materials would then be taken to a workshop for making into brooms of differing sizes and shapes.[46]

As the 18th century drew to a close, Horsham Town appeared to be a thriving market town, with a good trade to London in grain, poultry and rabbits, and with a variety of tradesmen and manufacturers providing leather, beer, brooms, sacks and hats for the local populace through local shops, fairs and markets. There is limited evidence that St Leonard's Forest was used as a commercial local resource, unlike the Wealden areas of Kent, as described by Thirsk who suggested that by the end of the 18th century in the Weald of Kent, forest resources offered occupations of timber felling, carpentry, woodturning, charcoal burning, iron smelting and cloth making.[47] It is not clear how much industry there was in St Leonard's Forest, apart from the early iron industry, charcoal burning, broom making and perhaps early brick making. There was however the presence of a large and easily accessible Common nearby. The acreage of the Common at the turn of the 19th century was estimated to be 689 acres with 58 acres already identified as encroached upon. The Common wrapped around the town from the north, butting up against the old boundary of the Borough of Horsham on its southern edge, up to the still existing Dog and Bacon public house, north through Little Haven and Roffey to the north east and then south, coming near to St Leonard's Forest at Compton Brow and Leachpool, and ending at the Brighton Road to the south east of the town, see illustrations 31 and 32: page 77.

In his Horsham town history, published in 1947, William Albery, a solicitor, wrote that the legal rights over the Common were based in the feudal Manorial and Burgage tenure system. The right of the soil of the Common lay with the Lord of the Manor, in this case the Duke of Norfolk, while the right of herbage and pannage lay with the burgesses, who were the legal owners, with their heirs, of ancient properties which made up the original 52 incorporators of the Borough. Although neither the Duke nor the burgesses could give freehold title to others to enclose areas of the Common, they could, and did, give leases for small enclosures, provided both were consulted and agreed.[48] It is estimated that in the late 18th century 50 people had been granted leases with 11 extra parcels of land, with the suspicion that the Duke had not always consulted the burgesses before issuing leases. It should be stated that the public had always had free access over the Common, so there was no crime of trespass in journeying over the Common. As noted, town events such as the St Leonard's Fair were held on the Common after moving from the Forest itself, and before its subsequent move to the Brighton Road. Sports such as bowling and cricket were held on the Common, and as the Napoleonic wars threatened, volunteer soldiers

46. Groombridge, G. (2010) A Short History of Brooms, Broom-making and Broom-makers, *Horsham Heritage, Issue No. 19*, Autumn, Horsham Museum Society, pp. 44-55.
47. Thirsk, J. (1984) *The Rural Economy of England, collected essays*, London: The Hambledon Press, pp. 224-5.
48. Albery, 1947, 169-185.

drilled and camped on the Common, while condemned prisoners were taken from the County Gaol and hanged there as a public warning and entertainment.[49]

Albery's map of the Common also shows four windmills. Champion's Mill had been granted leases on the Common from 1765 when it was stated that it had recently been erected by John Champion on half an acre. Near to Champion's windmill was Dr Lindfield's inoculation house where in 1774 John Baker, a solicitor living at Horsham Park House, had his servants inoculated against smallpox and they spent three weeks in isolation, with him bringing them warm punch and jelly to cheer them up. He was a kind and progressive employer, for although Horsham suffered from recurrent outbreaks of smallpox, the townspeople were suspicious and resistant to the idea of inoculation.[50] A Pest House for the isolation of people with communicable diseases is in fact noted on Albery's map but at a little distance from Champion's Mill.

It can be concluded that the Common was a particularly useful area into which Horsham town could place its dirtier and smellier manufacturing, away from the growing population in the town. Although there were fears of robbery at night, the height and openness of the heath was ideal for windmills, and a healthy safe place for an isolation house. The Common also offered opportunities to a bold and determined individual to enclose a bit of land on which to build a house and establish a smallholding or business, albeit on an agreed lease. St Leonard's Forest in contrast was largely in the hands of individual landowners, encroachments were unlikely, and as reported by Albery and Hurst, in the 18th century there were frightening stories of smugglers and robbers frequenting the Forest.[51]

Albery told of the notorious Shipley gang, formed from members of the Rapley family who would meet at Gosden Mill in the south of the forest to plan and deal with smuggled items. Albery's accounts are now disputed as inaccurate and exaggerated with the Shipley gang in reality being more petty thieves and burglars than smugglers.[52] However, Albery recorded the reminiscences of James Lindfield, who lived as a boy at New Lodge, the Aldridge mansion in the middle of the Forest. Lindfield remembered often having to go to Burnt House in Cowfold for bottles of brandy, and once discovered 40 casks of spirit concealed in a hedge and covered in grass. He also remembered having seen Thomas Walter, Excise Officer for Horsham with his own militia, going through the Forest and out towards Pease Pottage. Yet another incident reported by Albery was that on 7th May 1792 a lone smuggler, with his horse loaded with four tubs of spirit, was found drowned in one of the hammer ponds. Presumably he had become lost, or perhaps sampling his contraband, stumbled into the pond on his way through the Forest. [53]

Finally, Hurst, writing in the mid-19th century, reported that St Leonard's Forest was a famous place for smugglers to rest between the coast and London. She wrote that Mr Al-

---

49. Bowen, E.J. (2007) *The Enclosure of Horsham Common*, Horsham Museum Society, pp. 12-15.

50. Crook, D. (2006) *Defying the Demon, Smallpox in Sussex*, Lewes: Dale House Press, pp. 74-5.

51. Albery, 1947, pp. 245-251 and Hurst, 1868, pp. 162-3.

52. Wickens, C. (2001) The Terror of the County – a history of the Shipley Gang, *Horsham Heritage*, Issue No. 3, Spring, Horsham Museum Society, pp. 3-23.

53. Albery, 1947, pp. 474-501.

dridge, and one can assume she meant Robert Aldridge (1801-1871) remembered that when he was a boy it was a common for 30 to 40 armed men to ride up the avenue to the house. Suppers would be laid out for them, and fresh horses made available in the stables, which suggests some complicity and perhaps financial gain from the smuggling business. However, isolated unprotected houses had little choice but to comply, and indeed although Robert Aldridge's father, John Aldridge, had been a local Magistrate and a Captain in the Royal Sussex Militia, he died in 1803, leaving the household particularly vulnerable to the smuggler gangs.[54]

Winslow wrote that before 1740 there had been a Sussex custom amongst the wealthy, landowners and farmers of smuggling wool to avoid export tax, with the poor of Sussex considering it a legitimate part of the local economy. Only later, with the illegal import of tea and brandy of a much higher value, did the business turn particularly violent and was met by the full force of the militia and revenue officers. A two-year campaign instigated by the Duke of Richmond in 1748 followed the brutal murder of Galley and Chater, a customs officer and informant respectively. This resulted in 35 people being hung after five trials, although as Winslow points out, many benefitted from smuggling, but only the poor went to the gallows.[55]

A Footpath Dispute

In the latter part of the 19th century, growth in population and urbanisation in the United Kingdom was accelerating. The period from 1851 to 1914 saw the population of England and Wales double, and remarkably their living standards doubled as well, whilst the number of people living in towns trebled. London's population doubled between 1801 and 1831, and again between 1851 and 1901 to reach 6.5 million inhabitants due to both net in-migration and natural increase, so that in the late 19th century it was the world's largest metropolitan centre.[56] These figures were sustainable due to an increase in industrial output, which quadrupled over the same period, and increasing trade - particularly the import of cheap food. There was, however, growing concern in some quarters over the importance of maintaining open spaces in the face of this enormous tide of urbanisation. Along with this was an increasing interest in footpath walking. Macfarlane cites George Barrow in the early 19th century who inspired a surge in footpath following and later writers such as W. H. Hudson and Hilaire Belloc who made walking paths an attractive pastime.[57]

By 1812 Horsham Common had been enclosed, and in 1813 and 1815 a Parliamentary Act allowed landowners to close any footpath if agreed by two JPs at a Quarter Session.

54. Hurst, 1868, pp. 161-8.

55. Winslow, C. (1975) Sussex Smugglers, Hay, D., Linebaugh, P., Thompson, E. P.(eds) *Albion's Fatal Tree, Crime and Society in Eighteenth-century England*, New York: Pantheon Books, pp. 119-166.

56. Black, J. (2009) *London, a History*, Lancaster: Carnegie Publishing Ltd., pp. 230-5.

57. Blunden, J. & Curry, N. (eds)(1985) *The Changing Countryside*, Milton Keynes: Open University with Croom Helm Ltd., pp. 72-5, and Macfarlane, R. (2013) *The Old Ways*, London: Penguin Books Ltd., pp. 18-27.

Although this does not appear to have been used by the Aldridge family on St Leonard's Forest, it caused concern in towns, and was condemned by many including Edwin Chadwick, the social reformer. The first response was in York in 1824 with the setting up of the Association for the Protection of Ancient Footpaths, this was followed swiftly by a Manchester version, but it was not until 1865 that real progress was made in the protection of rights of way with the founding in London of the Commons Preservation Society which fought long legal battles for public rights over Epping Forest, Banstead Downs and Berkhamsted Common in the 1870s and 80s. At its annual meeting in July 1899 it voted to merge with The National Footpath Preservation Society to become the Commons and Footpath Preservation Society, thereby combining forces to campaign for the protection of open spaces and public access. Short notes that by the 1870s disputes over common rights in English forests, chases and parks was not new, but the middle classes and intellectuals now felt the need for the preservation of open spaces, along with the flora and fauna. The Ashdown Forest case (1876-1882) was another similar type of struggle for access to resources on common land.[58]

An important response by the Government to public concern regarding access to footpaths and open spaces was the Local Government Act of 1894, Section 26, which stated that a district council, with agreement from the county council, could aid persons in maintaining rights of common where, in their opinion, losing the rights would be prejudicial to the inhabitants of the district. In order to do this the district council could institute or defend any legal proceedings, and in fact take any steps that they felt to be expedient. This allowed Horsham Rural District Council, in concert with the Urban District Council to defend the legal action when the footpaths through St Leonard's Forest were threatened by their new landowner, Edmund Molyneux, who had recently bought the core of the Aldridge estate, 1731 acres in four lots, when it had been put up for sale in 1896.[59]

It was reported in newspapers in May 1899 that certain paths through St Leonard's Forest had been obstructed, and pedestrians ordered off the estate. This had been brought to the attention of Horsham urban, rural and parish councils and an inquiry was held on 16th May 1899, in the Town Hall, to establish the precedents for the rights of way over 12 footpaths through the forest. On hearing the oral evidence both for and against, the councils were convinced that the rights of way were correct and should stand. They therefore removed the obstacles in the footpaths, and according to *The Times* court report they had dug earth, filled trenches and pulled down fences. A month later, the Commons and Footpath Preservation Society, Horsham Centre, organised a mass ramble through the Forest with an estimated 120 walkers taking part. According to evidence from Richard Francis, 59, they walked via Herons Copse path past the Grange up to the top of Mick Mills Race and then down past Mill Farm by The Goldings.[60]

58. *The Morning Post,* (London, England) Friday July 14 1899, p. 6 Issue 39659 and Solnit, R. (2001) *Wanderlust, A History of Walking,* London: Verso, pp. 159 – 168, and Short, B. (1999) Conservation, Class and Custom: Lifespace and Conflict in a Nineteenth-century Forest Environment, *Rural History,* Vol. 10.2, pp. 127-154.

59. Local Government Act 1894, Chapter 73, 56 and 57 Vict. Part II S26 (2)(3).

60. *The Times*, 19 July 1900, Issue 36198, and WSRO MS RD/HO24/2/1.

The response from Molyneux was to instigate proceedings against Horsham Rural District Council in the Chancery Division of the High Court, claiming that the alleged public rights of way did not exist, and thus claiming an injunction restraining the defendants, or their agents, from trespassing and demanding damages for trespass. The case came to the High Court in front of Justice Kekewich on 20th June 1900. It was agreed that documentary evidence could not be supplied, and in fact it later transpired that proof of footpaths stretching back to before the Aldridge's occupation was required by law due to the estate being entailed from father to son rather than in fee simple, that is disposing of the estate at will. Such a task was impossible, and so local people were called to give oral evidence as to their knowledge of use of the 12 footpaths in dispute. Not surprisingly, small details of everyday life were given regarding the work and leisure practices and these give a glimpse into Forest life as far back as the late 18th century.[61] The oral evidence also gives credence to the *The First Report of the Commissioners on the Employment of Children, Young Persons and Women in Agriculture 1867-8* reports of leasing and subleasing Forest land, which had led to a large number of cottages and turf huts each on an acre of land which had appeared in the Forest. [62]

James Langley, 66, stated in Court to be a grocer and dealer living in Colgate, (the 1901 census a year later has him living at the Mars Chapel on his own means), said that his father had worked for Thomas Broadwater at Holmbush and that there used to be more people living in Colgate, and that he could show where 50 little farms had been given up. When asked if a good deal of wood had been taken from the estate he agreed and said that also a lot had also grown up, but it had been let to run to ruin and the little farms cut off and gone. He also thought that the footpaths were ten times better 30 years ago. Edward Gates, 60, carpenter and steam sawyer, said his father had worked for Squire Aldridge as a woodman, and his grandfather as warrener on the estate. He noted that 'a great many people lived in the Forest years ago, not in houses but in huts' and he remembered that as a boy these people were charcoal burners and small farmers. Alfred Greenfield, 57, said that before 1881 there had been a lot of little holdings on the eastern side of the estate and these tenants used the footpaths, although others did as well. Thomas Gent, 77, thought that by far the greater number of people using the footpaths were not tenants and gave examples of people he knew who had used Mick Mills Race in the course of deliveries as there was a waggon road that linked to the Race. However, he also said that 'in those days there were about four times as many people in the Forest as now, I have known 25 houses, or huts, down where there are none now'. Many of the farms he said had 'gone destitute' and the roads kept in order by the farmers had been left alone. William Gates, 47, said he knew most of the people of the farms and they had to use the footpaths to get to Horsham, as did people from Handcross.[63]

---

61. HM MSS 2917 1-2 which are two note books written by C. J. B. Hurst, Barrister-at-law, who observed the case for local landowner R. H. Hurst, MP, and recorded evidence from 23 local people, and also collected newspaper cuttings of the trial, which are not individually referenced, and WSRO MS RD/HO24/2/1.

62. P.P. 1867-8, XVII, p. 82.

63. HM MSS 2917 1-2.

33. Post card of 'Mike' Mills Race with clear straight track, date of post mark on reverse unclear but, given Forestry Commission (Forestry England since 2019) planting, after 1919.

The evidence clearly showed that the footpaths were used for work, such as for the carting of dog food and bird feed to the Kennels by New Lodge before the Grange was built. Underwood and heath was carted past the Grange and through Spurs Orchard. Bricks were carted to Colgate and Crawley, and apples were carted from Slaugham to Roffey, all on the footpaths. William Gates said that he had seen carts on the race and knew that they were not connected with the estate. A blacksmith, James Mitchell, 49, remembered shoeing horses for Colonel Aldridge and walking all over the estate via the footpaths, and as a boy he had accompanied a vet on his work through the footpaths. Labourers spoke of using the paths to get to work cutting wood, harvesting, tending birds, and digging potatoes while Jesse Norman, 53, who lived at Holmbush Potteries was sent as a boy to collect debts at Plummers Plain, Nuthurst, Leonardslee and other places and used the footpaths. William Jupp, 45, distinguished between the keepers and watchers on the estate who had a right and duty to be there and the general public. Several people mentioned the keepers but no one seemed to know how many there were. However, Alfred Greenfield said he had been employed as a keeper and walked the whole of Molyneux's property, saying that the keepers' paths were between the central paths and were used for feeding and shooting. Jesse Norman had said that Colonel Aldridge kept beagles for hunting hares and rabbits, and pheasants were also kept on the estate. Laurence Lovegrove, 77, remembered his father's body being carried from Roffey through Hampers Lane, past the Sun Oak to St. John's Coolhurst for burial, and Edward Gates remembered a corpse being carried to the church from Whitevane pond via the footpaths.

The only woman recorded by Hurst to give evidence, Elizabeth Wickham, 46, said she had lived all her life in the Forest and walked to Sunday school at St. John's as a child. She also said she frequently used two different paths through the Forest to get to Horsham, and that others had accompanied her to shopping in Horsham.[64]

The footpaths were also used for leisure purposes, as noted by Albert Etheridge, 46, who worked in the brickyard on the south side of Forest Road, west of Colgate, and said he used the paths for pleasure. He admitted to playing in a summerhouse on the estate many times as a boy. Several pieces of evidence were given referring to pleasant times had in the summerhouse, including courting. It appeared to be on Herons Copse path which ran from New Lodge-Grange-Mick Mills Race, and was approached through a keeper's garden. David Price, 42, a stationer and printer interested in entomology, said that when he was a boy he remembered it as a favourite walk; people would take refreshments and go into the summerhouse. He told the Court he had gained permission from the Aldridges to pursue his hobby and remembered capturing a rare moth in the neighbourhood of Roosthole pond. He said that on his walks through the Forest he met people he knew from Horsham, London and Brighton and various other places.[65]

The Lily Beds were another popular destination for local walkers. William Simmons, 61, who had been a gardener to Colonel Aldridge for over eight years, said that when the Lily of the Valley were in flower he had to stop people from pulling up their roots, but they were a great sight with acres of them in bloom. Richard Francis, 59, a shoemaker, said he had been in the Horsham Union Workhouse at Roffey when he was an eight-year-old, and remembered using the paths in the forest for pleasure. He also told the Court that the workhouse children used to bathe in Whitevane pond; he did not know whether the Squire had given permission, but a schoolmaster accompanied them and those who would not go in were thrown in. Reading the notes on this oral evidence, the impression is of footpaths constantly busy with people, and with Mick Mills Race being used as almost a road or track from north to south through the Forest.[66]

Up to - and indeed following - the time of the Court hearing, negotiations had been progressing between the Joint Committee of the district councils and Molyneux. Molyneux had conceded the footpath from Goldings Bridge up past the Sun Oak and his carriageway to New Lodge, or St Leonard's, and out at Upper Park pond towards the town, and by this point the Joint Committee had prepared a map of the estate, edged in blue, with the footpaths accepted by the councils marked in red. It is not clear what the green lines indicated, although they were clearly paths of some sort, see illustration 34: page 86. Molyneux proposed conceding two more paths but the council felt it could not let all the others go, and made a counter proposal. However, this was not accepted and the Court had to sit for five days hearing all the oral evidence. At this point another offer was made by Molyneux, and with further negotiations by the council for adding a small but important footpath linking Town Copse with a footpath through Leechpool Woods towards Horsham, this was accepted. A second map was made by the council to confirm the footpaths which would be

64. HM MSS 2917 1-2.
65. HM MSS 2917 1-2.
66. HM MSS 2917 1-2.

34. Local authority map indicating footpaths agreed after initial local enquiry. Footpaths identified by letters. West Sussex Records Office MS RD/HO/24/2/1.

35. Local authority map indicating footpaths agreed after negotiations with Molyneux bringing court case to a close. West Sussex Records Office MS RD/HO/24/2/1.

accepted by both parties, although surprisingly this left out Mick Mills Race, see illustration 35: page 87. The conclusion to the dispute in the form of this compromise came on the 18th of July, 1900, when the defending council informed the judge of the agreement reached.[67]

The Horsham Centre of the Commons and Footpath Preservation Society had its third annual meeting on the 12th June, 1901, under the chairmanship of Rev. J. J. Marten in which minutes of the annual report outlined what had been happening that year and the 'grave danger to many public rights of way' in the district. Details of the conclusion to the St Leonard's Forest footpath dispute was outlined and it was hoped that:

'—a portion of this old Forest might be secured for the public before the inevitable alternative of enclosure for private villa and paddock occupation shall have monopolised its entire area, and have irreparably destroyed its wild and sylvan character'

The Secretary commented that it had been difficult to get evidence given that Colonel Aldridge invited all and sundry to walk all the paths, and 'had a great fancy for shifting paths, and as far as one could make out there was scarcely a path in the whole Forest he had not shifted from one line to another'. Added to this was Robert Hurst's evidence that there was a ring fence at some time around the Forest, in which he may have been referring to John Speed's map of 1610, or perhaps early references to Lord Erskine's Holmbush estate. The Commons and Footpaths Preservation Society felt that given these problems the compromise was a good outcome.[68]

Edmund Molyneux remains a difficult figure to find, not assisted by the fact that he is referred to as both Edmund and Edward in official documentation. He does not appear on the 1901 or 1911 census in the Horsham area, although in letters to Robert Hurst at the time of the footpath dispute he has the title of Captain, so it is likely he would have been caught up in the First World War, from which he may, or may not, have returned. The Land Valuation Survey of 1910-15 shows him as the freehold owner of a large portion of the Forest, with the notes of inspection dated 18th February 1914. These inspection notes show him as owner of Forest Grange with 1,307 acres, the Home Farm with smithy, saw mills, barn and carpenter shop, and 185 acres of Forest land with cattle yard and shed. No other occupier is noted for these properties. As the Land Valuation Survey allowed landowners to offset tax by listing Rights of Way through their land, it is interesting that a large number of footpaths were still there in 1914 with 28 claimed through Forest Grange land. The Land Valuation field books also showed that Harold Dennis had bought the Aldridge mansion, New Lodge - also known as St Leonard's - with 122 acres, freehold. Again, tax relief on 30 footpaths is noted on this land, and 25 on an adjoining 53

67. WSRO MS RD/HO/2/1

68. WSRO MS RD/HO/2/1

69. 1911 census accessible through: http://interactive.ancestry.co.uk and Knight, J.(2008) Horsham's History, Volume 3 1880-1913, Horsham District Council, p. 269, and WSRO Hurst MS ACC 3296/146 and TNA IR58/94086.

acres, clearly more than the 12 that were agreed at the footpath dispute. Perhaps old habits die hard for the people living in the Forest, and the landscape of the forest paths had not in fact been much changed by the 1900 dispute.[69]

The contrasting evidence from the official census and oral remembrance shows two sides of development in the Forest landscape during the 19th century. There was the early leasing, and almost uncontrolled subletting of tracts of land in the St Leonard's Forest estate which had encouraged small farms and huts, or hovels, to be thrown up on this marginal land. Such temporary structures left little evidence so they and their occupants melted away as the agricultural boom years from 1815 to the 1870s gave way to depression. Nervousness amongst the upper classes and the clergy as to what was really going on in the Forest, plus their anxiety of losing potential congregations to the nonconformists, encouraged the building of churches and schools by the local landowning patrons. It was this that effectively created the villages of Colgate and Lower Beeding in the Forest, which then attracted new residents to settle in a rural area with good access to London, Horsham and Brighton, which will be explored in the next chapters, although first one needs to look at the ownership of the Forest estates.

Mountain Ash or Rowan, *Sorbus aucuparia* by Dr Maggie Weir-Wilson.

Chapter 5

The Forest Estates

Introduction

I have looked at the five main private estates that have formed the main part of St Leonard's Forest since the 18th century. The exact boundaries have been difficult to fix without access to detailed estate maps and archives which remain in private hands, however public archives have been very useful. One could imagine that some of these

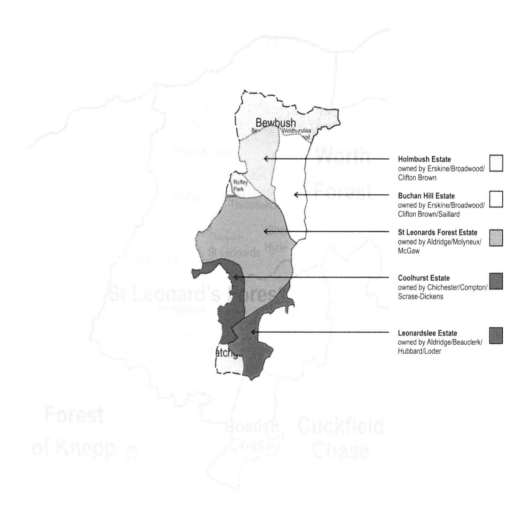

Holmbush Estate
owned by Erskine/Broadwood/
Clifton Brown

Buchan Hill Estate
owned by Erskine/Broadwood/
Clifton Brown/Saillard

St Leonards Forest Estate
owned by Aldridge/Molyneux/
McGaw

Coolhurst Estate
owned by Chichester/Compton/
Scrase-Dickens

Leonardslee Estate
owned by Aldridge/Beauclerk/
Hubbard/Loder

36. Sketch map of the approximate positions of the five estates within the Forest. It is indicative rather than actual and the light green areas to the north, west and south probably fell outside these particular estates.

37. St Leonard's House, originally known as New Lodge, part of the Aldridge forest estate

estates follow the old internal boundaries of the Forest chase given that many footpaths and roads show continual usage through centuries, but this is speculation.

New Lodge, or St Leonard's

The St Leonard's estate with its mansion of New Lodge remained in the Aldridge family from 1760 to 1906, almost 150 years, but it began to be slowly eroded as large parts were leased and then sold off from the turn of the 19th century. The estate was considered of poor-quality soil, not fit for agricultural use, and the policy of the family, set out in a Trust, was to sell or lease land in order to provide annuities for the family. The first major sale, of approximately 1,000 acres to the south of the estate, was to Charles George Beauclerk in 1803. Previously, in 1801, the lease of 3,000 acres to Railton and Hulls had been completed which opened the central area to subletting. In June 1837 *The Brighton Patriot* advertised for sale a 'valuable leasehold estate' of 68 acres in St Leonard's Forest.

---

1. *Brighton Patriot and South of England Free Press* (Brighton, England) Tuesday, June 6, 1837, issue 120. This was a very radical paper which indicates left wing politics so perhaps Railton and Hulls were driven to issue numerous small leases through political ideology rather than financial gain.

This was described as '13 acres of meadow and pasture, the remainder woodland principally Birch and Alder, well adapted as a game preserve.'[1]

Leasing and subletting continued through the 19th century; for example, in 1862 Carter's Lodge and Newstead Farm, together with 782 acres, were leased, mortgaged, and a schedule of 14 subleases listed all with 20 and 21-year leases. In 1865 21 tenancies on this same land were noted, and some of these were to the same people as noted in the previous leases. Six of these names can be found in the 1871 census and it is interesting to note that one of these, Thomas Gent, settled in Tattletons Farm where seven other families were also settled, including the family of Thomas Light, a pedlar, in a caravan on the farm with seven children.

The other families reported to be on this farm were three agricultural labourers and four identified as farmers, with the acreage of their farms helpfully being noted as 25 acres, 20 acres, 11 acres and nine acres, so quite small farms. Of the named lessees, Thomas Gent, 45, at Tattletons was an agricultural labourer, with seven children, the eldest two being boys aged 16 and 17, who were agricultural labourers. Thomas Agate was a

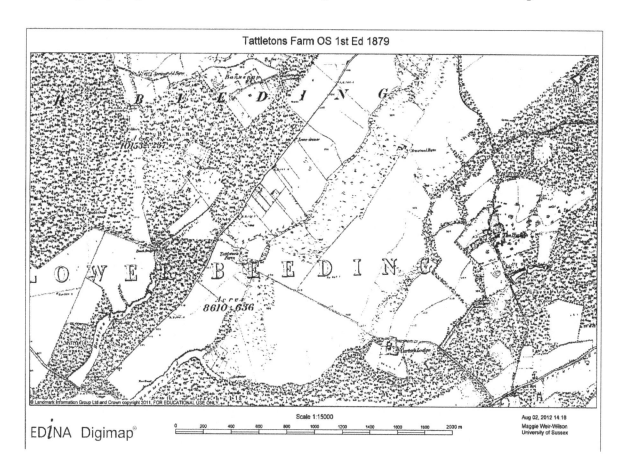

38. Tattletons Farm (between the B and E of Lower Beeding) with smallholdings running east west in the centre, Barnsnap to the north and Carter's Lodge to the south east. OS County Series 1:10560, 1st Edition, 1879, reproduced with permission of Edina Historic Digimap.

39. Map of New Lodge also known as St Leonard's, OS County Series, 1:2500, 1st Edition, 1875, reproduced with permission of Edina Historic Digimap.

gamekeeper with wife and small son at Grouse Road; William Gent was Thomas Gent's brother, both having been born in Cudham, Kent, and he was at Black Hill near Colgate, a sawyer with three children, his eldest a 16-year-old agricultural labourer. Henry Etherton, 46, was an agricultural labourer at Barnsnap also with a 16-year-old son who was an agricultural labourer and four other young children; likewise, Christopher Jupp at Barnsnap was an agricultural labourer, his eldest son of 14 was an agricultural labourer and he had five other children. Most of these men and their wives came from the local area, except the Gents from Kent. As agricultural labourers and small farmers they would not have been well off and would have suffered in the subsequent agricultural depression that swept many of these workers off the land.[2]

Further evidence of leasing and subletting is supplied by the 1867-8 Report on the Employment in Agriculture which looked at the Parish of Lower Beeding as one of the ten parishes that formed the Horsham Union. It noted that Lower Beeding was a 'wide scattered parish of 10,000 acres, sparsely peopled with 4000 acres of uncultivated and wood land.' Although the report wrote that the condition of the cottages in the south of the parish was deemed to be fair, in the north their condition was described as bad and overcrowded. The report commented on the subletting, mentioned earlier, of 3,000 acres of St Leonard's Forest in 1801 by Railton and Hulls, and how cottages and turf huts of a 'very inferior condition' were allowed to be built, and that about a dozen of these cottages still remained in 1867 in their original condition, which was clearly a worry for the Commissioners.[3] However, it is of note that the Chair of the local Commissioners who had been engaged for the report was E. M. Smith Bigg of The

---

2. HM MSS 3132, 3135, 3138.

3. House of Commons Parliamentary Papers (1867-8) *The First Report of the Commissioners on the Employment of Children, Young Persons, and Women in Agriculture*, pp. 81-2 (hereafter Employment in Agriculture 1867-8).

4. HM MS 3124.1.

Hyde in the nearby Parish of Slaugham, who had also been involved in mortgaging, with the Strong family, 1950 acres of Carter's Lodge and Great Warren. It seems unlikely that he would not have known what was happening and the poor conditions of the cottages and huts.[4]

New Lodge was the original name of the mansion built by Abel Aldridge in the mid-18th century, possibly on the site of a previous lodge house, as the name would suggest, although the name does change through the decades. Horsfield wrote that Robert Aldridge was the principal proprietor of St Leonard's Forest and his residence was called St Leonard's Forest.[5] Elwes, writing later, referred to the residence as St Leonard's and noted that it was still sometimes called New Lodge, and that it was sited in a park of 250 acres.[6]

Gardner and Gream's Sussex map of 1795, illustration 29: page 72, shows the site of New Lodge as a rectangular enclosure with paths radiating out over the Forest. This remains clear in the OS Old Series 1813 map, although the main southern drive takes precedence and four meadows or fields to the south west have appeared, illustration 30: page 72. The later OS 1st edition 1875 map, illustration 39: page 94, shows a modest footprint of the house, some large stables or barns to the north and between them the divided square of what looks like a walled garden or kitchen garden. The original rectangular enclosure is no longer delineated, but the house appears set in a lawn of mixed deciduous and conifer trees with a drive to the easterly front of the house, and a long avenue lined with trees running down to the south to meet Hammerpond Road.

Dorothea Hurst wrote in 1868 that this house was approached by an 'avenue of ancient Spanish Chestnuts and in the garden is one of the largest rhododendron plants known.' She also commented that the park which surrounded the house was noted for fine old Birch trees. Other features that can be seen on the 1875 map are two ponds immediately to the south of the mansion, an orchard and a Laurel Walk to the south east, with a small cottage called Turfplain Lodge to the south on an area called Turf Plain, which is shown wooded and cut through with a grid of paths in the later 1897 OS 1st Revision map.

An interesting report comes from *Albery's Recollections of Henry Burstow* who described how, as a boy, he watched the St Leonard's Forest Races which occurred on Tuesday, 15th September 1835. To illustrate his report, he reproduced the programme of the races in good detail. He wrote that the course was one and a half miles in circumference and situated on the west side of the big house, New Lodge. By checking the OS 1st edition 1875, illustration 39: page 94, one can see a clear, almost circular, area of parkland of about one quarter of a mile in diameter from the back of the house to the edge of the property and a band of trees. This area is not large enough to encompass such a large

5. Horsfield, T. W. (1835) *The History, Antiquities and Topography of the County of Sussex*. Vol. 2, Lewes: Sussex Press, p. 222 (hereafter Horsfield, 1835).

6. Elwes, D. G. C. & Robinson, C. J. (1879) *A History of the Castles, Mansions and Manors of Western Sussex*. London: Longman, p. 27 (hereafter Elwes, 1879).

40. Photograph of Colonel John Aldridge 1868 reproduced from Albery's Parliamentary History, p. 287. © Horsham Museum & Art Gallery, (Horsham District Council).

circular race track, although it may not have been circular or oval as are today's race courses.

According to Albery, Burstow remembered that the first race meeting had been held the previous year in 1834 and was fairly small, but that the 1835 meeting was a 'grand event: early in the morning every approach to the forest was crowded with vehicles of all kinds, and with people on foot and on horseback.' He added that by ten in the morning when the first race was to start, it was estimated that 12,000 people and 1,000 horses were present. To add to the festivities a Race Ball and supper were held in the evening at the King's Head Hotel in Horsham. The following year the races had been fixed for 10th May but were postponed for a month due to the 'sudden and dangerous illness of Robert Aldridge' steward and owner of the park. However, it commenced on his recovery, and the *Hampshire Advertiser* reported that 'about 1500 persons were present. The company, on the whole, consisted of the most influential and wealthy in this part of the county'.[7]

These races were very popular and ran for seven years, and despite the 1836 meeting raising over £200 towards the building of a new church, St. John's at Coolhurst, just beyond the southern edge of the estate on Hammerpond Road, the local clergy were very against such 'betting, drinking and swindling.' So, they complained to Robert Aldridge as to the presence at the races of 'so many undesirable characters, hawks and pigeons, sharps and flats, bounders, boozers and harpies of all sorts' and so this brought about its early demise. No doubt the many people and horses would have had a detrimental impact on the St Leonard's parkland which could not have supported any ornamental garden into the 1840s, and there is little evidence of it later. However, there is comment that Robert Aldridge did try to improve the estate by laying down tile drains, and this had more success than previous attempts by Sir Richard Weston to improve the soil.

Intriguingly there are hints of financial problems and family disagreements amongst the Aldridge family. During the first attempt to sell the bulk of the estate in 1878, No.6 of the Conditions of Sale reported that on 21st February 1873 a bill was filed in the Court of Chancery in suit of Aldridge versus Aldridge. This apparently had been instituted for the purpose of obtaining legal consent to enable the Trustees to raise money for enlarging, repairing and improving the mansion. This was granted but no decree was made and the bill was dismissed in June 1875. Robert Aldridge had died in 1871 aged 69 and the estate was inherited by the eldest son of seven children, Major

---

7. *The Hampshire Advertiser and Salisbury Guardian* (Southampton, England) Saturday 7 May 1836, Issue 668 and Saturday 18 June 1836, Issue 674.

8. Ellis, W.S. (1925) *The Parks and Forests of Sussex, Ancient and Modern*, Lewes: H. Wolff. p. 247 (hereafter Ellis,1925).

John Aldridge (1832-1888). As noted in Ellis, the parliamentary return of 1875 lists Major Aldridge as holding 5,739 acres of land with a gross annual rental of £3,164. In comparison with other landowners in Sussex who held over 1,000 acres of land, this was a very respectable acreage for someone not of the aristocracy, although a lower rental ratio to acreage probably reflected the poor quality of the arable land. [8]

Major John Aldridge (1832-1888), later a Colonel in the Royal Sussex Regiment, see illustration 40: page 96, married the widow of Thomas Broadwood of Holmbush, Maria Althea Matthew, and together they had four sons and one daughter. Colonel John Aldridge contested the Parliamentary seat for Horsham in the notoriously corrupt election of 1868, tying with Robert Hurst and both taking their seats in the Commons. This result was vigorously contested by both men crying foul. Eventually the result was overturned with Hurst retaining the seat and Aldridge withdrawing. Colonel John Aldridge also stood for the 1874 election but again lost out to Robert Hurst. However, he was on the Board of Guardians appointed to manage the running of the Horsham Union Workhouse, and was one of the senior Magistrates of whom it was said 'His zeal was great to discharge the duties of a Magistrate, whilst at the same time he always strove to combine mercy with justice'.[9] All their sons were soldiers in the South African wars, and their eldest son, Robert Beauclerk Aldridge died unmarried in 1892 at the age of 27. Their second son, Charles Powlett Aldridge (1866-1907), Captain in the Royal Sussex Regiment for all of his adult life, made the major sale of the estate in 1896.[10] After his death in 1907 Sussex Genealogies shows that the inheritance of St Leonard's Forest fell on the youngest son, John Bartelott Aldridge (1871-1909) who died at Bangalore in India aged 37, leaving three young sons aged nine, seven and four.[11] Of the previous generation, three uncles, brothers of Colonel John Aldridge, also died young. Robert Bartelott Aldridge (1835-1863), Henry Aldridge (1842-1876), and Charles Compton Aldridge (1839-1866), who was in Holy Orders.

It is therefore not surprising that in the latter part of the 19th century the Aldridge estate was beset by death and taxes. Although Colonel John Aldridge had improved the estate by building new properties and improving roads, he must have felt compelled to put a large part of the estate up for sale in 1878. Two years beforehand, the *Hampshire Telegraph and Sussex Chronicle* noted that a military camp was to be formed in St Leonard's Forest, the seat of Colonel Aldridge, although there is little evidence that this did actually happen.[12] However, 1878 was not a good time to sell. In the earlier part of the 19th century demand for land had been maintained by large landowners consolidating their holdings, and new wealth like Holmbush's Broadwood and Clifton Brown founding landed families with all the social position and political influence that brought. However,

9. From newspaper cutting in the archive of the Rev. Bloxham, Magdalen College, Oxford. MS 741.

10. Boorman, D. & Djabri, S.C. (2009) Country House Cricket at St Leonard's Forest. *Horsham Heritage*, Issue No. 18, Horsham Museum, pp. 46-59 (hereafter, Boorman and Djabri, 2009).

11. Comber, J. (1931) *Sussex Genealogies (Horsham Centre)*. Cambridge: W. Heffer & Sons Ltd., pp. 8-12.

12. *Hampshire Telegraph and Sussex Chronicle*, Saturday 27 May 1876.

13. Thompson, F.M.L. (1968) The Land Market in the Nineteenth Century, Minchinton, W. E. (ed.) *Essays in Agrarian History*, Vol. II, Newton Abbot: David & Charles, pp. 50-4.

the Reform Acts took away automatic opportunities for political power, and so, as Thompson noted, by 1878 the landed aristocracy were at 'territorial saturation point'. Another development was that the laws on entailment, where the land remained in one family, began to be loosened. To make matters worse for sellers there was an agricultural depression, rents were falling and there was no sign of them levelling out.[13].

On Tuesday 30th July, 1878, 3,400 acres of the St Leonard's Forest Estate came up for auction in eight lots. The sales particulars give a very useful snapshot of the estate at this time. The position of the estate appeared to be an important selling point as it was noted that it was two miles from Horsham station with the advantage of two lines of railway into London. The sale was clearly aimed at those wanting to retreat from the expanding city of London, and there were no shortage of newly wealthy merchants and business people who wanted their own piece of the peace and quiet of Sussex. The sporting opportunities were also emphasised, such as in Lot 5 which included 900 acres surrounding Hammer and Hawkins Ponds and other 'ornamental sheets of water of great extent, affording capital fishing, boating and water fowl shooting'. The whole estate, it was noted, 'presents a magnificent sporting property'.

In addition, opportunities for building were made clear. Not only were there resources for building on site due to 'valuable quarries of stone, good building sand, and excellent brick earth on the estate also good gravel for roads', but suitable sites for development were suggested. It was reported that care had been taken with the division of lots to present 'beautiful sites for the erection of superior residences ... with frontage to the capital roads.' Finally, the picturesque nature of the estate was emphasised, as it was described as having 'some of the most charming views in the county' and that the hills and valleys over the whole four-mile length of the estate presented sites for building. The sales particulars do confirm that for some years the owner, Colonel John Aldridge, had made improvements, both by ornamental planting, drainage and fencing and by the building of roads. This can be further confirmed by enclosure orders in 1869, 1871 and 1878 awarded to John Aldridge for land drainage, improvement and road building, thus making the estate more productive and accessible. Mingay, writing about the English Agricultural Revolution, suggested that it was only after the mid-19th century with steam power and the invention of cheap ways of making pipes and tiles that large scale land drainage could take place, but that it was one of the most important improvements to agricultural production.[14]

In examining the details of the eight lots for sale it is possible to come to some conclusion about the character of the central part of the Forest at this time. There are 19 properties identified as farms, although one called Monks Gate is clearly not, given the small acreage and lack of farm facilities, so it is not included in my calculations, but another two properties clearly are, Plummer's Plain House and Woodlands, so they have been included in this brief analysis. Of the 20 farms thus identified, six are above 100

---

14. HM SP203, and McGaw Collection MSS 3293, 3294, 3295 and Mingay, G.E. (1968) *The Agricultural Revolution in English History: A Reconsideration*, Minchinton, W.E. (ed.) *Essays in Agrarian History*, Vol. II, Newton Abbot: David and Charles, pp. 10-22.

acres. The largest, Dockers Lodge Farm, has 311 acres and the smallest, Woodlands, has 115 acres. The 14 farms below 100 acres have between 22 and 89 acres each. An approximation of the acreage of the farms from a total of the estate of 3,400 is about 2,136, or just under two thirds.

Although one cannot be sure that all the animals and buildings are accounted for in the sales particulars, there is a good indication that they were all small mixed farms. For example, of the six larger farms all had horses, and all but one had cattle, four had pigs and four had chickens, two had dairies and only one had a bake house, or a brew house or an orchard. Of the 14 smaller farms, 11 had horses, ten had cattle, nine had pigs, two had chickens, and one had pheasants. Altogether there were two dairies and six orchards. Stabling for 18 horses within all the farms can be identified, although there may have been more given that horses would have been used for transport as well as for the plough. This gives a picture of a busy farming area around the edges of the forest, with animals, people and associated buildings.

Taking only the acreage in the calculation of the six larger farms it is indicated that about 80% of farm acreage was in arable cultivation, 18% in pasture, grass and rough pasture, and just 2% was woodland. A similar calculation for the smaller farms produces almost the same result, 75% arable, 22% pasture including orchards, and 3% wood. It is not explicit what is grown in the arable fields but several farms have granaries, often above stables, which would indicate wheat and/or oats for the horses. Also, there is mention of water from Hawkins and Hammer ponds being let for Mill purposes to a yearly tenant, which would also indicate wheat being grown and milled for flour from across the area. However, with the number of cattle being kept, the arable could also be for root crops and cattle feed. It does appear to be a particularly high proportion of arable, given that land use crops for Sussex as a whole taken from tithe reports circa 1836 give figures of 43.8% arable, 34.9% grass, 15.1% wood and 2.8% common. However, it should be remembered that the comparison is between the whole of Sussex and a very small area. It was noted in these 1836 reports that on clay soils a four-course rotation was grown of wheat, oats, seeds and fallow, either tares or beans. On the better soil turnips were grown, whilst on the lightest poorest soils seeds were allowed to lie for two or three years.[15] It could be that the sales particulars exaggerated the amount of land under arable cultivation, or that it was later reduced as yields reduced on poor soil despite attempts by Col John Aldridge to drain, enclose and improve the land. Deputations from the 1901 Footpath Dispute tend to indicate a reduction in the number of small farms (see Chapter 4).

Apart from the farms there were a number of cottages, tenements and larger residences included in the estate sale dated 1878; in fact, most of Lower Beeding and Colgate villages were included, plus a new road with a strip of houses or plots south of Colgate. Eleven newly erected properties were described, including five cottages, two farmhouses, and two residences plus two sites of farm buildings. These represented a significant capital outlay if paid for, or mortgaged, by Colonel John Aldridge.

---

15. Kain, R.J.P. (1986) *An Atlas and Index of the Tithe Files of Mid-Nineteenth Century England and Wales*. Cambridge University Press, pp. 102-111.

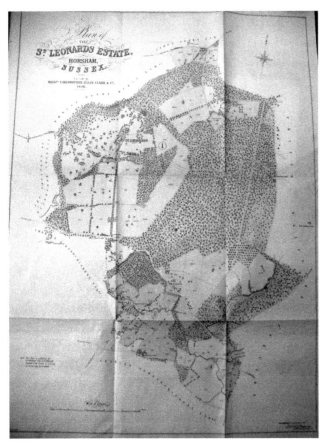

41. Plan of St Leonard's Forest Estate, coloured according to the four auction lots, and attached to sales particulars SP 230, dated 1896. Horsham Museum & Art Gallery (Horsham District Council).

Although the farms had a small percentage of woodland, between two and three percent, there was still enough to promote some parts of the estate as good for shooting. This is confirmed by what seems to be a business carried out by John Boyd. The new cottage by Holy Trinity Church in Lower Beeding was let to him annually and he had sporting rights over five acres of Holme plantation woods. Boyd was also named as renting the Pheasantry at Buckshead Farm and had shooting and fishing rights over 425 acres, mainly of woodland, in the centre of the estate such as Race Hill, Barnsnap and Cinderbank. Another 243 acres of woods to the north of the Horsham-Colgate-Pease Pottage road, and to the west of Tower Road in Lot 7 was again let to him on a yearly notice. One would therefore assume that John Boyd ran and stocked shoots over 673 acres of woodland in St Leonard's Forest at this time.[16]

It appears that little was sold in this 1878 sale, or perhaps much was withdrawn, as most of the property came back onto the market three years later. It may have been, as suggested earlier, that the 1870s was a particularly poor time to sell land. Colonel John Aldridge put it all up for sale again on 13th July, 1881, this time in 56 lots and including other land he possessed in Warnham and Roffey, making 3,200 acres in all. Demand for land did not pick up until the early 1890s, however despite demand still being slow in the 1880s, this time the estate did sell. Knight commented that this was one of the largest land transactions carried out in Horsham's modern history, and this echoes *The County Times* report three days after the auction which noted that it was the largest and most important sale of land that had taken place in Sussex for some years.[17] The amount of money raised by the sale from the 56 lots amounted to £35,000 and the individual lots varied according to acreage and buildings. For example, the most expensive was the newly built residence of Woodlands, along with Lower Grouse Farm with its newly erected cottage and numerous tenements, altogether about 200 acres, which sold for £6,500. On the cheaper end were four new cottages in Colgate which sold for a total of £145 and

16. HM MS SP203.

17. Knight, J. (2008) *Horsham's History Volume 3 1880 to 1913*. Horsham: Horsham District Council, pp. 24-6 (hereafter Knight, 2008).

18. HM MS SP218.

small plots of building ground in Colgate from 10 shillings to £50, £70, £77 and £100. The Dragon Public House in Colgate sold for £120 and the brickyard with five acres, a good cottage, extensive shed and good supply of brick earth sold for £530.[18]

The newly wealthy were acknowledging the 'very exceptional advantages for the erection of a residence of a high character' outside of London, and yet within easy commuting distance, much as they would today.[19] For the generation of John Ruskin and William Morris, the Sussex Weald remained a surviving medieval landscape with its 'close-set fields, crumbling manor houses, lichened castles, ivy-covered churches'. This view contributed to the revival of handicrafts and the valuing of vernacular architecture within its garden or parkland, particularly in south-east England and within reach of London.[20] The garden historian Quest-Ritson cited economic and political changes that impacted large landowners at the end of the 19th century, such as the depression of agricultural rents and prices, new taxation and death duties. He noted that spending thus passed to the newly rich and that most of the major gardens of the 20th century were made by people who bought land in the depressed years from 1885 to 1925. The newly wealthy certainly looked to the Sussex Weald and bought up property around Horsham, such as the Messels at Nymans, the Godmans at South Lodge, the Loders at High Beeches and Leonardslee, and the Millais at Comptons Brow.[21]

The remaining mansion and the surrounding park of St Leonard's estate amounting to 1731 acres was put up for sale on 16 July 1896 in four lots, see illustration 41: page 100. This sale was triggered by two unexpected deaths, that of Colonel John Aldridge at the age of 57 in 1888 who was 'seized with a fit' after addressing the Board of Guardians.[22] The second unexpected death was that of his eldest son, Robert Beauclerk Aldridge at the age of 27 in 1892. Although death duties were not enacted until two years later in 1894, there would still be estate duties to pay and this would have been a burden on the family's finances.

In this 1896 sale, the first lot was the largest section of 1,422 acres which was described in the sales particulars as 'a charmingly rural and particularly attractive freehold residential and sporting estate ... only one mile from the pleasant country town of Horsham'. Railway links to the City and West End in under an hour were emphasised plus links to the south coast towns and north to Guildford, and to the south west. More comprehensive train links than we have today.

The sales pitch praised the lovely sylvan (woodland) views, and noted that the estate was within walking or riding distance of a number of other gentlemen's estates, which was important for the socially ambitious. The very exceptional sporting amenities were noted and the 800 acres of extensive woodland were said to be well suited to a large herd of game. To further entice the hunter, it was noted that the estate fell within the area patronised by the Crawley and Horsham Hunt, and that there were two other meets of

19. HM MS SP218.

20. Brandon, 2010, pp. 34-5, 141-4.

21. Quest-Ritson, 2003, pp. 220-3.

22. From two newspaper cuttings in the archive of Rev. Bloxham, Magdalen College, Oxford. MS 741.

foxhounds and staghounds locally. A map of the hunts was provided with the sales particulars to further emphasise this advantage. In addition, other sporting facilities were listed: fishing, boating and wildfowl shooting on the lakes, plus for 'those fond of the now fashionable game of golf' the park offered a 'natural golf links'. The new owner of The Grange and the eastern part of the estate, Edward Molyneux, did in fact establish a golf course at Mannings Heath to the south-east of the estate, which is still in existence today although now part of a wine estate which also owns Leonardslee.[23]

The sales particulars also show that in the main house there were 16 bedrooms, including those of the servants, a drawing room, panelled boudoir, dining room, library and study. The domestic offices included butler's pantry and bedroom, servants' hall, kitchen scullery, housekeeper's room, store room, larder and lamp room. In the basement were two wine cellars, two beer cellars and a furnace room. The outhouses consisted of a game larder, knife room, coal house, oil store, two wood houses, workshop and two servants' toilets. Stabling was to the rear of the house, and comprised a four-stall stable, a loose box with loft, harness room, groom's room, three more loose boxes and a large coach house. Apart from the pleasure grounds of lawn, rhododendrons, cedars and other specimen trees, the rose garden, laurel walk woodland and two tennis lawns, there was a walled kitchen garden with fruit trees and a large range of glasshouses within the walls. The glasshouses consisted of a vinery and a heated conservatory and peach house. Nearby was a mushroom house, orchard house, a gardeners' yard and store room, potting shed and tool shed. Two modern stone-built cottages were also nearby for the coachman and gardener.

Although this appears to be a fairly comprehensive list of assets for a working estate, there was more at the Home Farmstead, which the sales particulars noted were 'fully adapted to the requirements of a gentleman fond of farming' and it is interesting to see the beginnings of mechanisation through use of steam power on the farm. There were four yards, a complete fully tiled dairy and wash room with hot and cold water and two good cottages. There was the Bailiff's house with gardens, more stock yards and sheds. There was an estate timber yard with carpenters' and painters' shops, blacksmith's forge, saw pit and shed, steam sawing shed, portable engine adjoining a machinery house on two floors which housed a beanmill, root pulper, chaff cutter and cake breaker, presumably all for dealing with animal feed and all worked from the steam engine. A food steaming apparatus was listed which again one might assume was for cattle feed. There were two more cottages and a bake house. There was also a laundry in the centre of the estate with a good drying ground, a garden, orchard and woodland. Inside was an ironing room, a Benham's drying closet and an ironing store, wash room with large copper washing bins and rinsing tub.[24] Finally were listed: dog kennels, brick and enclosed runs, a chicken house and pheasantry in three divisions, a Keeper's cottage with garden and orchard. The

23. Edward Molyneux is referred to in the Court of Chancery during the 1901 Footpath Dispute as Edward, but in other archival evidence such as the Land Valuation Survey 1910-15 as Edmund Molyneux.

24. John Lee Benham (1785-1864) set up as a furnishing ironmonger in 1817. The company moved to Wigmore Street in London and his three sons joined him. They produced a large range of domestic ironware for houses and institutions, supplying the Australian colonial market and exhibiting in International exhibitions. Five successive generations of the family managed the company until it was taken over by Thorn EMI in 1965.

impression one is left with is of a large self-sufficient estate employing a variety of locally skilled people, both men and women.

Also included in the sale of Lot 1 was The Grange, garden and park making up 17 acres but let for life to the elderly Mrs Aldridge. Although she does not appear on the 1901 census, her four female servants do: the cook, parlour maid, house maid and a 17-year-old kitchen maid. The Grange had probably been built in the mid-19th century, close to the main mansion, as a dower house for single female members of the Aldridge family. Mary Alethea Aldridge, widow of Colonel John Aldridge, died there in 1908 at the age of 80, having seen all of the Aldridge lands sold, the final tranche in 1906. When he bought the estate from Molyneux, McGaw rebuilt the Grange in a Jacobean style. He renamed it, somewhat confusingly, St Leonard's Forest, and lived there rather than the old St Leonard's mansion.[25]

It was recorded in Court during the Footpath Dispute hearing that the plaintiff, Edward Molyneux was the owner in fee, meaning he was in complete possession, of the St Leonard's Estate comprising over 1,731 acres in the parishes of Lower Beeding, Nuthurst and Horsham. As noted in chapter 4, the dispute with the Horsham Rural District Council regarding the public rights of access over Forest footpaths would have cost him dearly. It was in the Chancery Division of the High Courts of Justice with two Queen's Counsels and a Barrister at law prosecuting for Molyneux; however, in the end it was settled out of Court. Perhaps this soured the ownership of the estate for Molyneux, for it was sold, probably before 1913, to John Thoburn McGaw (1872-1952) known as Jack, the son of an Irish landowner and entrepreneur who had built up large wealth from sheep and minerals in Australia. The estate may have been empty for a time as both the 1905 and the 1911 *Kelly's Directory of Sussex* does not mention Molyneux as an owner but rather the Trustees of Robert B. Aldridge as lords of the manor and one of the principal landowners in Lower Beeding. However, in the 1911 directory J.T. McGaw is noted as a principal landowner with H. E. Dennis as resident at St Leonard's Park. Moreover, the 1911 census has no mention of Molyneux in the Forest at that time.[26]

The 1910-15 Land Valuation Survey gives a clearer picture of land ownership and the value of the St Leonard's Forest estate, and how it was broken up into smaller estates. On 1 September 1913 it was noted in the field books, which were prepared from notes taken on site by inspectors, that Harold E. Dennis owned the freehold of the mansion land and sporting rights of St Leonard's Estate which amounted to 122 acres. It was valued 'as found', the inspector noting that the house had been much improved since 1909 although a prior value could not be given, but this rather indicates that Dennis had bought around 1909. The gross value of the estate was estimated to be £17,883, and this was made up of £12,083 for the buildings, £500 for timber, and £250 for fruit trees and £1,000 for other things growing on the land, which were not detailed. Additions were made of £300 for public rights of way, footpaths, and £83 for tithes. A sketch was made of the building with measurements and description of building material, mainly stone and tile, the condition of

25. Boorman and Djabri, 2009, pp. 46-59.

26. HM MS 2917.1-2, and *Kelly's Directory of Sussex* 1905 and 1911, accessed through: www.historicaldirectories.org. (hereafter *Kelly's Directory of Sussex* 1905 or 1911).

27. TNA, IR 124/9/116 and IR 58/94086.

which was given as 'good'. A semi-circular rose garden was drawn in the eastern corner of the front courtyard. There were five parts to the estate, and included in the valuation was a dairy, wash house and woodland, all without tenants, and then 53 acres of grassland rented out from September 1908 for £40 a year and valued at £2,514 over and above the mansion valuation. [27]

So, it appears that the old St Leonard's Forest mansion, New Lodge, now known as St Leonard's Park, had been bought freehold around 1908 or 1909 by Harold Egerton Dennis of the Dennis Bros Ltd motor car and bus pioneers of Guildford. However, The London Gazette of 1915 shows him in the Royal Naval Volunteer Reserve as a Lieutenant, so presumably Dennis served in the Royal Navy in the First World War and did not return to the Forest.[28] It certainly appears that McGaw owned the whole estate including St Leonard's Park and the Grange around 1913, although as this is the date of the Land Valuation Survey it may well have been later, particularly if Dennis served in the First World War and did not return. Once McGaw had bought the estate he lived with his family in the rebuilt Grange, and - confusingly, given the date – is noted in *Kelly's Directory of Sussex* 1911 as a principal landowner in Lower Beeding along with Saillard of Buchan Hill and Loder of Leonardslee. Jack McGaw continued to live at St Leonard's Forest in some style, establishing a private cricket ground on the estate and developing a talent for watercolour painting, exhibiting at the Royal Academy and founding the Association of Sussex Artists. He died in 1952 and the estate was sold by his family.[29]

Holmbush and Buchan Hill

Thomas Broadwood (1786-1861) bought the Holmbush estate, between Forest Road and the A264, in 1824-5. He was the third generation of piano manufacturers, John Broadwood & Sons, whose manufacturing site was based in Horseferry Road, London.[30] It was a very successful company supplying their own upright and grand pianos both in the United Kingdom and abroad. By 1840 the company was said to be one of the 12 largest employers of labour in London producing 3,000 pianos a year at its peak. As a young man, Broadwood had met Beethoven when visiting Vienna on a European tour, and wrote that Beethoven had played for him despite the fact that he was deaf and unwell. In 1818 Broadwood had sent him a gift of their newly improved triple stringed Broadwood piano, which was apparently later owned by Liszt, and is now in the National Museum of Budapest. It was said that other famous composers such as Chopin and Haydn all played on Broadwood pianos.

---

28. *The London Gazette* 8 June 1915 Issue 29186 p. 5513.

29. Boorman and Djabri, 2009, pp. 46-59 and *Kelly's Directory of Sussex* 1911.

30. References vary as to when Thomas Broadwood actually bought the estate, for example Pike and English Heritage give 1823 while Burke and Noel-Paton give 1824. Since the Peel letters (see chapter 3) show the estate was still up for sale in the summer of 1824, it seems likely that it was bought towards the end of 1824 or early 1825.

31. One sheet of notes and diagram of garden entitled *A Short History of Holmbush House* by Duncan Noel-Paton of Holmbush House, undated, distributed at Sussex Garden Trust visit on 14.5.2011. (hereafter Noel-Paton, 2011). Also Byrne, H. (2005) The Broadwood Family and their local connections, *Horsham Heritage*, Issue No. **13**, Autumn, pp. 29-39 (hereafter Byrne, 2005) and Mould, C. (2004) *Broadwood, Henry Fowler*, Oxford Dictionary of National Biography, accessible through: www.oxforddnb.com.ezproxy.sussex.ac.uk (hereafter Mould, 2004).

42. Copperplate engraving of Holmbush, built in 1826, illustrated in *Horsfield The History, Antiquities and Topography of the County of Sussex*, Vol 2, p. 222. Horsham Museum an Art Gallery (Horsham District Council).

Thomas was a partner in the company with his elder step brother, James Shudi Broadwood who, while keeping a house in London, moved to Sussex in 1799 and bought Lyne Farm near Rusper.[31] Thomas followed his brother's example by keeping an existing property in London, and buying an additional country estate. He first purchased Juniper Hall near Dorking with 47 acres and a farm of 78 acres. The property had been auctioned in 1814 and he may well have been the purchaser at that time. Timbs wrote in 1822 that Broadwood was the owner of Juniper Hall and had designed and built a tower of flint near the summit of Box Hill probably as an observatory or 'prospect-room', and most likely 'suggested by the well-known tower on Leith Hill'.[32]

Thomas Broadwood sold Juniper Hall to a Miss Beardmore and on her death it was bought by F. Richardson.[33] In 1824-5 Broadwood bought the much larger Holmbush estate and employed the architect Francis Edwards to design his new mansion. Holmbush was a two-storey castellated mansion with octagonal turrets, described by Horsfield somewhat damningly as 'domestic Gothic'. It stood high on the forest ridge and to the north the mansion looked over a rich valley towards Rusper where his brother had his country retreat, and in the distance Box Hill and the Surrey Hills; perhaps Broadwood could see his Juniper Hall tower there.

32. Timbs, J. (1822) *A Picturesque promenade round Dorking in Surrey.* London: John Warren, p. 12.

33. J.S. Bright (1884) *A History of Dorking and Neighboring Parishes*, London: Simpkin, Marshall & Co., p. 146.

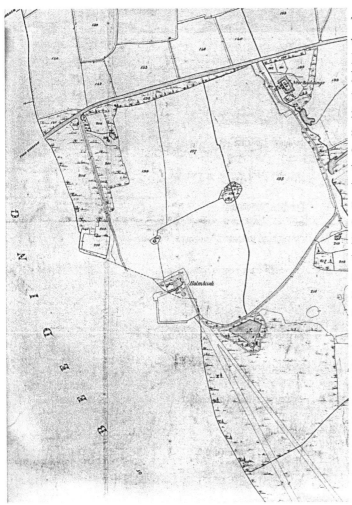

The back of the house faced south, with a good view of the garden and Forest. Early engravings show a very large fountain in the garden behind the house which must have been an impressive feature, illustration 42: above. Burke noted that to the north of the house, in the kitchen garden, were the springs of the Arun River which drained south, and to the south of the house were the springs of the Mole River which ran north into Fox Hole Pond, and that there was no lack of water on the estate, one lake being of 50 acres and three more lakes plus ponds of a lesser extent. As has been noted in chapter 1, the Forest was the watershed for these two important rivers, the Arun draining south and the Mole north. It can be confusing that Burke described the springs that fed the rivers rising in relation to the position of Holmbush House which is on a high point, although noting correctly that the river Arun drained south and the Mole to the north.[34]

43. Lower Beeding (Bewbush Tithing) Map 1841, 26.6 in to 1m., showing part of the Holmbush Estate. West Sussex Records Office TD/W160.

Horsfield, writing in the 1830s, noted that the turnpike road from Horsham to Crawley, which had been of concern to possible purchasers of the estate due to its proximity to the old house, was moved further from the mansion to the bottom of the hill, having been funded and completed by Thomas Broadwood by employing Macadam. The estate, Horsfield wrote, was '3033 acres ringed by a fence; fir trees grow well and contrast with the glittering sheet of water that is the lake'. He praised Broadwood for the greatly improved landscape scenery and commented that 'the garden and pleasure grounds are judiciously laid out, and the various productions raised in the garden have gained notoriety at the different horticultural shows of the county. Dahlias of every variety are raised'[35]. A native of Mexico, the first hybrid Dahlias had been introduced from France in 1815 and five years later they were the smart flower to have, along with geraniums and clematis. By 1839

34. Burke, B. (1852) *A visitation of the seats and arms of the noblemen and gentlemen of Great Britain and Ireland.* Vol. 1, London: Colburn, p. 24. (hereafter Burke, 1852).

35. Horsfield, T. W. (1835) *The History, Antiquities and Topography of the County of Sussex,* Vol. 2, Lewes: Sussex Press, p. 222 (hereafter Horsfield, 1835).

36. Stuart, D. (1988) *The Garden Triumphant, A Victorian Legacy.* London: Viking, p. 162.

there were more than 500 cultivars of dahlia but their popularity was beginning to wane, albeit that by the 1850s they were still very present in the autumn flower shows.[36] Quest-Ritson noted that by 1875 there had been a revival of interest, and this is confirmed by Robinson who, writing in the 1880s, was enthusiastic about the many beautiful varieties of dahlia, and noted that the newly introduced cactus and single varieties were, by then, taking over the shows.[37]

The Bewbush Tithing Map of 1841 encompasses Holmbush House and the eastern part of the estate, illustration 43: page 106.[38] The mansion is seen set in one acre of garden including pathways from the back of the house and its eastern side. In front of the house between the turnpike and the house are three fields identified as park and meadow of 88 acres, with the pump and small ring of plantations and outbuildings. On the west side is a driveway down to the turnpike, with a garden and orchard near the mansion and nine acres of birch coppice. At the end of the drive by the turnpike is what is described as a toy cottage and garden, small pond, and orchard. On the other side of the drive is another cottage and garden which is more like the gate house. To the south of the mansion house, garden and fountain, a garden path runs in a large loop, around to the east past the ornamental lake. It continues past Rose Cottage with a plantation and garden, and alongside a stream from Fox Hole Pond down to one acre of new buildings, tenements and yard at the turnpike.

The ornamental lake had a small island at the southern end and a 'cottage' which may well have been the boathouse. Between the lake and Fox Hole Pond are two arable fields of 11 and three acres each, but from the other side of the lake two wide rides cut through the Forest of 224 acres to plantations of 49 acres bordering Forest Road, the Horsham-Colgate-Pease Pottage road. This appears to be the extent of the pleasure grounds in the 1840s. According to the Tithe map, the estate also included the properties of Little Buckwood, Lower Baybush (Bewbush), The Hopper, Great and Upper Baybush. However, Kilnwood Farm with 173 acres to the north of the turnpike road to Crawley was not shown as being owned by Thomas Broadwood at this point, although it later appears to be part of the estate.

Burke, writing in the early 1850s, appeared impressed with the pleasure grounds. He suggested that the soil was particularly suited to growing American trees and plants. He cited the avenues of spruce firs and rhododendron which were growing to an enormous size, and one particular rhododendron he noted had reached a spread of 120 feet (36.5 m).[39] Quest-Ritson commented that the rhododendron became so fashionable towards the end of the 19th century that they became a mark of social respectability, and in fact the

---

37. Robinson, W. (1883,1903) English Flower Garden. London: John Murray, pp. 512-6 (hereafter Robinson, 1883) and Quest-Ritson, C. (2003) The English Garden, a Social History. London: Penguin Books Ltd., p. 206 (hereafter Quest-Ritson, 2003).

38. The relationship of this Tithe map of the Parish of Upper Beeding (Detached) or Bewbush to the untithed forest, and the Tithe Commutation Act of 1834 will be explained in Chapter 6.

39. It should be noted that the genus rhododendron is a large one, and although most come from China and the Himalayan region, some azalea types come from the eastern and southern United States.

40. Quest-Ritson, 2003, p. 207.

41. Burke, 1852, p. 24.

new wealth looking for a country residence would first check that the soil was suitable for the growing of rhododendrons before purchasing an estate.[40] Burke wrote of the Holmbush estate that the combination of natural advantages and money, meant the pleasure gardens were exceedingly beautiful. Gardens and pleasure grounds at this time offered the chance for new money to enter society, to demonstrate taste and gardening skills, and, not least, the size of the owners' bank balances.[41]

Situated in the south of the Holmbush estate was the tower, illustration 44: below, which Hurst records was erected in the summer months of 1855-7 by a man named Sumner, his son and another man called Cox. She wrote that the stone was dug on the estate, prepared during the winter and laid by Sumner in the summer. It was 106-foot-high (32.3 m) and built on the old site of the Napoleonic beacon, and when Hurst was writing about ten years later the tower was open to the public, for a fee, with a woman living at the bottom.[42] Later, in the early 20th century, it was lived in by the estate gardener and his family. The recollections of the gardener's son were of a nine-floor tower, from the top of which it was possible to see Crystal Palace on Sydenham Hill, London, and the south coast through the Shoreham Gap of the Adur valley.[43] The Ordnance Survey map of 1876 clearly shows the position of the tower at the end of one of the main rides through the Forest, illustration 45: below, labelled Beacon Hill and

44. Postcard dated 21/12/1906 showing the Holmbush Tower on the Holmbush estate, taken from Faygate Road.

45. Holmbush mansion and estate, OS County Series 1: 2500 1st Edition, 1876, reproduced with permission of Edina Historic Digimap.

42. Hurst, D. E. (1868, 1889) *The History and Antiquities of Horsham.* Lewes: Farncombe & Co., p. 164, (hereafter Hurst, 1868).

43. Pers. Comm. Gordon Isted of Ifield, Crawley, 19.4.2009 (hereafter Pers. Comm., Isted).

44. Burke, 1852, p. 24.

46. Postcard showing the fish pond and summer house on the Holmbush estate, date unknown, from West Sussex Record Office PH1095.

47. The square clock tower folly in the garden of the Holmbush estate.

Holmbush Tower. Thomas Broadwood clearly enjoyed towers and the views they provided, as he had built his first flint tower at Box Hill. This tower is still standing today, unlike Holmbush Tower which was dismantled in 1943 after it became unsafe following the bombing of Colgate during the Second World War.

An examination of the OS 1876 6 inch to one-mile map, and consultation of the accompanying Book of Reference to the Plan dated 1874, shows a considerable development of the pleasure gardens when compared to the previous 1841 Tithe map, illustration 43: page 106. It is striking how many more trees are indicated in the later map, and as mentioned in chapter 4, Burke noted that the owner had planted more than a million trees of larch, fir, oak, sweet chestnut and other varieties, which is well reflected in the later 1876 map.[44]

The looped path, clearly marked in the 1841 Tithe map, from the turnpike to Holmbush and around past the pond and Rose Cottage and back down to the turnpike, has been downgraded in the later map, and the link between Holmbush and Rose Cottage is filled with ornamental grounds and pasture. On the 1876 map the pond is called a fish pond with sluices, summer house and boat house, illustration 45: page 108. Paths lead from Holmbush House to the fish pond and south into 40 acres of woodland. There is a circular bed with a central point which may have been a statue or fountain, and what would appear to be a double circular ring of shrubs or flowers.

A short distance to the west, two wide and long rides from the house are clearly indicated on the 1841 Tithe map, the most easterly being labelled Church Walk and leading directly to the back of St. Saviour's Church in Colgate. This church was not in fact established until 1871, ten years after Thomas Broadwood's death. However, it is likely that it was built on the site of a small chapel which had in fact been built by Thomas Broadwood for himself and his family, given that the nearest church at that time was either at Crawley or Horsham.[45] Girouard, in his book on *Life in the English Country House* wrote that in the larger country houses regular family prayers became popular during the Victorian era, 1837-1901, with family chapels being built or the whole household assembling in the hall or dining room each morning for morning prayers. On Sundays the household walked through gardens or parks to the church, often 'newly built or restored at the pious expense of the owner of the house'. The family walked too, so that grooms and coachmen could observe Sundays by not working. One can imagine the Holmbush Church Walk serving exactly this purpose.[46]

Another wide ride, which would have been further east and off the edge of the 1841 Tithe map, ran from the house to Beacon Hill and Holmbush Tower. Here a bench mark height of 482.3 feet above O.D. sea level is given at the entrance to the tower on the 1876 map. Situated directly south of the circle bed and on Church Walk is the meeting of five paths with a statue indicated in the middle. According to an oral report, this statue was known as the White Man, but it seems nothing more is known about it.[47] At the back of the house there are two clear enclosures of garden, gated from the parkland beyond. These appear to be the pleasure gardens with woodland and lawn with a large fountain. There are also four small rectangular flower beds or tanks., To the west of the house on the 1876 map is the stable block and beyond that a large two-acre plot identified as 'garden' with a tank, probably walled with glasshouses; this would be the kitchen garden of which Burke had said that an equal degree of attention had been bestowed on it as the pleasure gardens.[48]

The three gates entering and exiting the gardens - the Blue, Green and the Stag Gates - were probably designed and built at the same time as the house and gardens were laid out and built by Francis Edwards for Broadwood. It is likely that the follies were also built in Broadwood's time, but whether initially or later is not known. The follies echo Broadwood's interest in towers in that there are the square clock tower, illustration 47: page 109, the round summerhouse and the small tower folly at the edge of the more formal garden to the west of the house. All of these are marked on the 1876 OS map but not labelled as such until the 1976 OS map, which then allows one to locate them on the 1876 map from their shape and position.

Thomas Broadwood was in the vanguard of wealthy London manufacturers and merchants who began to see value in the Sussex Weald, and who poured money in to create their country retreats. Others were to follow over the coming decades; estates were divided to enable smaller affordable country seats and landscape gardeners and architects were employed to recreate a tamed 'medieval' landscape. The Weald, and St Leonard's

45. Hudson T.P. (ed.) (1987) Churches, *The Victoria History of the County of Sussex* Vol. VI Pt. 3., The Institute of Historical Research by Oxford University Press, p. 27 (hereafter VCH Vol. VI.3).

46. Girouard, M. (1978) *Life in the English Country House.* New Haven & London: Yale University Press,

p. 271.

47. Pers.Comm. Mr Noel-Paton telephone call 16.3.2012, origin of statue not known but confirmed there were remaining plinths of other lost statues either side of the ride to the Blue Gate.

48. Burke, 1852, p. 24.

Forest, were ideal for this purpose, being wild and picturesque with the desirable acid soils for rhododendrons and yet, thanks to better communications via railways and roads, convenient to the new wealth, as either weekend retreats or as comfortable family homes.[49] Byrne noted that the Broadwood family loved sport, and indulged in hunting, shooting and fishing on their properties, for which Holmbush was ideal with its long vistas and rides, and it was in fact promoted as a sporting estate in 1824 with an abundance of game.[50]

Thomas Broadwood died in 1861 having done much to impose his idea of an ideal landscape on his part of St Leonard's Forest, of which a surprising amount has survived into the 21st century. He had designed a park of avenues, towers, gates and statues, more structured than the parkland of Capability Brown and reminiscent of the early Italianate pleasure park and garden, with elements of the picturesque in composition and scenic views. His estate was inherited by his eldest son from his first marriage, also called Thomas, but this Thomas moved to his uncle's house in Rusper, Lyne House, although he also spent much time on his yacht. The second son, John Jervis Broadwood, moved to nearby Buchan Hill, to the east of the estate, and did much to improve the building, but he did not live long and died in 1868. The piano business was inherited by Henry Fowler Broadwood who was the third son of James Shudi Broadwood, Thomas's half-brother and father of Lucy Ethelred Broadwood (1858-1929). Lucy lived at Lyne House and was a gifted pianist and singer in her own right. She travelled widely in England, collecting folk songs in the field, and contributed to the Folk Song Society founded in 1898. She was a friend and neighbour of the composer Ralph Vaughn Williams who grew up at Leith Hill Place in Surrey, and in 1910 performed his *Fantasia on a Theme by Thomas Tallis*, inspired by English folk songs. The Broadwood Morris Men established in 1972 honour Lucy Broadwood in their name and dance every May Day at Lyne House in her memory. The Broadwood family sold Holmbush House and pleasure grounds, firstly, unsuccessfully to a Mr Van-Agnew who was declared insane in 1864. Secondly, in 1868, they sold the estate, complete with Buchan Hill, to Colonel James Clifton Brown (1841-1917), younger brother of Sir William Brown, and grandson of Sir William Brown, 1st Baronet, Liverpool banker and merchant.[51]

Colonel Clifton Brown sold off the Buchan Hill part of the estate of over 1,000 acres to Philip F. R. Saillard, who built a new house on the site in 1882-3 designed by George and Peto. Saillard was born and educated in France and was a Liveryman of several city companies, master of makers of playing cards and merchant in Ostrich feathers. Lowerson noted that Saillard was proud of his origins and decorated part of the interior of his mansion with ostrich feather motifs in plaster.[52] *The Sussex: Historical, Biographical and Pictorial* book published for subscribers in 1907 was effusive of Buchan Hill which it stated 'is situated amidst some of the most picturesque scenery which all Sussex can boast' and noted that since Mr Saillard had owned it he had proved 'how greatly natural beauties may

49. Brandon, P. (2010) *The Discovery of Sussex*. Andover: Phillimore & Co Ltd., pp. 34-5, (hereafter Brandon, 2010).

50. Byrne, 2005, p. 31.

51. Noel-Paton, 2011.

52. Pike, W. T. (ed.) (1910) *Sussex in the Twentieth Century, Contemporary Biographies,* Brighton: W. T. Pike, p. 294, and Lowerson, J. (1980) *A Short History of Sussex*, Folkestone: Wm Dawson & Sons Ltd., p 167.

be improved as the result of constant and careful attention and far-seeing expenditure'. It is clear from this quote that a considerable amount of new money was being poured into the Buchan estate. It appears that a chain of ponds was created from the north to the south of the estate, and an aviary for pheasants. The 1897 OS map shows the four named ponds, three with fish, and formal parterre gardens to the west of the house. A very large walled garden with beds and sheds or glasshouses is shown plus another small fish pond. At least seven gardeners were employed on the estate, and Saillard appears to have achieved what many of the new wealthy London merchants and manufacturers were looking for: a country estate for status and relaxation.[53]

Saillard's landed wealth is also evident by looking at the Land Valuation Survey of 1910-15. This was a land valuation introduced by the Finance Act (1909-10) 1910 in Lloyd George's 'People's Budget' in order to raise taxes on the increase of land values from a base in 1909 following a sale or other change of ownership, somewhat like a present-day capital gains tax of 20% on land. The new tax was to raise revenue for social projects espoused by the 1906 Liberal government. Land ownership was still in the hands of the few: for example, an 1873 survey had found that in Sussex 25% of landowners held 97% of the land area. However, the legislation ran into considerable opposition and was repealed in 1920.[54]

The field book which included Saillard's land holdings estimated the gross value to be £85,225, considerably more than Clifton Brown in Holmbush at £41,718 (although additional properties made this £57,366), Dennis in St Leonard's Forest at £17,883 and Molyneux in The Grange at £30,527. The notes on Buchan Hill indicate considerable purchases after 1913, as the acreage is amended in red ink from 85 to 1,170, although there is no amendment to the gross valuation. The original valuation of £85,225 was made up of buildings and structures £47,200, timber £10,000, fruit trees £500 and other things growing on the land which was a catchall category, £5,000.

Valued separately, but also owned by Saillard at this time, was Bewbush House, or Manor House, buildings and land. Again, the original 195 acres have been amended in red ink to 215 acres, with six cottages. All these buildings were described as in very fair condition and consisted of a large eight bedroomed house with a dairy and cow stall for 50 cows, stabling, piggeries, calf pen and a large barn, total gross value was £7,525. Saillard is noted as the owner and occupier although he was also noted as the owner and occupier of Buchan Hill.[55]

Land ownership by Clifton Brown was quite widely spread to the north of Colgate. The main mansion of Holmbush was described as built of stone and slate, with numerous rooms for the family and their servants, a coach house, stabling, two cottages and a hovel, glass houses and potting sheds with 942 acres. The whole came to a gross value of

53. Editor not identified (1907) *Sussex: Historical, Biographical and Pictorial,* London: Allen North, published only for subscribers, no pagination.

54. Short, B., Reed, M., Caudwell, W. (1987) The County of Sussex in 1910: Sources for a New Analysis. *Sussex Archaeological Collections,* 125, pp. 199-224, and Short, B. (1997) *Land and Society in Edwardian Britain,* Cambridge: Cambridge University Press, pp. 9-37.

55. The National Archives (TNA) IR 124/9/114 and IR 58/94087.

£41,718. The valuation of £12,000 for the timber is striking and reflects the amount of mature woodland on the estate. As with Bewbush and Buchan Hill, the value of the timber in the north of the forest was greater than in the middle or south of the forest. Also estimated with this valuation was woodland of 614 acres, a gravel pit, water and sporting rights over 27 acres.

Other properties recorded as owned by Clifton Brown as part of the estate were Rose Cottage, described as a dairy with one acre and occupied by David Gibson. The 1911 census records David Gibson as the farm bailiff, 46 years old living with his 34-year-old wife, Mary and five children. The field notebook show S. Jupp occupying Home Farm and smithy. The other buildings which were identified in the field book were Home Farm with 156 acres and three cottages on a yearly rental to W. A. Jolliffe for £125. There was also Holm Farm occupied by Frederick Crook, a farmer in his own right. Black Hill House was also separately assessed. It had 26 acres and was rented out yearly. Next was Upper Bewbush Farm with land of 101 acres, later amended to 99 acres and rented yearly for £43 by J. Brooker from 1899. The 1901 census showed Jesse Brooker as a 47-year-old farmer on his own account, living with his wife of the same age, Mary, and their 12 children, eight sons and four daughters aged from 22 to two, with the eldest six appearing to work on the farm with their parents. Of necessity it was a large farmhouse with six bedrooms.

Finally, in the portfolio of Clifton Brown properties are Kilnwood Farm and Kilnwood House. The brick and tile farm house of Kilnwood farm had two reception rooms, kitchen, larder, four bedrooms, box room and lavatory. There were cow stalls for 24 cows, an eight-stall stable, piggery, barn, cart shed and hovels. The house and two cottages with 195 acres, amended from 131 acres, were rented yearly to Edward Barns at £85 per year and the gross value was estimated to be £3,390. A sketch map indicated that the condition was mainly good. *Kelly's Directory of Sussex 1911* shows the Barnes as a large local farming family. Frank and Albert are noted as farmers and Philip and Ernest are noted as poultry farmers at New Barn.

Kilnwood House is noted as brick and part tile, part slate, house of a good size for a middle-class family. It contained a library, smoking room, drawing room, telephone room, dining room, five bedrooms and two dressing rooms, nursery, four servants' rooms with their own hall, pantry and scullery. Outside there was a loosebox, and one stall, electric light generator, motor garage, glass houses, cottage and potting shed. According to a note attached to the field note book this house was furnished with shooting rights over 700 acres. The gross value was £5,200 and although the estimate of rental was £200 per year, no leasee was identified and the 1901 census has just a butler, two housemaids and a footman in residence, with coachman, groom and gardener in the stables. However, in the 1911 census it appears to be occupied by a Mr W. M. Scott and this is confirmed by *Kelly's Directory of Sussex 1911* which shows William Marten Scott living at Kilnwood.[56] Today, Kilnwood Vale is a large development of new houses, which is expanding over previous farmland, engulfing these old properties.

---

56. TNA IR 124/9/113 and IR 58/94086 and Kelly's Directories accessible through: www.historicaldirectories.org

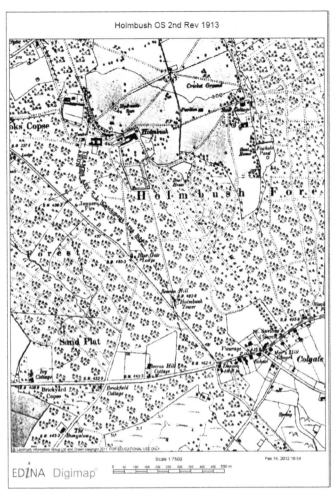

Holmbush OS 2nd Rev 1913

EDINA Digimap

48. Later map of the Holmbush mansion and estate, OS County Series 1:10560, 2nd Revision, 1913, reproduced with permission of Edina Historic Digimap.

The OS 1913 map, illustration 48: left, confirms that Clifton Brown kept Broadwood's basic design for the gardens, although the circle bed and statue in the five ways appear less prominent. Writing in 1905, Goodliffe commented on Holmbush Tower, which adjoined a tiny lodge at the entrance to the grounds of Clifton Brown's 'beautiful residence'. Having made the steep ascent of the tower he is repaid with a magnificent panorama and wrote that a finer view from the vantage point among the many trees of the forest could not be found elsewhere the country.[57] A postcard dated from 1906 shows the tower much as Goodliffe would have seen it, just near the side of the road to Faygate from Colgate, illustration 44: page 108. The development of this road, known as Tower Road, is clear on the 1913 map, with the entrance to the Holmbush Tower as well as that of the Blue Gate lodge clearly marked, this latter being only an unnamed gate on the previous 1876 map.

The fountain at the back of the house is no longer marked and had presumably gone by this time. In later modern maps there is a curious set of tiers, or terracing, on the back lawn which Noel-Paton believes to be Victorian due to photographs in his possession, however they are not indicated in maps of the time, and their exact purpose is unknown. The kitchen garden is less cultivated than previously, although the garden enclosure appears similar with fewer trees indicated. A very clear development is to the front of the house, between the house and the Horsham-Crawley road, and that is a cricket ground and pavilion.

The very striking Stag gates were embellished with the two stag sculptures, cast from zinc alloy by Joseph Winn Fiske at his ornamental ironworks in Chicago and imported by

57. Goodliffe, W. (1905) *Horsham and St Leonard's Forest with their Surroundings*. London: The Homeland Association, p. 54 (hereafter Goodliffe, 1905).
58. Noel-Paton, 2011.

49. The stag gates, Holmbush estate.

James Clifton Brown for his gates from the garden into the parkland or forest.[58] These were set on the original pillars of the gates and follow a hunting theme.

James Clifton Brown appears to have lived the life of a country gentleman at his Holmbush estate. He and his wife, Amelia Rowe, brought up nine children there, five boys and four girls, a sixth boy died. He was the Liberal MP for Horsham from 1876-1880, and served as Lieutenant-Colonel of the 1st Lancashire Royal Garrison Artillery and after retirement was given the title of honorary Colonel of the 2nd brigade Lancashire Division. In 1888 he was appointed High Sheriff of Sussex and served as a Justice of the Peace. Both he and his wife were great advocates for homeopathy, giving talks in support of it and sponsoring the Homeopathic Convalescent Home in Eastbourne and the London Homeopathic Hospital.

Like Broadwood before him he was clearly a keen sportsman, from sailing to shooting. He was a regular visitor to Southsea in the 1890s when two of his yachts, the 'Argula' and 'Petrel', took part in races and regattas.[59] With regard to shooting he took estates in Scotland for the season as the *Dundee Courier* noted in 1885 that 'the extensive deer and

---

59. *Hampshire Telegraph & Sussex Chronicle* (Portsmouth) Jul 7 1894, Jun 19 1897 and Aug 1898.
60. *Dundee Courier & Argus and Northern Warder* (Dundee) Feb 27 1885 issue 9862.

grouse shootings of Tulchan, belonging to the Earl of Airlie, have been let for the coming season to Mr J. C. Brown of Holmbush, Horsham Sussex. The rent is between £1200 and £1500'.[60] The slaughter at these shoots was quite breathtaking as noted by *The Hampshire Telegraph* which in its gossip column informed the reader that by renting Erchless Castle in Invernesshire one could kill a considerable amount of wildlife. As proof it wrote 'the Erchless bag last season, when Colonel Clifton-Brown had the place, comprised nearly eight hundred brace of grouse, thirty stags, nineteen woodcocks, nineteen roe deer, and nearly eight hundred head of miscellaneous game'.[61] From today's perspective one wonders what on earth they did with all that meat, and hope that it was not wasted.

Hunting and shooting were clearly important to Clifton Brown and so it is not surprising that he was attracted to Holmbush with its abundance of game, although perhaps this was decreasing - certainly the Black Grouse had gone. Noel-Paton wrote that after losing his seat as the Liberal MP for Horsham in 1880, Clifton-Brown became a farmer on a large scale and a successful breeder of cattle and horses. James Clifton Brown died in 1917 and his estate passed to his eldest son Howard Clifton Brown whose eldest daughter, Elizabeth, married Edmund Calvert and it remained in their family into the 21st century.[62] Continuation of ownership has an impact on this landscape. The rents from the farms and houses maintain an income for the landowner, and little change has occurred in the layout of the park and gardens. However, sales of land for development are now changing the wider estate landscape, as with Kilnwood Vale, a large new housing estate on the opposite side of the A264 to Holmbush House, with the promise of more to come.

Coolhurst

The Coolhurst estate lies to the south of St Leonard's estate, between Doomsday Green and Mannings Heath. In 1830, Arthur Chichester sold the Coolhurst estate of about 55 acres to Mary Compton, the Dowager Marchioness of Northampton.[63] According to Horsfield, the Marchioness spent a considerable amount of money improving the property, and he wrote that she had the main part of the house demolished and rebuilt by the architect P.F. Robinson of London, with the remaining offices improved and altered. It was rebuilt in the Elizabethan style, with the south front extending to 70 feet, opening onto a terrace protected by a gothic balustrade with steps in the front and at each end leading onto the lawn. The flower garden was at some distance from the house but 'enriched by magnificent timber trees and very fine rhododendrons' which, Horsfield wrote, added greatly to the beauty of the spot, illustration 50: page 117.[64]

The Marchioness died in 1843 and the Coolhurst estate passed to her daughter, Lady Frances Elizabeth, who married Charles Scrase Dickins. The Coolhurst estate has remained largely in the hands of this same family up to the present day, although the main house was sold in the 20th century. Hurst, writing in the 1880s, noted that at that time the

61. *Hampshire Telegraph and Sussex Chronicle* (Portsmouth) April 20 1889 Issue 5627.

62. Noel-Paton, 2011.

63. Hudson T. P. (ed.) (1986) *The Victoria History of the County of Sussex*, Vol. VI Pt. 2., The Institute of Historical Research by Oxford University Press, p. 165 (hereafter VCH Vol. VI.2).

64. Horsfield, 1835, p. 265.

Coolhurst. Engraved for THE GARDEN from a photograph. (See p.

51. Engraving of Coolhurst taken from *The Garden*, Vol. 31, 1887, showing the larger house and more mature garden. RHS Lindley Collections.

50. Engraving of Coolhurst before alterations, reproduced from Horsfield, (1835) *The History, Antiquities and Topography of the County of Sussex*, opposite p. 264. Horsham Museum an Art Gallery (Horsham District Council).

owner was Lady Frances Elizabeth's grandson, Charles Robert Scrase-Dickins (1857-1947) who was the present owner's great uncle. His obituary in *The Times* noted that he died in his 90th year, had attended Eton and Oxford, and was President of the County Hospital in Brighton as well as serving on the Almoners' committee of Westminster Hospital, and as a local Magistrate. It was suggested that he would be remembered 'as the creator of what is probably the most perfect, as it is certainly is the most natural, of wood gardens in a county where such places abound'.[65] This comment is interesting as the garden today is largely forgotten and yet less than a century ago it was regarded as a classic woodland garden.

According to John Newton, Chairman of the Shepherd's Cot Trust, the Scrase-Dickins family is fondly remembered in Crouch End, North London, for their generosity in donating land for the building of a new church, Christ Church, by the gothic revival architect A. W. Blomfield. It appears they had leased Shepherds Cot Farm, part of the 294 -acre Rowledge Farm in North London. It is not entirely clear what other connection the Scrase-Dickins family had with this area, although the name of Coolhurst remains there today as the name of the road leading up to where Shepherds Cot Farm used to be, and also in the name of a well-respected local tennis club.[66]

Dorothy Hurst, writing in the second edition of her book dated 1889, on Coolhurst noted that the house was a fine specimen of the Tudor style of architecture. Unusually around the top of the house was a carved Latin frieze of the first verse of the 127th psalm, which translates to 'Except the Lord build the house, they labour in vain that build it'.

---

65. The Times, Sept 06 1947 p. 7, issue 50859.

66. With thanks to John Newton, Chairman of Shepherds Cot Trust, February 2020

67. Hurst, 1889, pp. 145-6.

Hurst also noted that in the grounds azaleas, rhododendrons and other shrubs 'flourish in great beauty' and that a fine sheet of water was formed from the river Arun.[67]

At the beginning of the 20th century, Goodliffe wrote about his walks through this part of the Forest. He described how he had walked past Hammer and Hawkins ponds, and the large house called The Goldings, he then reached the head of Coolhurst pond on the left with St Leonard's Lodge on the right with a quarry and the Sun Oak, which he describes as 'one of the grandest specimens in the forest', see frontispiece. He commented on the fine woods of Coolhurst and their abundant treasures of specimen larch, pine, beech and oak. Near the forest church of St John, built in 1835, he saw a magnificent Californian redwood, *Sequoia sempervirens*, which he estimated to be 70 to 80 feet high. He then described what he guessed, from its attractive garden, was the gardener's cottage in whose care, he wrote, was a beautiful collection of bulbs and herbaceous plants. In the private grounds he noted huge azaleas and rhododendrons and the 'graceful foliage of a well grown *Fagus asplenifolia*, or fern-leaved beech'.[68]

The Ordnance Survey map 1st Revision of 1897, illustration 52: page 119, clearly shows the small Coolhurst estate south of Hammerpond Road with the entrance to the Aldridge estate to the north east, St John's Church in Coolhurst wood and the mansion of Coolhurst itself with orchard and large kitchen garden. The large area marked as Coolhurst woods between Hammerpond Road and Mill Pond show paths through planted woodland and a series of small ponds on the eastern side linking with the Mill Pond. These were used to great effect to grow water lilies by Charles Scrase-Dickins according to his great nephew. Immediately south and west of the house is the parkland, giving good views to the water over a ha-ha, or designed ditch, with Coolhurst Farm to the west.[69]

Pike's Blue Book of 1899-1900 recorded that the gardener on the Coolhurst estate at that time was Andrew Kemp. In addition, there was William Weller in Coolhurst Lodge, Charles Reynolds was the bailiff and Henry Peacock the coachman. The later 1901 census provides a bit more detail in that it shows Charles Reynolds, aged 61, living at Coolhurst Farm, with his wife, Elizabeth, 59, working in the dairy with her single 36-year-old daughter and 80-year-old mother. In West Lodge was Anne Peacock, 64, and her husband, Henry, 60, who is shown in the main house where he was working as coachman. They had four adult sons and daughters living with them, all single. The eldest daughter, 39, was not noted as having any occupation, but the eldest son was a carrier, the youngest daughter, 32 a court dressmaker, the youngest son was an engine cleaner, and lodging with the family was a 25-year-old boarder who was a baby linen maker. By this time, 1901, it appeared that William Waller had died, and his widow, Susan, 77 was the lodge keeper in her own right, with her single daughter, Helen, 40.

In another lodge was William Pronger, 38, gardener, with his older wife, Eliza, 48. There were two young men, John Edwards, 25 and Charles Wells, 19, both gardeners, and

---

68. Goodliffe, 1905, p. 48.

69. Personal discussion with Major Mark Scrase-Dickins, great nephew of Charles Robert Scrase-Dickins, at Coolhurst, on 6.3.2012 (hereafter Pers. Comm. 6.3.12).

as their address was Coolhurst Gardens, they were perhaps lodged in a bothy. Andrew Kemp, 60, was in Coolhurst Cottage, not noted as a gardener but rather lodge keeper with his wife, 67 and two single daughters, Jessie aged 24 and Jeannie, 20. Jessie was a teacher and Jeannie a maker of some description, possibly dressmaker but difficult to decipher. The Kemp family were all born in Scotland, and Andrew Kemp was noted in *The Garden* journal of 1887 as previously the gardener for 'Mr Cunningham, of Orchid renown in Scotland and well known to be one of the best Orchid growers in the country'. Kemp was clearly a respected and skilled gardener, one of a growing profession who would be valued by the estate owner and enthusiast. Finally, there was another cottage with a widower, James Cook, 61, a gamekeeper, and his 25-year-old son who was a house painter. In the main house itself the Scrase-Dickins family were not resident on census day, and could perhaps have been staying on their Irish estate, but there were two young laundry maids in residence, Emily Jones, 28 and Lizzie Turner, 21, along with Henry Peacock the coachman. Thus, it can be seen that a total of 24 people lived on the estate, however only half of them were employed by Coolhurst, that is seven men and five women.[70]

The 1901 census shows that Coolhurst is a much smaller estate than St Leonard's Forest which had raised £35,000 in its sale of 1881. The Coolhurst estate, with its emphasis on gardeners, had an older community of workers, with single adult children living with their parents but working outside the estate, and with no younger children. Although only a snapshot in time it is not quite what one would expect, for example, there is a high number of older single women working in a variety of trades. The Valuation Survey of 1910-1915 shows the Coolhurst estate with house, garden, stabling, park, dairy farm with 17 cows, garden cottage and the three lodges, south, north and west, to have a

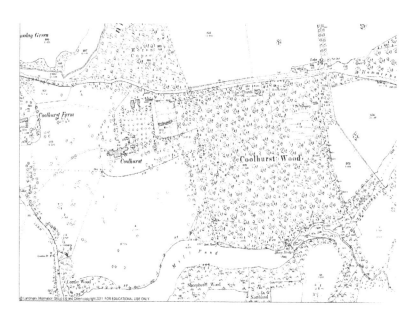

52. Coolhurst estate and wood, OS County Series 1:2500, 1st Revision, 1897, reproduced with permission of Edina Historic Digimap.

70. *Pike's Blue Book* 1899-1900, Horsham, Crawley and District, and Goldring, W. (1887) Coolhurst, Sussex. *The Garden*, Vol. 31, p. 25, and Census of England and Wales, 1901, Sussex, Reg. Dis. 13.

53. Photograph of Coolhurst Mansion from the south, 2014.

gross value of £17,768 and to total 87 acres. This is an increase in acreage from the original 55 acres when the Scrase-Dickins family inherited the property in the mid-19th century.

The personal recollections of Major Mark Scrase-Dickins, who is still resident on the estate, suggested that the Coolhurst estate was in fact much larger than just the house, garden, park and farm. Additions had been made by the inheritance of land from the Aldridges through Charles Robert Scrase-Dickins' mother, Anna Maria Aldridge, daughter of Robert Aldridge, and also through acquisition which extended as far as the village of Mannings Heath.[71] The Valuation Survey Field Books confirm this further extent of the family's holdings at the beginning of the 20th century. When the details were recorded in 1913, Charles Robert Scrase-Dickins (1857-1947) is noted as the freeholder not only of the Coolhurst estate but also Coolhurst Mill Farm and Whitebridge, three Coolhurst cottages at Buchanbridge Hill, three cottages on Doomsday Green, Rickfield Farm, Lower Goldings Farm, Birchenbridge House and mill machinery, Mill Farm Cottage, Northlands woods and orchards, land and cottages at Mannings Heath, Holm Farm, Woolmers Farm, Newells Farm, Newells mansion and park, Seamans Farm, and Forest House. The vagaries of the field books allow for some duplication and omissions, but given this the freeholds amount to a further 585 acres at a further gross valuation of £51,592, which is a good accumulation of property over half a century.

71. Pers. Comm. 6.3.12.

The field books show how the value of the estate is made up. Arable is not mentioned apart from 'other things growing' and the crop is not specified. One comment related to Coolhurst Mill Farm is 'arable rather foul', although the grassland is in fair condition, grassland being sometimes mentioned in the comments. One can only assume that arable did not feature much in this estate although fruit production, mainly apples, was of some importance. From the total value of the whole estate of £69,360 the timber value was £1,923, fruit £953 and grassland £256. It appears that ownership of the estate and rents were of more importance than farm production; however, what is missing from this is the production of dairy cattle, the grassland was good grazing and Major Mark Scrase-Dickins recollected that the estate was an early breeder of Jersey cows. An interesting feature that does reoccur on these properties is that their state is mainly poor, particularly in the cottages, such as the Doomsday Green cottages, one of which, rented by a Frank Tanner, was 'partially falling down' the other two are noted as in 'poor condition'. It is perhaps an indication of the interest shown in the estate as a whole that a comment made by the valuation inspector of six acres of land and buildings at the Goldings is that 'owner is not certain where this is so has not given any other particulars'. It appears that the owner's interests lay in plant breeding and growing rather than maintaining the buildings on the estate.[72]

In 1934 Charles Robert Scrase-Dickins was awarded the Royal Horticultural Society (RHS) Victoria Medal for Horticulture as an amateur gardener and successful grower of difficult plants. It appears from journal articles thirty or so years earlier that he was indeed expert in the growing of camellias, lilies, orchids and early bulbs, using his house at Coolhurst and the gardens there to showcase his achievements. An entry in the 1885 edition of *The Garden*, an illustrated weekly journal of horticulture founded by William Robinson of Gravetye, Sussex, and author of well-known and innovative garden books such as *The Wild Garden* and *The English Flower Garden*, first shows an entry by Scrase-Dickins about the cultivation of camellias. He wrote an article about the cultivation and habits of the single camellia, a rare plant at that time, and replied to readers' questions. He noted that his own single camellias were too precious to test their hardiness, but saw no reason why, like the doubles (many petalled), they should not thrive out of doors, and in this he was proved correct. He had three distinct varieties of single camellia, a single white, a large pink colour and a red. These were drawn and painted at Scrase-Dickins' garden on 6 March 1885 and served as an illustration in *The Garden*, illustration 54: page 122. He wrote that a curious little form of the common single red grew at Coolhurst against an east wall, over 15 feet high and quite old. He thought it 'a jolly little thing, quaint and pretty for cutting'. A later article by W.G. Goldring suggested that Scrase-Dickins had 'undoubtedly the finest collection of seedlings in Europe'.[73]

William Goldring (1854-1919), journalist and landscape gardener, visited Coolhurst in June 1886 and his description and impressions were published in the January issue of The Garden the following year. Initially, Goldring was struck by the colour, scents, and sounds

---

72. Pers. Comm. 6.3.12, and TNA IR 124/9/120, IR 124/9/124, IR 58/94028, 94036, 94040, 94041, 94045, 94047, 94086, 94987.

73. Desmond, R. (1994) *Dictionary of British and Irish Botanists and Horticulturists.* London: Taylor and Francis and C.R. Scrase-Dickins (1885) Garden Flora, Plate 506, Single Camellias, *The Garden* Vol. 28, pp. 202-3.

The White Indian Azalea (A. Indica), in a wood at Coolhurst, Sussex.

54. Photograph reproduced from William Robinson's The English Flower Garden, 1883, 1903, John Murray, London, page 121.

of birds and insects which assailed his senses and which he thought was totally in harmony with the quiet country home that was Coolhurst.

He speculated that the garden remained much as it had a hundred years ago, avoiding the 'modern caprices' of fashion, and was satisfied that the only bedding out was in a tasteful stone edged parterre. He described how welsh poppies, yellow fumitories and wall ferns grew from crevices in the house walls and terraces, a very natural planting with a sense of the wild that would have pleased Ruskin. The lawn sloped towards the park and lake, separated by the ha-ha, and beyond was a dense wood. The lake was full of water lilies, and the park had many fine hawthorns including one of a pendulous habit. Goldring was impressed by the arboretum, and suggested that perhaps Bishop Henry Compton (1632-1713) of Fulham Palace, an ancestor of the Marchioness of Northampton, and an inveterate collector of exotic and unusual trees and shrubs, had helped to enrich the arboretum. Given the dates, this is unlikely, although the Marchioness may have had access to some unusual specimens through this family link.

Goldring's very thorough article named the varieties of tree and shrubs that he saw at Coolhurst. Of the non–native trees he wrote that they were mostly from North America, such as the false acacia, black walnut, hickories, magnolias, snowdrop trees and amelanchias. He noted the presence of some European trees such as evergreen oaks, silver leaved lime, wingnut and pear. The conifers also appeared to be mainly North American with the Canadian hemlock fir, Californian Cypress and Californian redwood, although Japanese red cedar grew well. Native beeches were the prevailing trees on the lawns, but there were also oaks and sycamores of remarkable size, wild service trees, mountain ash and yews, fine groups of scotch fir and old birches by the lake. The glory,

---

74. Goldring, W. (1887) Coolhurst, Sussex. *The Garden*, Vol. 31, pp. 21-2, 25.

according to Goldring, was the arboretum which in June of 1886 when he visited was 'aglow with fiery tints of azaleas and the air filled with their spicy fragrance'. He was impressed with the size, quality and colour of the azaleas and thought the rhododendrons were remarkable, but not so elegant or picturesque as the azaleas.[74]

William Robinson, in his book *English Flower Garden*, quotes Scrase-Dickins who recommended growing the white Indian azalea, which flowers early and grows well outside if sheltered and left to grow naturally. A photograph in this book shows *Azalea indica* in full bloom in a wood at Coolhurst, Sussex, see illustration 54: page 122. There was clearly some uncertainty at this time as to whether camellias and azaleas were hardy enough to be grown outside, and Scrase-Dickins was at the forefront of trying a variety of specimens in his woodland garden. Goldring noted that vases of Azalea indica were in the hall and dining room of Coolhurst when he visited, along with a 'grand specimen' of the orchid *Cattleya lobata* with three spikes of flower.[75]

A later journal article in *Country Life* in 1936, which focussed on the growing of lilies in garden and woodland, demonstrated what an expert Scrase-Dickins must have been in developing and growing a variety of lilies. In fact, he was invited to be one of the first amateur growers to join the RHS Lily Committee when it was set up in 1931. The article

55. Group of single camellias drawn at Coolhurst, 6 March 1885, artist unknown, and illustrated in *The Garden*, 28, page 202. RHS Lindley Collections.

---

75. Robinson, W. (1883, 1903) 8th Edition, *The English Flower Garden and Home Grounds*, London: John Murray, pp. 121-2.

76. Taylor, G.C. (1936) Lilies for Garden and Woodland, *Country Life*, 14 Nov 1936, pp. 507-9.

mentioned a very desirable white martagon lily growing in open woodland at Coolhurst, and a hybrid of the orange lily, *Lilium croceum* named Coolhurst Hybrid, which was found and developed at Coolhurst. Five of the six photographs in the article show different varieties of lily growing in the Coolhurst woodland garden.[76]

Leonardslee

As noted earlier, approximately 1,000 acres of the southern part of the St Leonard's estate was sold by John Aldridge in 1803 to Charles George Beauclerk who built a house on the land called St Leonard's Lodge, and set out an ornamental garden and kitchen, or walled, garden. Charles George Beauclerk (1774-1845) was the only son of Topham Beauclerk (1739-80) and Lady Diana Spencer (1735-1808). With these eminent, scandalous and profligate parents it is perhaps unsurprising that the quiet and retiring Charles Beauclerk should look to the secluded St Leonard's Forest to make his home.[77]

Charles was educated at Eton and Oxford and after graduating he was sent to Italy due to his poor health. He recovered well and married Emily (Mimi) Ogilvie (1778-1832) the first cousin of his close friend, the 3rd Lord Holland. She was the daughter of the Dowager Duchess of Leinster and her second husband, William Ogilvie, former tutor to the Duchess' 22 children. Lady Holland described Charles Beauclerk as intelligent but silent, suggesting that he was lost in shyness. Lady Holland also reported that he was spending far beyond his means and thought he would be half-ruined by the purchase of the southern portion of St Leonard's estate for which he had sold up his investments and also the crumbling ancestral home of Speke Hall in Liverpool. Initially, due to the costs of farming the new land, he could not afford to build a house, but Lady Holland reported later that in about 1808 he had completed the house and had fathered eight children in as many years, but she feared for Mimi's isolation in St Leonard's Forest.

Hicks noted in the epilogue to her biography of Charles' mother that Charles and Mimi went to live in Italy where Mimi became a noted hostess, friendly with Shelley, Byron and Trelawney. Djabri suggests that in fact it was only Mimi that went to Italy, taking her daughters with her and introducing them into society there. Indeed, one of her seven surviving daughters, Caroline Anne Beauclerk who married Robert Aldridge, heir of the St Leonard's estate, became a close friend of Mary Shelley and had been much admired by Edward Trelawney (1792-1881) the adventurer and biographer.[78]

The Beauclerk family were supportive of Mary Shelley, author of 'Frankenstein', daughter of Mary Wollstonecraft and second wife of Percy Bysshe Shelley, when she returned to England with their small son after Shelley's death. Caroline's sister, Georgina became her best friend and tried to intercede on her behalf with Sir Timothy Shelley, her father-in-law who lived at Field Place, Horsham, and who had not forgiven Mary for

77. Hicks, C. (2001) Improper Pursuit, *The Scandalous Life* of Lady Di Beauclerk, London: Macmillan Publishers Ltd., Diana's family tree (hereafter Hicks, 2001).

78. Hicks, 2001, pp. 254, 357 and Djabri, S.C. (2005) Charles Beauclerk of St Leonard's Lodge, *Horsham Heritage*, 12 Spring, pp. 31-45 (hereafter Djabri, 2005).

79. *The Morning Post*, London, England, Monday, April 29, 1839, Issue 21316.

eloping with his son and thereby abandoning his first wife and family. It seems Mary Shelley was fond of the eldest Beauclerk brother, Major Aubrey William Beauclerk, and had hopes of marriage to him, but he was five years her junior with two illegitimate children and he chose to marry the 19-year-old third daughter of a Baronet, Ida Goring. Ida later drowned in one of the ponds on the Leonardslee estate on 23 April 1839, when she was 24 years old. The inquest found she had probably been 'seized with giddiness' and accidentally fallen in.[79] Mary Shelley offered comfort and sympathy to the widower Aubrey Beauclerk but marriage still did not come her way and instead Aubrey turned to her young friend, Rosa Robinson.[80]

When first at St Leonard's Lodge, Charles Beauclerk had been enlisted as a Captain and was then promoted to Major in the Sussex Volunteers, commanding three companies in the Northern Division. This force had been set up to defend the homeland from Napoleon Bonaparte and was disbanded when peace came. When war in Europe ended Mimi felt able to go abroad, and perhaps Charles joined her for at least some of the time, although there is no evidence of this. There is, however, evidence in *The Morning Post* of 1826 that the Duke of Rutland was residing at 'the seat of Mr and Mrs Beauclerk in St Leonard's Forest', perhaps as a guest or leasee, but that in 1827 the Duke was due to dine with Mr Beauclerk at his seat there.[81] It must have been around this time that Charles put his energies into developing the basics of a great garden at St Leonard's Lodge. Later, after Mimi's death in 1832, he moved to South Lodge, just across the road from St Leonard's Lodge. The 1841 Census records him living there by himself with two male servants and two female servants. This was the property of Henry Boldero (1788-1859) the member of a military family who had shooting rights over the St Leonard's Lodge estate let by the Beauclerk's on an annual basis. This move had allowed his eldest son, Aubrey William Beauclerk, to live at St Leonard's Lodge with his first wife and then, after she drowned, his second wife, Rosa, where the 1841 census records them with five young children and seven servants.

There is a hint of how productive the estate was in a comment made in *The Hampshire Telegraph and Sussex Chronicle* of 1833, which discussed the poor harvest of that year and compared the previous year's production when the estate of Mr Beauclerk of St Leonard's Forest produced 6,000 bushels of apples compared to the current several hundred.[82] Further evidence of this comes after Charles Beauclerk's death in 1845 from the detailed sales particulars of 1852 when the estate was sold by his eldest son, Aubrey. The sale was presumably in an effort to honour the codicils of his will, given that there was an order from the High Court of Chancery to sell following a court hearing of Perry and Another versus Beauclerk and Others.[83] The 1852 sales particulars state that for sale were 1,919 acres of productive arable meadow and woodlands with some thriving plantations including 96 acres of valuable orchard in a high state of cultivation. The annual income value given for this estate was £1,638 13s 9d with an extra £27 7s 0d for ground rent on

80. Seymour, M. (2000) *Mary Shelley*. London: John Murray (publishers) Ltd., pp. 414-426.

81. *The Morning Post*, London, England, Monday April 10, 1826 Issue 17256 and Saturday May 19, 1827 Issue 17606.

82. *Hampshire Telegraph and Sussex Chronicle*, Portsmouth, Monday July 8, 1833, Issue number 1761.

83. *The Standard*, London, England, Saturday May 15, 1852, Issue number 8663.

84. East Sussex Record Office, SAY 2831.

long leases of 999 years.' Another attraction emphasised in the sale particulars was the accessibility of the estate, about 37 miles from the metropolis. It was noted that the estate was only four miles from a railway station at Horsham, and five miles from a station at Haywards Heath, allowing easy access to London, and demonstrating the suitability of the estate for the new London wealthy and their need to escape from the city.[84]

As can be seen from the plan of the estate attached to the sales particulars, illustration 56: left, the estate was split into four lots, to be sold separately or together. Lot one consisted of St Leonard's Lodge, the mansion house, park, meadow, pasture, woodland and plantations, sundry cottages and houses and an estate on the northern edge of 48 acres known as Stonewick. The whole of lot one amounted to 955 acres and brought in an annual income of £803 in rentals. The mansion house in stone and slate with eight bedrooms was described as suitable for a family of distinction and 'delightfully situated on table land reigning over well-timbered

56. Plan of the St Leonard's Lodge (Leonardslee) estate attached to the sales particulars of 1852, East Sussex Records Office SAY 2831.

park and beautifully undulated domain, lake, valley, picturesque and extensive views of Weald of Sussex with the renowned south down hills in the distance'.

Descriptions of the pleasure grounds near to the house show how much Beauclerk must have been the initiating force for the laying out of the garden. The gardens are described in the sales particulars as being very ornamental, interspersed with walks beneath luxuriant growing Beech and other timber and comprise the American Garden containing magnolias, rhododendrons, azaleas and other flowering shrubs in great luxuriance, of great height, growth and beauty. This would indicate a reasonably mature garden already set out with exotics. The American Garden is identified on the map to the north of the mansion house amid a maze of paths. Hurst recorded that the American Garden was planted by Beauclerk and was one of the oldest in the country, 'having

---

85. Hurst, 1889, p. 167

magnolias of different kinds, rhododendrons and similar shrubs of great height and size'. The Wellingtonias, *Sequoiadendron giganteum*, which are still standing today, having been introduced to the UK in about 1853.[85]

The kitchen garden was situated a short distance from the house to the east, part walled and extending to just over one acre, clothed with fruit trees, both bushes and standards, and including peach. Beyond the kitchen garden was the park of 32 acres, described as beautifully timbered, undulating woods and thriving plantations, with a winding and extensive lake timbered to the water's edge. There were the usual buildings of a thriving estate, the coach house, stabling, cow sheds, wood house, coal house, piggery, fatting sheds, barns, bark shed, carpenters' workshop, cider house, and ice house. In addition, were a number of cottages which included much of the village of Lower Beeding on the north-east side of the estate, beyond this still being owned by Robert Aldridge and the St Leonard's Estate. [86]

The 1852 sales particulars show that the central part of the estate of 955 acres, identified as Lot One, in the parish of Lower Beeding, was mostly garden, parkland and woodland with some arable fields growing wheat, oats, rye, barley and turnips. Around the edges of the estate was Lot Two to the south, Park Farm with 612 acres, Lot Three to the north east, Chase Farm with 184 acres, and Lot Four to the north west, Eastlands with 166 acres. Of note are the orchards of Park Farm which were 86 acres of mainly apples, with a cider and apple house amongst the barns. Chase Farm and Eastlands also had orchards of about ten acres between them. At Chase Farm value would have been added by the addition of a smart five-bedroomed residence with gardens and pleasure ground, with a tenant, and Eastlands had been improved with a range of new farm buildings for cattle and fattening.[87]

The estate was bought in its entirety by a wealthy merchant who traded with Russia, William Egerton Hubbard (1812-1883), and who was the younger brother of John Gellibrand Hubbard, first Baron Addington. It appears that Hubbard not only bought the whole estate but added 57 acres to it over the next two decades. The Parliamentary Returns of 1875 record a list of landowners in Sussex holding over 1,000 acres, and W. E. Hubbard is listed as having 1,976 acres, producing a gross annual rental of £2,188 21s 0d per annum.[88] Before purchasing the St Leonard's Lodge estate, which he renamed Leonardslee, he had been living and working in St. Petersburg with his family and had returned to settle in England in 1843. The family consisted of his wife, Louisa Ellen Baldock, four sons and three daughters. The eldest of the children, Louisa Maria Hubbard (1836-1906), was born in St. Petersburg and educated at home in Leonardslee. She grew up to be a great advocate of women's education and employment and was influential in increasing work opportunities for women, initially through the Anglican Deaconess

86. East Sussex Record Office, SAY 2831.

87. East Sussex Record Office, SAY 2831. The discrepancy of two acres between the total acreage of 1919 for sale and the individual lots of 1917 is made up by the rods and poles not noted.

88. Ellis, W.S. (1925) *The Parks and Forests of Sussex, Ancient and Modern*. Lewes: H. Wolff, p. 249.

89. *Oxford Dictionary of National Biography* entry for Louisa Maria Hubbard, accessible through: www.oxforddnb.com.ezproxy.sussex.ac.uk and Wojtczak, H. (2008) *Notable Sussex Women*. Hastings: The Hastings Press, p. 66.

57. Photograph of Leonardslee in 2009.

movement. She wrote and published pioneering works and was central in bringing about changes for the position of women in Victorian Britain through founding a teacher training facility in Chichester, and what later became known as the Royal College of Midwives.[89]

When Hubbard bought the estate his initial concern was with the house, St Leonard's Lodge, which although in a good position was in need of attention. Hurst wrote that the view from the house and grounds of Leonardslee were almost unrivalled in varied richness and beauty.[90] Thus the original house was demolished and a new Italianate mansion built of sandstone was erected on the site in 1855 to the design of T. L. Donaldson, and renamed Leonardslee. It does not appear that Hubbard added much to the garden that Charles Beauclerk founded, although clearly the gardens and grounds were being managed well by the gardeners. Short *et al.* note that a good variety of cooking apple, named 'Dr. Hogg' in honour of the Victorian pomologist of that name, was developed from a seedling of the variety 'Calville Blanc' by the head gardener of Leonardslee, Mr S. Ford, and it gained an RHS First Class Certificate in 1878.[91]

In 1876 Hubbard's youngest daughter, Marion, married into a local family, the Loders of High Beeches near Handcross, five miles from Leonardslee. Sir Robert Loder, Bt. bought High Beeches in 1847. His father had also been trading in St. Petersburg it is likely the families knew each other from this connection. Sir Robert was a keen gardener, exhibiting at horticultural shows including the Crystal Palace, and this interest was shared by several of his seven sons. The eldest brother, Edmund Loder (1849-1920), inherited the Baronetcy in 1888 and acquired Leonardslee the following year from his in-laws, the Hubbards, Marion's father having died five years previously.[92] One of the younger

90. Hurst, 1889, p. 167.

91. Short, B. with May, P., Vines, G., Bur, A-M., (2012) *Apples & Orchards in Sussex*, Lewes: Action in rural Sussex & Brighton Permaculture Trust, pp. 28, 36.

92. Thacker, C. (1994) *The Genius of Gardening, The History of Gardens in Britain and Ireland*. London: Weidenfeld and Nicolson, p. 262, (hereafter Thacker, 1994) and Loder, R., undated, Leonardslee, lakes and gardens. Guidebook published by Leonardslee, pp. 4-5 (hereafter Guidebook Leonardslee).

brothers, the fifth son, Gerald, began to create the gardens at Wakehurst in 1903, which are now part of the Royal Botanic Gardens at Kew. Wilfred, the second son, inherited High Beeches but it was his son, Giles, who was the enthusiastic gardener and continued the work of his grandfather from 1906.

On coming to Leonardslee Sir Edmund Loder brought with him gardening experience from his previous garden at Floore in Northamptonshire where he had lived with his family for 12 years. Here he had grown narcissus, cacti and tree ferns and had also built a rock garden. Sir Alfred E. Pease quotes in his memoir from Sir Edmund Loder's own notes which, as a meticulous naturalist and horticulturist, assisted him in the acclimatisation of exotic plants. He regularly noted rainfall, degrees of frost, minimum and maximum temperatures and described the situation of Leonardslee as 270 feet above sea-level, nine miles from the northern slopes of the South Downs and 13 miles in a direct line to the sea near Shoreham.[93]

Sir Edward Loder was not a public man. Although he served on the local Magistrates bench this was his only public duty. His friend and neighbour, John G. Millais (1865-1931), the fourth son of Sir John Everett Millais, painter and founder with Holman Hunt of the Pre-Raphaelite Brotherhood, and an expert on rhododendron himself, wrote that Sir Edmund Loder began collecting rhododendrons and azaleas, and then became more interested in the hybridisation, having been introduced to Harry Mangles who first hybridised them at Valewood House on the Surrey-Sussex border and was known as the 'high priest of the rhododendron cult'. Sir Edmund increased his knowledge of the subject by reading, corresponding with nurserymen and botanic gardens, and by visiting other enthusiasts such as J. C. Williams at Caerhays in Cornwall. After years of development he produced his most successful hybridisations which were the *Rhododendron loderi* group. Millais contributed to Sir Alfred Pease's memoir suggesting that the *Rhododendron loderi* was 'without doubt the finest hybrid rhododendron ever raised and one that as a hardy shrub is never likely to be surpassed.' Of the many varieties produced and named by Sir Edmund, Millais wrote that the variety most admired was 'King George.' He further noted that he grew the loderi group in his garden at Compton's Brow, Horsham, and its high quality stood out from the others.[94]

Sir Edmund Loder continued to plant in the American garden, or the Dell, and to increase the planting on the slopes and walks of the valley, paying attention to colours and grouping so that the woodland effect would be retained. By the turn of the century Leonardslee was being acknowledged as a superb garden. The head gardener, W. A. Cook, was publishing small pieces of horticultural interest in the *Gardeners' Chronicle* regarding plants and trees growing at Leonardslee. For example, in March 1907 he contributed the fact that there was a fine large 93-foot *Liriodendron tulipifera*, or tulip tree, growing at Leonardslee, and in the same month reported on the size and care of a magnificent

93. Pease, A. E. (1923) *Edmund Loder, Naturalist, Horticulturist, Traveller and Sportsman, A Memoir.* London: John Murray, p. 65-6, (hereafter Pease, 1923).

94. Pease, 1923, pp. 68, 303-6, and Brandon, 2010, p. 141.

95. Cook, W. A. (1907) Liriodendron Tulipifera, and A Large Camellia Tree out of doors. *Gardeners' Chronicle,* March 30 1907, pp. 208-9, Magnolias at Leonardslee, *Gardeners' Chronicle,* April 6 1907, p. 223.

58. Rhododendron loderi 'King George' with kind permission of Chris Loder, Loder Plants. See www.loder-plants.co.uk

Camellia near the house that had produced between 5,000 and 6,000 double pink flowers the previous year. The following month, in April 1907, he described 18 different species of Magnolia growing well at Leonardslee, with recommendations for care and maintenance.[95]

In October 1906, a lengthy article in *Gardeners' Chronicle* had extolled the excellence of the planting and the variety of plant species at Leonardslee, following a visit by the journal's writers, unidentified, to the gardens in June of that year. Their attention was first caught by the Palm Walk, winding away from the mansion on the west side and containing over 400 palms interspersed with bamboo and flowering shrubs such as camellia, deutzia and *Choisya ternata* and of course rhododendrons which featured throughout the garden. They commented how this planting gave the garden an 'unusually exotic appearance' given that the palms were large and could be seen from every viewpoint. However, they judged that the alpine garden and the shrubberies were the 'paramount features' of the garden. They noted the rock garden to the north-west behind the mansion. This was created in 1900 by James Pulham and Son from two types of their own artificial creation of rock called Pulhamite, and planted with azaleas and numerous varieties of alpines of varying habit such as the saxifrages. Walking from the rock garden to the American garden, or Dell as it later became known, they observed that there were fewer trees than formerly, and that the undergrowth consisted of choice rhododendrons and other flowering shrubs. A supplementary illustration of the American garden in the May 1907 issue, the photograph taken in January, showed the hardy palms amongst leafless deciduous trees and the comment was that the palms and bamboos were a foil to the colourful rhododendrons and roses of June and July.

After noting the collections of bamboos and heathers they commented that the kitchen garden had a warm south wall planted with a large selection of less hardy flowering plants for their protection. The vegetable garden was described as being a full five acres; the production looked promising, and included 500 apple and pear trees encompassing 120 different varieties. Indoor plants were also cultivated in the greenhouses and included chrysanthemums and over 2,000 carnations in 100 different varieties as well as soft indoor fruit. The end of the article emphasises that the success of this private garden reflected credit on its gardener, W. A. Cook, who clearly was very skilled and an asset to Sir Edmund Loder. However, Sir Edmund Loder was the driving force behind the

---

96. Anon., (1906) Leonardslee, *The Gardener's Chronicle*, October 13 1906, pp. 253-4 and continued October 20 1906, pp. 272-3. (hereafter *The Gardeners Chronicle*, 1906).

development of Leonardslee, and as *The Gardeners' Chronicle* noted he 'possesses zeal for everything concerned with its betterment'.[96]

Sir Edmund Loder was also well known in zoological circles as an enthusiastic naturalist and kept a variety of live animals in the gardens, and a collection of dead ones in the museum at Leonardslee. Goodliffe writing before 1905 noted that near the house to the west the turf was divided into paddocks in which grazed deer, antelopes, gazelles, ibex, springboks, mountain sheep, prairie dogs, wallabies and kangaroos, while on the other side of the valley amongst bracken and pine trees were fallow deer and Australian bush turkeys. In the ponds, beavers and beaver rats were kept. The 20th century guide book notes that historically Sir Edmund Loder kept antelopes, axis deer, beavers, bush turkeys and barasingha (also known as swamp deer from parts of India and Nepal, and prized for their antlers), capybara and cavies, kangaroos and kookaburras, moufflon, prairie dogs, wallabies and mountain goats.[97] It is good to know the wallabies, much loved by the public, survived into the 21st century.

The Land Valuation Survey of 1910-15 indicated that at this point in time the four original lots of the estate bought by Hubbard were still intact. Although W. E. Hubbard had died in 1883, his family still remained in the area for a short while. Goodliffe noted that W. Egerton Hubbard, presumably junior, was in residence at Selehurst and Miss

59. Photograph of Leonardslee in 2019

97. Goodliffe, 1905, p. 65 and Guidebook Leonardslee, p. 5.

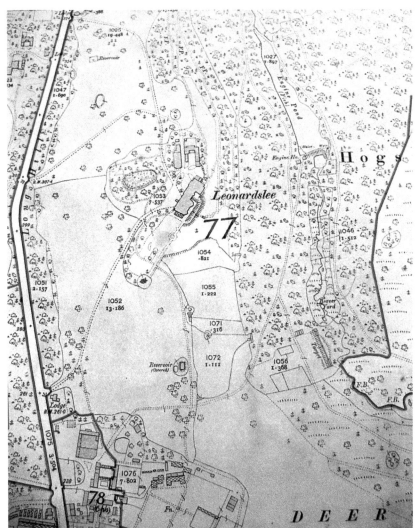

60. Plan of Leonardslee with beaver yard and ponds, target range, kitchen garden in the south, the museum behind the house, and rock garden to the west, from the Valuation Survey plan TNA IR 124/9/221.

Hubbard at Beedinglee. Both properties were owned by Loder when Goodliffe was writing. It is probable that the Miss Hubbard was Louisa. Pratt wrote that she stayed on the family estate until 1883 when, after her father's death, her brother built her a new home in Leonardslee. However, the 1911 census, as well as the Valuation Survey field books, no longer indicated any Hubbards on the estate in the first decade of the 20th century. The field books show Selehurst owned by Loder but leased to Basil Lang and Beedinglee also owned by Loder and occupied by a Mrs Rutherford.

The Land Valuation Survey confirmed that the value of the whole estate was quite considerable. Many of the cottages and small businesses in Lower Beeding and Crabtree were part of it, including farms such as Eastlands and Park Farm, and large houses such as Selehurst and Beedinglee. However, by far the most valuable property was Leonardslee itself, the mansion and gardens valued at £38,050 and noted in the comments as 'all garden pleasure grounds'. The value of the timber was given as £1,602 and fruit £300 but under 'other' was value noted as £5,000, presumably giving this value to the garden.

Park Farm and its 14 cottages were the next in gross value at £16,374, with fruit trees valued at £2,500. The total gross value of the whole Loder estate added up to £111,367, 10.4% of this value being in timber, with less than 3% in fruit, and so the building and the land made up the bulk of the value.[98] The Land Valuation Survey was dated 1910-15, when the estate was the most valuable in the Forest, clearly enhanced by the creation of the garden at Leonardslee. This was clearly just before the First World War and before the death duties that followed the loss of the next generation in Sir Edmund Loder's only son, Robin, in 1917, and Sir Edmund himself in 1920. In the 1924 *Country Life* article by Cox on Leonardslee, he wrote that the garden was a fitting monument to the late Sir Edmund Loder, and noted that 'his plan was the betterment of rhododendron hybrids in general and the adornment of his own woodland in particular'.[99]

Impact of 19th Century Horticulture on the Forest Estates

The layout of Holmbush parkland, designed by Thomas Broadwood and his architect Francis Edwards, tends to hark back to the geometric patterns of the early 18th century before such things were swept away by picturesque sensibilities and the simplicity of the lakes and pastural parks of Capability Brown. It is suggested by Tom Williamson that before 1750 the Italian influence was felt in the symmetry of line with prospects and terraces, sculpture, grottos and balustrading, the garden and pleasure grounds being considered together with the house for the first time. Status came from a demonstrable knowledge of classical allusion but also from the setting of a purely ornamental park. Early in the 18th century avenues planted with lime or sweet chestnut became distinctive of this period, often forming networks throughout the park with open ironwork grilles and gates set in the perimeter walls of the garden which allowed extended vistas down the length of the avenues, the widest and longest focused on the façade of the house.

All these features of an early 18th century landscape echo the manner in which Holmbush Park was laid out, although surprisingly this was sometime after the influence of Capability Brown (1716-1783) and so for this estate it demonstrates a return to structured order around the house and a delight in gardens and pleasure grounds. Thomas Broadwood must have enjoyed his avenues, towers and prospects, which were becoming more prevalent under the influence of designers such as Uvedale Price (1747-1829)[100] and Richard Payne Knight (1750-1824). Williamson writes that avenues had particular symbolic significance, in that they demonstrated the owner's possession of all the ground over which they passed and the enclosure and control of that land. One reason that this design appealed to Broadwood, and he planted many trees to create it, was that he could ride and hunt easily on the straight avenues, getting a clear shot at deer or grouse, something that would also have appealed to his successor Clifton Brown, illustration 61: page 134. Williamson wrote that 'the park was a landscape moulded by every aspect of the

98. TNA, IR 124/9/221 and IR 124/1/51, also IR 58/94086, 94087, 94089.

99. Cox, E.H.M. (1924) Leonardslee. *Country Life*, July 19, 1924, p. 98.

100. Everson, P. and Williamson, T. (1998) Gardens and designed landscapes, Everson, P. and Williamson, T. (eds) *The Archaeology of Landscape*, Manchester: Manchester University Press, pp. 139-165. (hereafter Everson and Williamson, 1998)

101. Williamson, T (1995) *Polite Landscapes, Gardens and Society in Eighteenth Century England*, Stroud: Alan Sutton Publishing Ltd., pp. 19-31, 140.

102. Hurst, 1898, pp. 148-9.

61. The avenue from Holmbush House towards site of the tower.

lifestyle of the class by whom it was owned' and this became very true of this part of St Leonard's Forest.[101] It should also be noted that Hurst refers to a fine avenue of ancient Spanish chestnuts in the main avenue up to New Lodge, the residence of the Aldridges, in the centre of the Forest.[102]

At the beginning of the Victorian era, John Claudius Loudon (1783-1843) was an influential garden designer and journalist, whose ideas impacted not only Victorian gardening taste, but also improvements in the education and status of gardeners. In 1832 he wrote for the first time about a concept he called the 'gardenesque', where each plant was displayed to its best advantage without competition. Simo wrote that Loudon was 'delighted to observe the beauty of each individual young plant as it made daily progress towards its ultimate perfection of form'. Loudon had a lifelong fascination with trees and enjoyed seeing them grown as specimens in this way so that their whole growth and shape could be appreciated. Perhaps the wonderful weeping beech tree at Holmbush, which Noel-Paton suggested is one of the largest in the country, was placed on the edge of the lawn to be seen and admired in just this manner, illustration 62: page 135.[103]

The gardenesque Victorian designs of Loudon arose as a reaction to the later 18th century landscape parks, and doubts as to what form of 'nature' was acceptable and should be followed. For example, William Gilpin (1724-1804) and his picturesque style required wild scenery with rocks or grottos artfully composed. Gilpin wrote that the picturesque was 'that kind of beauty which would look well in a picture', while John Ruskin (1819-1900) demanded nature in the raw, wild and unaffected by man.[104]

Glass houses were important in the production of new bedding plants. Perhaps unsurprisingly, there was also a growing interest in gardening journals which discussed the best methods of caring for and propagating plants. The status of the head gardener grew with the influx of exotic bedding plants and the increased skills needed to maintain them. W. A. Cook of Leonardslee and A. Kemp of Coolhurst were examples of these skilled and valued head gardeners. Kitchen gardens were also a feature of all of the five St

103. Simo, M. L. (1988) *Loudon and the Landscape, From Country Seat to Metropolis* 1783-1843, New Haven and London: Yale University Press, pp. 33-6, 87, 165-170, (hereafter Simo, 1988).

104. Elliott, B. (1986) *Victorian Gardens*. London: B. T. Batsford Ltd., pp. 7-20 (hereafter Elliott, 1986) and Dixon Hunt, J. and Willis, P. (eds) (1988) *The Genius of the Place, the English Landscape Garden 1620-1820*, Cambridge, MA: MIT Press, p. 337.

Leonard's Forest estates, and good gardening skills were essential to maintain the fruit and vegetables demanded by the Victorian household, family and staff. The kitchen gardens were separate enclosures surrounded by ten-foot walls, and included glasshouses, frames and pits.

Both Coolhurst and New Lodge had kitchen gardens near to the house for convenience, suggesting they had been built before the early 18th century, as later in the century it was thought preferable to have them sited away from the mansion house, by this time they were busy workplaces, full of the noise and smells of horticulture. However, Everson and Williamson suggest this has been much exaggerated, most kitchen gardens being directly accessed from the ornamental

62. Weeping Beech on the lawn at Holmbush.

pleasure grounds as part of the principal walks from the house, and growing flowers as well as vegetables. Campbell noted that a one-acre (0.4 ha) kitchen garden could feed 12 people and required two or three gardeners to maintain it. Leonardslee's kitchen garden was in fact five acres. In 1852 it was described as partly walled and clothed with fruit trees, and in 1906 *The Gardener's Chronicle* article gave a good account of how the garden was used for fruit, vegetables and flowers. Acreage of the other kitchen gardens is not noted, but the sales particulars for New Lodge in 1896 described an excellent walled kitchen garden, planted with standard and wall-trained fruit trees and including a mushroom house and a range of glass houses which were used to cultivate vines and peaches.[105]

Coolhurst has no sales particulars to refer to - being in the same family now for seven generations. However, the Land Valuation Survey of 1910-15 did have a drawing of the Coolhurst kitchen garden. It showed three large brick, tile and glazed houses, within the garden on presumably the south facing wall, all of poor condition. There were three tall ten-foot sheds on the opposite wall, of fair condition, and two brick and glazed glass houses outside the walls, again south facing, of fair condition. The drawing also shows another two shed buildings outside the east wall, one of poor condition and one of fair condition.

Holmbush had little information about the kitchen garden apart from the fact that the Land Valuation Survey noted that there were eight glasshouses and four potting sheds, all of good condition. Buchan Hill had even less information, but the large kitchen gardens

105. Everson and Williamson, 1998, pp. 139-165, and Campbell, S. (1999) *Walled Kitchen Gardens,* Princes Risborough: Shire Publications Ltd., pp. 3-9.

can be seen on the 1st Edition OS map 1897 to the south of the main house. The provision and maintenance of kitchen gardens were perhaps less subject to garden fashions than the garden and park land, although exotic fruit and tender plants were reared in them. They were, however, a necessity for providing each estate with fresh food, and as long as these estates remained and there was labour enough to work in them, they survived.[106]

The mid-19th century saw the popularity of geometric and colourful bedding schemes but also the contrast of quiet winding woodland paths through shrubberies. Collections of trees, and the more formally arranged arboretum, were noted by garden writer Jane Loudon, wife of J. C. Loudon, in 1843, as a fashionable and effective way of achieving maximum enjoyment from a minimum of space. Although the terraces and bedding can be barely glimpsed in the garden of New Lodge on the 1875 1st Edition OS map, illustration 38: page 93, to the south east of the mansion is a clearly marked Laurel Walk. Although this sounds quite dull, the 1896 sales particulars describe Laurel Walk Wood as an extensive tract of woodland 'ornamented with very handsome beeches, intersected by winding walks, and charmingly planted with laurels, rhododendron etc'. It led down to Sheepwash Gill and the beds of wild Lily of the Valley, *Convallaria majalis*, which had established there.[107] Both Coolhurst and Leonardslee took their woodland walks to new heights in the second half of the 19th century when the organisation of arboretums gave way to a more relaxed woodland embellishment as promoted by William Robinson (1838-1935) of Gravetye in Sussex in his first book *The Wild Garden* published in 1870. This book advocated the 'naturalising or making wild innumerable beautiful natives of many regions of the earth in our woods, wild and semi-wild places'.[108]

However, it appears that it was not so much the new appreciation of gentler, naturalistic planting in woodland and border that was being applied at Coolhurst and Leonardslee, but rather a scientific enquiry regarding new plants and the possibilities for their care, maintenance and improvements in the climate and geology of their portion of Sussex, St Leonard's Forest. At Coolhurst, Scrase-Dickins had hybridised successfully *Lillium croceum* and experimented with growing what were thought to be tender varieties of camellia and azalea in his woodland. Although he was a naturalist and horticulturist, as were his near neighbours the Loders, Millais, du Cane Godmans and Stephenson-Clarke, he does not appear to have mixed easily with them socially or professionally, possibly because he was not of the hunting and shooting fraternity. Also, both Millais and Loder were particular experts in the rhododendron. John Guille Millais (1865-1931) produced a seminal book on the subject *Rhododendrons and their Hybrids*, published in 1917 after many years of work in his 16-acre garden at Compton's Brow on the north-east edge of St Leonard's Forest. In the preface to his book he acknowledged the 'tutelage of my friend and neighbour, Sir Edmund Loder, who at all times has given me the benefit of his great

106. Campbell,1999, pp. 3-9 and HM, SP230; *The Gardeners Chronicle*, 1906, and TNA, IR 124/9/114 and IR 58/94087.

107. Horsham Museum, SP 230.

108. Elliott, 1986, p. 94, and Elliott, P., Watkins, C. Daniels, S. (2007) 'Combining Science with recreation and . Pleasure': Cultural Geographies of nineteenth-century arboretums, *Garden History*, Vol. **35**: Supplement 2, pp. 6-27, (hereafter Elliott *et al*, 2007).

109. Watson, J. N. P. (1988) *Millais: Three Generations in Nature, Art and Sport*, London: The Sportsman's Press, pp. 116-7, 164-5.

knowledge of the genus'. Millais advocated less space in a garden given to lawns, borders, roses and herbaceous plants and more space given to beds and woodland walks of flowering shrubs, exactly as had been developed at Coolhurst and Leonardslee.[109]

The naturalist F. du Cane Godman lived opposite the gates of Leonardslee at South Lodge, and his interest was in collecting rare plants, which included the rhododendron, and developing orchids and carnations. In 1895 a journalist for the *The Gardeners' Chronicle* wrote of seeing not only a large and pretty rock garden but a 'lofty winter garden filled with giant specimens of Indian rhododendrons and their hybrids already exhibiting many hundreds of large trusses of delightfully fragrant flowers'. It is interesting that Pease noted that in fact the Loderi hybrids were developed from crosses of 'exceptionally fine sweet-scented R. *fortunei* and a very large flowered R. *Griffianthium* that existed in Mr Fred. Godman's green-house at South Lodge'. Perhaps it is not surprising that this group of enthusiasts shared their plants as well as their knowledge.[110]

Goodliffe had mentioned the fine woods at Coolhurst and specified particular outstanding trees. However, this was the only garden of the five St Leonard's Forest estates that had been described as an arboretum, and this was by Goldring in his article in *The Garden*, 1887, as noted earlier in the chapter, in which he wrote that this was the 'glory' of the Coolhurst garden. Clearly, Leonardslee also had a collection of exotic trees which began with Beauclerk's American garden early in the 19th century, but it is not certain whether it was ever scientifically arranged and called an arboretum. American gardens were a development from mid-18th century shrubberies which were planted with newly imported North American flowering trees and shrubs, and were perhaps the precursor to the 'wild garden' of Robinson. The American shrubs included magnolia, kalmia, azalea and rhododendron as well as cistus, arbutus and ericas, all of which were at home on the slightly acid and increasingly humus-rich soil of St Leonard's Forest.[111]

Arboretums gained in popularity from the 1830s, encouraged by J. C. Loudon's great work on trees called the *Arboretum et Fruticetum Britannicum*, published in eight volumes in 1838. As Jane Loudon had recommended, arboretums were regarded as suitable additions to private gardens, as well as parks and botanical gardens, as they were collections of both deciduous and evergreen trees, mainly exotic, one specimen of each and systematically displayed in order to better study the acclimatisation and growth of the trees. J. C. Loudon, who designed the Derby public arboretum which opened in 1840, also recommended growing native trees with exotics, as specimens in the gardenesque style for aesthetics as well as scientific enquiry. William Robinson, along with others, reacted against these collections of exotic trees and complained that many of the finest native varieties were not grown, whilst money was thrown away on worthless exotic trees like the Giant Redwood, *Sequoia wellingtonia*.[112]

110. Anon., (1895) South Park, *The Gardeners' Chronicle*, Vol. XVII Third Series Jan-June 1895, April 20 1895, London, Covent Garden, p. 485 and (1906) Vol. 39, Third Series Jan-June 1906, pp. 98-9, and Pease, 1923, p. 305.

111. Laird, M. (1991) Approaches to planting in the late eighteenth century: some imperfect ideas on the origins of the American garden. *Journal of Garden History*, Vol. 11 No. 3, pp. 154-172.

112. Hadfield, M. (1967) *Landscape with Trees*, London: Country Life Ltd., pp. 139, 155-183, and Quest-Ritson, 2003, pp. 203-4, and Elliott *et al*, 2007, pp. 6-27.

Tree collecting had of course preceded the fashion of arboretums, but the new species which increasingly came into Britain from the late 18th century encouraged this trend towards arboretums which became particularly popular from the 1830s. For example, when the American pacific conifers were introduced by David Douglas (1799-1834) and later by William Lobb (1809-1864) they caught the enthusiasm of landowners. In the Sussex Weald, Borde Hill, Sheffield Park, Nymans and Wakehurst, all participated in the collection of exotic trees in the latter part of the 19th century and beginning of the 20th until the First World War closed borders and trade. Elliott *et al.* considered arboretums to be one of the most important developments in landscape gardening in the 19th century. They suggested that as the Victorians and Edwardians strolled in a public park or through their own estate 'they reaffirmed a beautifully ordered conception of nature, whilst partaking of the triumphs of science, commerce and exploration, conquest and empire'.[113]

---

113. Elliott *et al*, 2007, pp. 6-27.

Sweet Chestnut with nuts, *Castanea sativa* by Dr Maggie Weir-Wilson.

Chapter 6

Society and Community

Diarists and their Leisure

The diaries that survive from the Georgian period clearly indicate that the Forest was viewed as a pleasant place to go for leisure, away from the cares of work and family. The agreement, or permission, of the owners of the Forest land, such as the Aldridges, would of course always be needed. There are two very different diaries from the 18th century that give a glimpse of life in and around Horsham and St Leonard's Forest after 1750. Sarah Hurst wrote her diary from 1759 to 1762 about her daily life and aspirations. At the time Sarah was writing she was a young woman working in her father's drapery shop in Horsham. She was hoping to marry a soldier, Henry Smith, thirteen years her senior and serving with the Marine Corps against the French in Canada during the Seven Years War struggle for colonial dominance.[1] The second diary was written from 1750 to 1779 by John Baker, a Solicitor who moved to Horsham as a mature man. In considering how far and in what ways St Leonard's Forest was used by the residents of Horsham, the diaries do give some clues for this section of society, showing that they used it for leisure, riding out and walking for their health and pleasure. It should be noted however, that unlike the Common where the public had free access across it, the Forest was private property, and although footpaths and routes through were well marked and presumably well used this would have been with the permission of the landowners, see chapter 4.

In June 1760 Sarah noted in her diary that she consulted the doctor for headaches and pain in her joints and he recommended exercise, so she rode out on horseback, and also went out in the 'chariot' sent to her by neighbour Mrs Tredcroft. She wrote of 'a pleasant ride in the forest' and at another time 'ride out in the forest, most delightfully pleasant'. In the July she was in better health and noted 'very busy in the shop all morning. Ride to the Hammer Pond in the afternoon with Sally Sheppard and her brother, Stringer. We drink tea there and then ramble about the forest, such excursions as these are vastly agreeable at this delightful season'. There is little doubt that the forest she refers to is St Leonard's Forest, because of the reference to the Hammer Pond. On a fine day in September 1760, she rode with her father to Slaugham, south east of the Forest, to visit the Rev. John Bristed, Rector of Slaugham from 1749 to 1783. Sarah wrote that they walked about the forest and observed the beautiful scenes and admired the 'paradise' in which God had

---

1. Djabri, S.C. (ed.) (2009) The Diaries of Sarah Hurst 1759-1762, Stroud: Amberley Publishing, pp. 16-20, 50. Sarah Hurst's Diaries and their transcriptions by Barbara Hurst are held by Horsham Museum MSS 3542-3 and 3541. (hereafter Djabri, 2009).

63. Postcard from 1900s. Hammerpond Lane with church wall on the left.

placed them. This certainly confirms that those who went to the Forest enjoyed the natural forest scenery.[2]

Another clue as to how the Forest scenery was regarded comes from a letter written at around the same time that Sarah was writing her diary entry, probably between 1758 and 1760, by Elizabeth Ingram of Hills, Horsham, to her sister in law, Frances Ingram, later Lady Irwin, at Temple Newsam in Yorkshire. In the letter she wrote 'We have a forest near us that is beautiful without the help of art and where we go a airing thro' rides of two or three miles. Mr Wicker (of Park House, Horsham) has sent us a key of a part of the forest call'd Leech Poole that is beyond description pretty and full of stately oaks and ponds with the large and noble carp'.[3]

In his book *Landscape and Western Art*, Andrews writes that by the end of the 18th century natural scenery had become a valuable commodity, an amenity, and this had an impact on heathland and waste areas, such as St Leonard's Forest, that had previously been seen as of little value.[4] In 1792 the Rev. William Gilpin described two types of landscape, one round and smooth as in chalk downland, the other varied and wooded, such as the Weald, and he praised this latter type as more aesthetically pleasing and desirable. This demonstrated a change in perceptions from a fear of the dark wooded places to valuing them for their romantic natural scenery, a picturesque landscape which was rocky, wooded and well composed 'as if by art'. The French and Napoleonic Wars had brought an end to the grand tours of Italy and the continent of Europe which had

2. Djabri, 2009, pp. 150-3, 209-10.

3. Djabri, S. C. (ed.) (2002) *A Little News from Horsham, Some 18th century letters from Hills,* Horsham: Museum Society, pp. 34-5 (Hereafter Djabri, 2002) and HM, MS 792.2.

4. Andrews, M. (1999) *Landscape and Western Art,* Oxford: Oxford University Press, pp. 55-75.

been such an essential part of a wealthy education. The upper classes now turned to British landscapes for education in aesthetic appreciation, and found it amongst places in the Lake District and the Weald, comparing the views with many in Italy. This also began to bring within the sphere of the growing middle classes the opportunity to attain and develop 'picturesque estates', thus demonstrating their own good taste and growing affluence.[5]

John Baker was a wealthy man. His fortune was made through a well-judged marriage and through his professional work as a solicitor. In 1771 he came to live at Park House in Horsham, a large mansion previously owned by John Wicker, with parkland on the edge of town and land on the east of the Forest called Leechpool. It is from that date that his diaries illuminate 18th century life in Horsham for the minor gentry. Within a mile or two of Park House were his neighbours, minor Sussex landed gentry such as the Shelleys, Tredcrofts, Eversfields, Aldridges and Blunts. He wrote in a mixture of English, Latin and French, and from extracts published by his descendant, Wilfrid Scawen Blunt, in 1909, one can see how time was passed by this class. Blunt is quite critical of the lifestyle saying 'it shows the very material life led by the Sussex gentry of the day, the limited interest taken by them in public affairs, and the trifling nature of their amusements … neither hunting or shooting being seriously pursued … contenting themselves with heavy eating and drinking, much card playing and occasional entertainments at the Horsham public rooms'.

W. S. Blunt (1840-1922), in contrast to his ancestor John Baker, was not only an energetic hedonist and poet but achieved much in his lifetime, as did his wife, Byron's granddaughter Lady Anne. She learnt Arabic, published travel books, and established an internationally renowned stud of Arabian horses at Crabbet Park, Crawley, whilst he entered politics after travelling widely in the diplomatic service, promoted anti-imperialism and supported Egypt, India and Ireland in their efforts for independence. So, they were clearly a very active couple but living at a very different time than Baker.[6]

John Baker passed his time by visiting friends, drinking and eating with them, listening to music, attending fairs, shooting, and watching a lot of cricket on the Common before its enclosure. Like Sarah Hurst he wrote of riding in the Forest, although not so often as her. He noted that he had walked in the Forest and that his family had ridden in the Forest and met their coach at the Aldridge's. With regard to his friends' houses and gardens he showed some interest in garden design. When visiting John Shelley's estate at Field Place, Warnham, he described two swans on the water, thickets and fields of wheat and a large pleasant level field at the end of a thicket with a fine smooth green walk. John Shelley had created an early American garden at Field Place, possibly for his mother who was born in New Jersey.[7]

---

5. Brandon, 2010, pp. 23-36.

6. Blunt, W. S. (1909) Extracts from Mr John Baker's Horsham Diary, *Sussex Archaeological Collections*, Vol. **52**, pp. 38-82, and Oxford Dictionary of National Biography entry for Blunt, Wilfrid Scawen and Blunt (née King) Anne Isabella Noel, accessible through www.oxforddnb.com.ezproxy.sussex.ac.uk.

7. Pers. Comm. Djabri 13.5.2012.

64. Reproduction of a drawing by S. H. Grimm of New Lodge House, about 1787 BL Add MS5673

American gardens began to appear in the late 18th century and were simply areas in the garden given over to the new plant and tree introductions from North America and Canada such as rhododendrons, which did not all come from China at that time. In June 1773, Baker diarised that while drinking tea with Lady Irwin he found out that Lancelot 'Capability' Brown was at their home, Hills Place, to oversee his landscaping of the parkland, including widening the river Arun and creating ponds and cascades. Such a venture not only provided the status of a modern and expensive setting in which to socialise, but it underlined the move from formal gardens to a more confident picturesque style of parkscape with vistas on the grand scale.[8]

A welcome mark of status for the Aldridges must have been a visit from the artist John Claude Nattes on 30 August 1784. He completed a pencil sketch of New Lodge, erected by John Clater Aldridge, probably about ten or 20 years earlier, which showed a small Georgian style mansion surrounded by pine and deciduous trees with small gate posts and drive. It does look like a house in a forest, but the detail is limited and it would have been good to see an illustration of the garden, as the only evidence that there was a formal design lies in the Gardner and Gream map of 1795, illustration 29: page 72. John Claude Nattes' drawing of New Lodge is now in the Royal collection.[9] In 1787 another artist, S. H. Grimm, produced a portfolio of Sussex drawings, within which is a tinted drawing of New Lodge. This is somewhat similar to the Nattes drawing, and shows a small Georgian stone mansion, decorative garden fence and views to the east, illustration 64: above.[10]

By the end of the 18th century and beginning of the 19th century, a qualitative change in labour relations was underway, with the labourer becoming more independent and able to choose his work and employer. Commercialisation and the dominance of monetary payments were becoming the norm, or as Thompson puts it 'economic rationalisation had long been nibbling through the bonds of paternalism'.[11] Nevertheless, old-fashioned

8. Mowl, T. (2000) *Gentlemen & Players, Gardeners of the English Landscape*, Stroud: Sutton Publishing, pp. 149-162, (hereafter Mowl, 2000).

9. The sketch of New Lodge by Nattes resides in the collection of H.M. The Queen, and was on loan to Horsham Museum for the 2011 exhibition entitled 'Forgotten Views of Georgian Sussex: The Drawings of John Claude Nattes'.

10. BL, Add MS 5673, f68, image 123.

11. Thompson, 1993, p.38-9.

paternalism still survived at this period of time, not only in the management of estates, but in attitudes and largesse, for which there is the example of the Aldridges of New Lodge.

The occasion for this largesse, was reported in *The Morning Post* at the time, were the celebrations for the coming of age of the young Robert Aldridge. His mother, Anna Maria Aldridge, bore two sons. The first died in his first year,1801, and then Robert was born the same year, and it is noted in the newspaper report that for many years he was of such delicate health that he was hardly expected to reach the age of 21. An additional reason for celebration of this birthday was that Anna Maria had been widowed when Robert was two, and so this was an end to her guardianship of the estate.[12]

The celebrations began on Monday 24 June 1822 with peals of Horsham town bells and the town band walking, before daylight, out to the Forest and New Lodge to rouse the family and their visitors with

Donkey Racing
AND OTHER AMUSEMENTS
New Lodge St. Leonard's
on Tuesday the 25th June 1822,
To Start at Five

A MATCH FOR *Three Guineas*
BETWEEN
Mr. Aldridge's Frolic , 6 years old – Colour Blue
Mr. J. Erskine's Lady Jane, 4 years old ditto Pink
START AT HALF PAST FIVE

FOR A HAT
Mr. W.B. Smith's Whiz Gig, - Colour Green
Mr. D. Erskine's Moses, - ditto Red.
Mr. Aldridge's Frolic, - ditto Blue,
Mr. J. Erskine's Lady Jane, - ditto Pink
START AT SIX

FOR A BRIDLE
Take Notice, Persons wishing their Donkies to start, must have their names entered at the Crown Inn, on or before six o'Clock on Monday evening, or at the Starting Post at four o'Clock on Tuesday with the Names and Colours of the Riders.

Chemise to be run for by Ladies

A Soaped tail Pig

Jumping in a Sack for a pair of Shoes.

CLIMING A POLE FOR HATS AND BLUE RIBBONS

BOBBING MATCH FOR PAIR OF WHITE STOCKINGS

Driving a Wheelbarrow Blindfolded for a Silk Handkerchief

Jingling Match for a Round Frock

Women to Walk Blindfolded for a Gown and Jingling Match for Caps and Blue Ribbons

Eating Rolls and Treacle for a Hat

Young gentlemen cannot be admitted as Candidates whose mouths exceed Seven Inches and One-Quarter

Dipping for Money in a Flour Tub

Walking the Bowsprit,
Grigg's Mare to be shod for a Silk Handkerchief,
FOR HAT AND WHITE STOCKINGS
Ladies and Gentlemen Candidates for the above Prizes need be under no apprehension of hurting themselves in the event of a Fall there being a sufficiency of Mud in the Pond to prevent any unpleasant consequences,
The Sports commence at Five o'Clock precisely,

Phillips, Printer, Horsham

65. Copy of poster announcing the second day's celebrations for Robert Aldridge's 21st Birthday, © in private collection.

'cheerful and patriotic airs'. As this was midsummer it must have been very early in the morning. Visitors arrived throughout the day and included most of the 'rank and fashion of the county'. *The Morning Post* reported that nearly 300 people 'formed a display of elegance and beauty seldom equalled, assembled in a temporary ball-room' - presumably some sort of marquee on the lawn. The Sussex regiment military band played and from London came 'Collinets's celebrated Quadrille players' to lead the dancing. Cooks from London and Brighton provided the finest meal in another temporary room decorated with plants and flowers. Dancing continued into the late hours of the following morning.

The next day another party was held for 500 Horsham residents including the poor of the neighbourhood; however, status was not forgotten as the newspaper report tells that superior tables were provided for tenants of the Aldridges and respectable tradesmen

---

12. *The Morning Post* (London, Eng.) Tuesday July 02 1822 Issue 16005.

who then presided as carvers of meat for the inferior tables. A Baron of Beef surmounted by the royal standard was ushered in by the Horsham Band playing 'The Roast Beef of Old England' and a copious supply of ale crowned the feast. The Sunday school children were given cake and ale, and games took over the afternoon until fireworks concluded the event, illustration 65: page 145. Another supper and ball was prepared for the following Thursday for the 'respectable tenants and tradesmen to be given in the supper rooms'.[13]

By any standard this does appear to have been a particularly generous sharing of a family celebration with Horsham town and employees on the estate, although class status was clearly maintained. Anna Maria Aldridge was only to live another three years and died in Paris on 25 June 1825 and therefore did not see her son, Robert, marry his near neighbour, Caroline Anne Beauclerk, at Cowfold on 20 October 1829. Caroline was the eldest daughter of Charles George Beauclerk of St Leonard's Lodge and granddaughter of the Duchess of Leinster.[14]

Religion and Morality

An important impact on the Forest, and in particular the formation of the two villages within the Forest, was that of the drive to build churches in what was seen as an ungodly forest area. Hurst refers to the Forest as a 'country so wild and lawless' that it was no surprise to her that superstitions and legends were rife.[15] The antiquarian, Rev. J.R. Bloxam, who was the friend and companion of Cardinal Newman and a Fellow of Magdalen College, Oxford, was also vicar of Upper Beeding from 1862 to 1891. He collected letters and documents, and made notes of relevance to his large parish. These archives are now held by Magdalen College, Oxford.

Research of this archive shows that the clergy from the surrounding parishes of Horsham and Rusper, Cowfold, Nuthurst and Ifield felt compelled to take action to 'civilise' the wilder residents of the Forest, and so in the early 1820s they sent a letter signed by them all to the President and Fellows of Magdalen College, Oxford. It was noted in the previous chapter that on the demise of Sele Priory in 1459, its property was transferred to Magdalen College, newly founded by William of Waynflete, Bishop of Winchester, with the result that Magdalen College became responsible for the religious life of Lower Beeding, which included St Leonard's Forest. Hence the concerned clergy of the northern part of Beeding, without a parish church, wrote to Magdalen College outlining the pressures of a growing population in the area of 'Upper Beeding' which they said now contained above 400 inhabitants.

Lower Beeding was originally part of the ecclesiastical parish of Upper Beeding, although separated by eight or nine miles. However, for civil purposes such as poor law administration, land tax and census, it was a civil parish in its own right until 1838, when it became a proper ecclesiastical parish with a parish church. The area of Lower Beeding

---

13. A 'baron' of beef was a very large double Sirloin joint of roast beef.

14. *The Morning Post* (London, Eng.) Tuesday July 02 1822 Issue 16005, and also Wednesday July 06 Issue 17018 and Friday October 23 Issue 18366 for death and marriage respectively.

15. Hurst, 1868, p. 162.

was virtually coterminous with the core area of St Leonard's Forest and so any statistics on Lower Beeding are relevant to the Forest. In the West Sussex Land Tax records of 1785, it is stated that in the Land Tax administrative area of Lower Beeding, an area of 10,152 acres which was more or less the area of the Forest, there were 12 landowners and ten different occupiers, although sadly the lands owned and occupied are not noted, and of course the poor and landless are not included.[16]

The first census of 1801 was purely a counting exercise of the people actually resident in a particular place at a particular time, so there is not the extra detail of later census. However, the Table of Population extracted from census data and published in *The Victoria History of the County of Sussex* as a comparative table shows the civil parish of Lower Beeding as having an acreage of 10,152 and populations of 230 in 1801, 274 in 1811, and 405 in 1821 making a population increase in 20 years of 76%, which explains the concerns of the clergy who were writing in the early 1820s. From the same census data, a further abstract of answers and returns shows that ten years later in 1831 there were 90 houses in Lower Beeding housing 97 families, 80 of these families being engaged in agriculture, 14 in trade, manufacture and handicraft and three in other activities. Of the total population of Lower Beeding of 533 in 1831, there were 261 men and 272 women. A rough and ready calculation therefore gives an average family size of 5.5 people, which was not large at this period of time.[17]

In their first letter of the early 1820s, the local clergy pointed to an influx of settlers who were forced to travel to the outlying parish churches for marriage, baptism and burial, not only an inconvenience for those people but an added burden for the clergy ministering to them. However, the clergy felt that these problems 'sink into utter insignificance when compared with the frightful moral evils necessarily attendant on the state in which they are left. These wretched people have neither Pastor nor Church'. They also note that many of the inhabitants are not known to the few resident gentry, and thus appeared to be even further from a good moral compass. They end their letter by restating that the people in this unfortunate district 'are notorious for their disorderly and profligate conduct and it is the resort of the idle and worthless from the surrounding neighbourhood'. They even fear that the morals of their own parishioners may be contaminated by this unruly lot, and hope that some measure could be taken to provide the unfortunate inhabitants with the blessings of a 'resident Pastor, regular religious instruction, without which they will be making daily advance in disorder and depravity'. There was in this last sentence some sense of urgency and real concern.[18]

The Rev. H. J. Rose, Vicar of Horsham and Rusper, wrote a letter in his own right dated September 25th 1822 to the President and Fellows of Magdalen College in which he focused on the Forest area and said it was a deplorable case. He cited that the people were either dissenters or of no worship at all 'for they inhabit the wild and unfrequented part of

---

16. Readman, A., Falconer, L., Ritchie, R. and Wilkinson, P. (2000) *West Sussex Land Tax 1785,* Lewes: Sussex Record Society, **82,** p. 49.

17. Page, W. (ed.) (1973) Social and Economic History, Table of Population, 1801 to 1901, *The Victoria History of the County of Sussex,* Vol. II, The Institute of Historical Research by University of London, pp. 215-228 (hereafter VCH, II).

18. Magdalen College, Oxford, MS741.1.

66. Photograph of St John's Church, Coolhurst, built 1839.

St Leonard's Forest, their habits are peculiarly lawless and need peculiar pains and attention' and he wished to remedy these 'crying evils'. The Rev. Rose suggested that the common land where the Barracks had been built, and dismantled shortly after 1815, now in Worthing Road, could be used to build a church to take 'the spiritual charge of the forest part of Beeding' and he suggested that he begin to obtain subscriptions for such a church. This letter and the previous one from the local clergy, appeared to set in train negotiations over tithes, land and church which was ultimately to lead to the withdrawal of Magdalen College, Oxford from the spiritual responsibility and collection of tithes, and to the building of three churches, the creation of the Parish of Lower Beeding in 1838 and Consolidated Chapelry of Saint Saviour, Colgate in 1871. [19]

There is limited additional evidence for the moral state of the population in Lower Beeding, and what gave rise to such concern. However, a glimpse is given by the *First Report of the Commissioners into the Employment of Children, Young Persons and Women in Agriculture 1867-8*. It shows that on November 7th 1867, in a meeting at Horsham with representatives from Horsham, Nuthurst and Lower Beeding parishes, it was reported that 'In 1800, 3,000 acres of St Leonard's Forest, in the centre of the parish (which was then a rabbit warren) was let on 100 year lease, and several cottages, turf huts, were allowed to be run up (erected) by the lessee, of a very inferior condition, which were let with an acre of land at £1 a year. About a dozen of these cottages still remain in their original condition, about half of which are occupied by Irish families'. This may go some way to explain the sudden increase in the population in Lower Beeding, and the fact that many were Irish Catholic which may have caused anxiety to the protestant clergy, who were also under pressure from the increase in dissenters, i.e. Baptists, Quakers, and Unitarians. [20]

At this time Horsham and Lower Beeding women appeared to be quite assertive in expressing their anger with regard to what they saw as government interference with their food. The new 1800 Brown Bread Act (repealed in 1801) was in response to shortages of white wheat flour at a time of war and poor harvests. It required millers to sell only wholemeal flour, which was often adulterated to make it go further. The story first

19. Magdalen, MS741.2.

20. Royal Commission on the Employment of Children, Young Persons, and Women in Agriculture, 1867, First Report (P.P. 1867-8, XVII), pp. 81-2. (hereafter P.P. 1867-8, XVII).

appeared in the *Sussex Weekly Advertiser*. A number of women descended on Gosden Mill in the south of the Forest, abused the miller for selling them brown flour and seized the cloth he was using which they then cut into 'a thousand pieces', threatening to do the same with other tools of his trade. The report then said that 'The Amazonian leader of this petticoated cavalcade afterwards regaled her associates with a guinea's worth of liquor at the Crab Tree public-house', in Lower Beeding. This event gives an indication that the poor of the Forest were not content with their situation and equally not afraid to do something about it. One can indeed imagine some rather nervous clergy reflecting on this local popular protest, led by women, behaving independently and in a manner at odds with the expectations of the clergy and gentry.[21]

A hidden population which is not easy to trace is that of the travellers and gypsies who would have frequented the Forest, more so after the commons was enclosed in the early 19th century. Ellis quotes in part from Murray's *Hand Book of Kent and Sussex* that:

> 'the forest was much resorted to by tramps and gipsies who could easily knock down a rabbit or hare, and kindle a fire to make the pot boil, and living within its precincts for weeks together, "lose and neglect the creeping hours of time", not knowing, as I have been assured, the day of the week or of the month.'[22]

This type of lifestyle would presumably have concerned the clergy as not conforming to the morality of the day or the protestant work ethic. Bovill wrote that the gypsies suffered particularly from the enclosure of the commons as these were their principal homes, living wholly in tents, and it was the loss of their traditional camping grounds that led them to adopt caravans at the end of the 19th century.[23]

Politics and Economics

In the late 18th and early 19th century, war, enclosure and civil unrest were the factors affecting Horsham and the Forest communities, and the Forest landscape to a limited extent. War with France over the Canadian colonies started in 1756 and continued for seven years. The American Revolution in 1775 resulted in war, blockade and the loss of America as a colony. The French Revolution occurred in 1789 with the French King and Queen executed in 1793. A French Republic followed, and subsequently war with Europe for the following twenty years. In response to British government policy, barracks were built in Horsham in 1796 and an extra 960 young men added to the town's population.[24] To add to the country's difficulties in the last decade of the 18th century, there was not only the fear of war and invasion but poor harvests and food shortages. An Icelandic volcano, Laki, had erupted in 1783 and its effects on the atmosphere were well described by Gilbert White of Selborne as a 'peculiar haze, or smokey (*sic*) fog that prevailed for many weeks'. The eruption lasted eight months, and the climatic impact caused a run of

21. Griffin, C. J. (2014) *Protest, Politics and Work in Rural England, 1700 – 1850,* Basingstoke: Palgrave Macmillan, pp. 106, 203.

22. Ellis, W. S. (1925) *The Parks and Forests of Sussex, Ancient and Modern,* Lewes: H. Wolff., p 176, footnote 111 (hereafter Ellis, 1925).

23. Bovill, E. W. (1962) *English Country Life 1780-1830,* Oxford: Oxford University Press, p. 26 (hereafter Bovill, 1962).

24. Knight, J. (2006) *Horsham's History, Volume 2, 1790 – 1880,* Horsham: Horsham District Council, p.16.

poor harvests in the northern hemisphere with subsequent higher corn prices. However, the influx of the soldiers to the town with wages to spend helped the shops, markets and public houses in Horsham to cope with these hard times. Albery noted that the soldiers were not always appreciated, with bad behaviour and theft being common, but he wrote that 'the extraordinary escapades and goings on of some of the soldiers at Horsham Barracks certainly prevented the town from getting dull'.[25]

During the period of 19 years from 1796 to 1815, after which the Barracks were dismantled, Horsham was the home, at different times, to 69 separate regiments or battalions of soldiers. Even before the Barracks were built, soldiers camped and drilled on Horsham Common. They were reviewed and inspected there by the Duke of Cambridge in 1805 and the Duke of Norfolk in 1808. There appears to be no evidence that the Forest was used by the Militia. This was mainly because it was divided into private estates, but also because the large area of open common was very suitable for military use and still freely available. In any case, before the 20th century the military avoided using woodland because of the difficulties it caused to the movement of men and supplies. It was only later with the development of aircraft and aerial surveillance that wooded areas became useful cover for soldiers and armaments.

The presence of the military in the town came to an end with the cessation of the Napoleonic Wars in 1815. Around the same time Horsham's large common met its demise. Property prices were rising at the beginning of the 19th century, mainly due to population pressure for housing, manufacturing and the consolidation of farms. In addition, there was political pressure to enclose arising from the political ambition of the 11th Duke of Norfolk. The property-owning burgesses of Horsham town, who had rights of herbage and pannage on the common, also had political rights to vote for their Member of Parliament. The power to elect the town's representatives in Parliament had long been held by the Irwin's of Hills Place due to their tight hold on the largest number of burgages. Throughout most of the 18th century the number of genuine independent burgages had declined through purchase of the freeholds by landowners like the Irwin's and Norfolk's determined to increase their political power. There remained only eight burgages, out of the original medieval 52, by the turn of the century.[26]

The last, and politically astute, Lady Irwin died in November 1807 and her two sons-in-law, the Marquis of Hertford and Lord William Gordon inherited her property, however they had little interest in the town, apart from agreeing a good price for their inherited property. The Duke of Norfolk took this opportunity to buy their burgages for the inflated price of £91,475 in 1811 and so secured for himself control over two seats in parliament. He then turned his attention to enclosing the Common. There were now only six individual Burgesses to deal with and the Duke of Norfolk had by far the overwhelming amount of property. He petitioned for an Act of Parliament to enclose the common for the improvement of the wasteland. Notice was posted in the *Sussex Weekly*

25. Horn, P. (1980) *The Rural World 1780-1850,* London: Hutchinson & Co. Ltd., pp. 37-68, and White, G. (1788-9, 1977) *The Natural History of Selborne,* Harmondsworth: Penguin Books Ltd., p.265-6, and Knight, J. (2006) *Horsham's History, Vol. 2 1790 – 1880,* Horsham: Horsham District Council, pp. 15-6, and Albery, 1947, pp. 511-520.

26. Bowen, E. J. (2007) *The Enclosure of Horsham Common,* Horsham Museum Society, pp. 23-34 (hereafter Bowen, 2007).

Advertiser in September 1811 of the intention of 'dividing, allotting and enclosing Horsham Common' with no mention of the Duke of Norfolk as promoter and beneficiary of this move. Those that benefited most from Horsham Common enclosure were undoubtedly the Duke of Norfolk as Lord of the Manor of Horsham, and Robert Hurst, brother of Sarah Hurst the diarist, who was accumulating wealth. The ambitious and those with some savings were given the opportunity to buy land and property that perhaps would not otherwise have come their way. Bowen wrote that the enclosure led to considerable land speculation, and the first house built on the old Common was 'Lynwood' on the Duke's land.[27]

With encroachments and the granting of leases it was perhaps inevitable that Horsham Common would not survive the 19th century, and Horsham town needed to expand. However, an aspect of loss that is sometimes discounted or forgotten is the loss of natural beauty in such an open or wooded landscape. Dudley brings this to our attention in a comment regarding the area around Coolhurst, to the south west of the forest and on the south-eastern edge of the Common. He wrote:

'the vicinity of this seat was lately rendered particularly interesting by a romantic and beautiful glen called Dubbin's Green, one of the wildest and most secluded spots in the district, but it is greatly to be lamented, the enclosing of the adjacent common, has almost entirely destroyed the beauty of the scenery, and robbed the visitor of a truly rural and picturesque treat'.[28]

Horsham was not the only place to suffer such loss of natural beauty at the hands of enclosure; John Clare (1793-1864) regretted the loss of both his natural and social environment around his native Northamptonshire village, Helpston. He expressed this through poems such as *To a Fallen Elm* and *The Mores* which illustrated such heartfelt regret.[29]

Hobsbawm suggested that in the three decades after Waterloo the populace of England were 'desperately dissatisfied' and large masses of them were feeling revolutionary both politically and economically.[30] Horsham was no exception to this. Although it had come through the wars reasonably well, with a productive agricultural hinterland, manufacturing of leather, brewing of beer, and a thriving market, several banks had failed in 1816 and 1817. Unrest was evidenced by a petition presented to the House of Commons on Friday, 7th March 1817 by Lord Folkestone. It was signed by 'many respectable signatures' following an 'orderly meeting' outside The Lamb public house in the Carfax. The petition related to a number of grievances, suggesting that the people were surrounded with difficulties and distress. The farmer no longer made a profit, trade was declining, and the labourer was becoming increasingly weak from lack of food and work, so it was difficult to

---

27. Albery, 1947, pp. 179-185, Bowen, 2007, pp 30-1, the author lives in one of the flats Lynwood Court, built on the site of Lynwood house.

28. Dudley, H. (1836, 1973) *The History and Antiquities of Horsham*. London, reprinted by J. Cramp Ltd., Horsham. pp 52-3.

29. Robinson, E. and Powell, D. (eds) (1984) *John Clare, Major Works*, Oxford: Oxford University Press, pp. xix, 96-8, 167-9.

30. Hobsbawm, 1968, p. 73.

bring up a family without parish aid. The petition asked for relief through lower taxes, which had brought much misery, increased by the sudden depreciation of paper money. They asked for a reduction in the state's shameful extravagance, such as the civil list and standing army. Finally, they asked for electoral reform; Horsham was a notorious rotten borough and they objected to the consequences of this which were 'bribery, perjury, rioting and drunkenness'.

It was a well written and persuasive petition, which was supported by Sir Timothy Shelley and opposed by Robert Hurst, both Magistrates in Horsham. However, the whole debate was somewhat undermined by Robert Hurst, the Duke of Norfolk's nominee in the House, who suggested that some of the signatures were in the same hand and therefore fraudulent, and the debate was thus side-lined into discussing the legitimacy of petitions and their signatories – a clever tactic of distraction from the real problem. It is clear however that there was real unrest in Horsham, which would increase in the following decades. Although the grievances were not targeted at the enclosure of the commons as such, this would have contributed to the impoverishment of the poor by removing useful free resources.[31]

People and the Parish

The Parish of Beeding, or Sele, as it was also known after the priory in Beeding, was a very extensive parish that was divided into two parts. The northern part was separated from the southern part by eight or nine miles and was known as Lower Beeding. It was called 'Lower', even though it was geographically the northern part, as in ecclesiastical terms the original medieval chapel in the Forest was a mission of Sele Priory and therefore a lower house. So, the Upper and Lower refers to status rather than geography, although Upper was only applied to the civil parish in the late 19th century, the ecclesiastical parish still being known as Beeding.

Horsfield described the northern part, or Lower Beeding, also referred to as St Leonard's Forest, as 'wild and sterile' when he was writing in the 1830s and he clearly regarded it as a rather desolate empty Forest. However, as mentioned earlier, the population was growing and according to the decennial census statistics from Lower Beeding, taken from the registration district of Horsham, there was a 370% increase in population over the 50 years, from a population of 230 in 1801, to a population of 1,081 in 1851.[32] As noted, this growth in population worried the local clergy as there was no church in the northern part of the extensive parish of Beeding. The nearest churches were

---

31. Commons Sitting on Friday, March 7, 1817, House of Commons Hansard, First Series Vol. 35 accessible through: ProQuest, House of Commons Parliamentary Papers, and Albery, W. (1927) *A Parliamentary History of Horsham 1295-1885*, London: Longmans, Green and Co. Ltd., pp. 260-3.

32. For population figures see Page, W. (ed.) (1973) Social and Economic History, Table of Population, 1801 to 1901, *The Victoria History of the County of Sussex*, Vol. II, The Institute of Historical Research by University of London, pp. 215-228 (hereafter VCH, II). Notes acknowledge that the 1801 boundaries of civil parishes, although virtually co-terminus with the ecclesiastical parishes could be affected by the Divided Parishes Acts of 1876, 1879 and 1882 which dealt with detached parts of civil parishes, as well as the Local Government Act 1888 which altered and amalgamated civil parishes. Upper Beeding and Horsham appear to have been affected by the Divided Parishes Acts but not every detail of change was obtained, thus figures for 1891 and 1901 were difficult to ascertain and were partially estimated.

in Horsham, Cowfold, Nuthurst, Rusper and Ifield, all bordering parishes with their own churches and clergy.[33]

At the beginning of the 19th century there was concern generally in England about the growing urban population and the lack of religious provision, particularly in London and the new industrial towns of the north, but also in the Sussex coastal towns of Brighton and Hastings. Concern was such that in 1818 The Church Building Act was passed in which state funding was made available under the guidance of Commissioners to identify gaps and build new churches. Under this Act 214 churches were built and £6 million spent by the Commissioners in what were known as Commissioners' churches. It is perhaps not surprising therefore that the vicars of Horsham and Rusper, Cowfold, Nuthust, and Ifield thought the time was right to press for a new church in Lower Beeding itself.[34]

These particular clergy therefore wrote a joint letter in the 1820s to the President and Fellows of Magdalen College, Oxford, who were responsible for the advowson and tithes of the Forest, requesting that a pastor and regular religious instruction be provided in this area. The Rev. H.J. Rose of Horsham parish followed this up with his letter in 1822 stating that a church was desirable and suggesting a site plus a subscription for funding. Magdalen College was perhaps concerned by the cost of this and so looked to the tithes that they were clearly not receiving from Lower Beeding. Cartwright had noted that 1,300 acres of Holmbush and Bewbush paid tithes but as for the rest of the Forest, no tithes had been claimed, as in the past a buck and doe were given annually to the vicar of Beeding in lieu of tithes, although the *Victoria County History* noted that this was commuted to between two and ten guineas in the 17th century.[35]

The result was a demand for tithes from Magdalen College to the landowners in St Leonard's Forest who had not previously been paying. In September 1834 an alphabetical list was produced by the college of 25 landowners in the area, the largest being the Aldridges at New Lodge and the Broadwoods at Holmbush. Against each name was the type of land owned, whether arable, pasture or heath, the acreage of that land, and the annual tithe due. For example, the first landowner noted is Robert Aldridge at New Lodge and farm with a total of 1,060 acres, 57 acres of this being arable, 30 acres new pasture, 125 acres old pasture or park, ten acres being meadow, 18 acres being pasture, 20 acres being deer park and 800 acres being heathland, for all of which a tithe was calculated to be £25 16s 6d. Added to the main Aldridge landholding was Millfield Farm, 45 acres of arable with a tithe of £6 15s 0d and Holm Farm, 100 acres of arable and six acres of meadow attracting a tithe of £13 2s 0d, making a total demand of £45 13s 6d. So it is little surprise

33. Magdalen College, Oxford archives, MS 741 Correspondence, and Horsfield, T. W. (1835) *The History, Antiquities and Topography of the County of Sussex,* Vol. II, Lewes: Sussex Press, p. 222, (hereafter Horsfield, 1835). For population figures VCH, II, pp. 215-228 and Vickers, J. A. (1989) *The Religious Census of Sussex 1851,* 75, Lewes: Sussex Record Society, p. 123 (hereafter Vickers, 1989).

34. Elleray, D. R. (1981) *The Victorian Churches of Sussex,* Chichester: Phillimore & Co. Ltd., pp. 2-3, (hereafter Elleray, 1981), and Snell, K. D. M. (2006) Parish and Belonging: Community, identity and welfare in England and Wales 1700 – 1950, Cambridge: Cambridge University Press, pp. 393-405.

35. Magdalen College, Oxford archives, MS 741 Correspondence and notes, also Cartwright, E. (1830) *The Parochial Topography in the Western Division of the County of Sussex,* Vol. II, London: J. B. Nichols & Son, p. 365, and Hudson, T. P. (ed.)(1986) *Victoria County History of Sussex,* Vol. VI Pt. 3, p. 26, Institute of Historical Research by Oxford University Press , p. 26 (hereafter VCH VI.3).

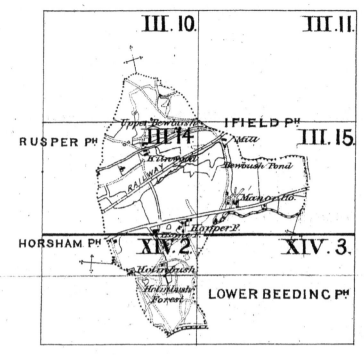

that the landowners suddenly presented with this sort of annual bill objected strongly, particularly as there were no churches or services being provided for such tithes. The total demand from the College from all the landowners was £252 17s 9d which would be about £21,000 in today's money. However, tithes as a method of taxation were becoming increasingly anachronistic and the cause of disputes. The Whig government thus introduced the 1836 Tithe Commutation Act which efficiently systematised the conversion of tithes into a rent-charge payment. The amount was agreed between landowners and assistant commissioners based on the price of grain,

67. Map of the Parish of Upper Beeding (Detached), index to sheets, OS 1875 showing surrounding parishes and area of the Holmbush estate. West Sussex Records Office.

wheat, barley and oats, as published annually in the *London Gazette*.[36]

One solution to the Forest tithe dispute was either the creation of an ecclesiastical parish of Lower Beeding with tithes being paid when a church was erected and endowed, or the establishment of a Chapelry for the outlying areas of Beeding parish. Consequently, in 1838 a Private Bill was introduced in the House of Lords for the erection and endowment of a Chapelry for the district of Lower Beeding, meaning a chapel of ease, or new church, to service the outlying parts of the parish of Beeding at Lower Beeding. However, it appeared that Thomas Broadwood at Holmbush did not agree with this solution, as he excluded Holmbush, Kilnwood and Bewbush from the new chapelry of Lower Beeding by his own private Act of Parliament. This portion was known as Upper Beeding detached, or the Bewbush tithing, a small area of 1,542 acres. The reason for wanting this exclusion is unclear; he did have his own small chapel at Colgate where services were occasionally held for family and tenants, but it is more likely he would have attended the larger St. Mary Magdalen church at Rusper, which was attended by his relations at Lyne House. Generally, Victorian landowners were keen to add to their status and prestige by generous endowments to the local church or chapel, so it is surprising that

36. Magdalen College, Oxford archives, MS 741 Correspondence, and Kain, R. J. P. and Oliver, R. R. (1995) The Tithe Maps of England and Wales, Cambridge: Cambridge University Press, pp. 513-7, and Kain, R. J. P. and Prince, H. C. (1985) The Tithe surveys of England and Wales. Cambridge: Cambridge University Press, pp. 28-67, and Evans, J. E. and Crosby, A. G. (1978, 1997) *Tithes, Maps, Apportionments and the 1836 Act: a guide for local historians,* Salisbury: British Association for Local History, pp. 12-29.

Broadwood did not do this at Colgate. However, this task was taken on with great enthusiasm after 1868 by the next resident of the Holmbush estate, James Clifton Brown.[37]

The situation of the split parish of Beeding could not have been satisfactory from an ecclesiastical point of view, particularly as there was no church in Bewbush detached tithing, and it was at some distance away from the main parish church, St. Peter's at Beeding. Most references agree, and the Religious Census of Sussex 1851 confirms, that the Parish of Lower Beeding was separated from the older parish of Beeding under the authority of a local Act of Parliament September 1837-8 and that the Church of the Holy Trinity at Plummers Plain, Lower Beeding village, was built as the Parish church and consecrated in June 1840.

A year earlier, under the same Act, a chapel of ease to the new Parish church had been established at Coolhurst. Lewis noted that the chapel, dedicated to St. John, was erected on the Coolhurst Estate in 1839, at the expense of Charles Scrase-Dickins, who also gave the land, which included a cemetery. The site lay to the north of the Coolhurst estate on Hammerpond road, just west of the entrance to the Aldridge estate and the Sun Oak, thus being convenient to the family and staff of both estates. Robert Aldridge also contributed to the cost of building St John's church. The land had in fact been given by Scrase-Dickins' mother-in-law, the Marchioness of Northampton, and the building financed by Charles Scrase-Dickins and Robert Aldridge, so it had been planned before the Act of 1838 to build a chapel financed by the two families.

Having been built ahead of the Parish church, it was always well used and became known as the Forest Church, although remaining a dependent chapel of ease, served by the same vicar of the Parish church, Holy Trinity in Lower Beeding village, without further stipend. At the turn of the century Goodliffe describes the church as forming a charming picture in its woodland surroundings, illustration 68: page 156. The 1851 Religious Census gives the average attendance at St John's the same as the parish church of the Holy Trinity at 200 people.[38]

The Scrase-Dickins family continued to support the church through the following generations. In 1889 it was enlarged by Charles R. Scrase-Dickins, grandson of the founder and in memory of his father, with the addition of a new chancel and north aisle. Archival evidence shows that permission was sought from the Bishop of Chichester by the Rev. C. B. Knox, and the churchwardens Robert Aldridge and William E. Hubbard and also C. R. Scrase-Dickins on behalf of themselves and the other parishioners. It was agreed in the parish vestry meeting of 2nd April 1888 to take down the existing chancel and erect a new larger one, to erect an organ chamber on the north side of the chancel and a vestry on the south side, to construct new roofs to the nave transepts and porch. It was

---

37. HL/PO/PB/1/1838/1&2 V1n 110, accessible through: www.portcullis.parliament.uk and VCH VI.3, p. 26, and Baldwin, M. (ed.)(1985) *The Story of the Forest*, Parish of Colgate, pp. 1-3, (hereafter Baldwin, 1985).

38. Vickers, 1989, p. 123 and Lewis, S. (ed.) (1848) *A Topographical Dictionary of England*, pp. 194-9, and Hurst, D. E. (1889) *The History and Antiquities of Horsham*, 2nd ed., Lewes: Farncombe & Co., p. 162, (hereafter Hurst, 1889) and Goodliffe, W. (1905) *Horsham and St Leonard's Forest, with their surroundings*, London: The Homeland Association, p. 48, (hereafter Goodliffe, 1905).

68. Watercolour painting of St John the Evangelist's church, Coolhurst, 1871-1890, Artist unknown. ©
Horsham Museum & Art Gallery (Horsham District Council).

also agreed to renew all the seating, the communion table, choir and clergy stalls, reading
desk and pulpit, and to generally restore the interior and exterior. This was a considerable
amount of renovation after only 50 years of use. To justify this request the petition stated
that the population of the Lower Beeding Parish was 848, although only about 30 resided
near the church of St John. However, as it was a popular church they noted that the
attendances amounted to 230, and the renovation would see this number increased by ten.
The cost was estimated to be £3,300 and it was agreed that the cost of this would be paid
by C. R. Scrase-Dickins. This proposal was accepted, and plans drawn up by the architect
John Oldrid Scott.[39]

In 1840 the new Lower Beeding Parish church of Holy Trinity was erected at Lower
Beeding village, on Plummers Plain on the Handcross to Horsham road. Lewis recorded
in the late 1840s that the church had been paid for by subscription aided by a grant from
the Incorporated Society, although it is not clear who the members of such a society were.
The *Victoria County History* noted that the building of the church was paid for by a levy of
£1,000 on landowners and occupiers of the new parish of Lower Beeding, although
Elleray identifies it as one of the 'Commissioners' Churches' paid for out of government
funding. It is probable that a combination of both public and private money contributed

39. Hurst, 1889, p. 162, and West Sussex Record Office (WSRO) MS EPISC II/27/273.

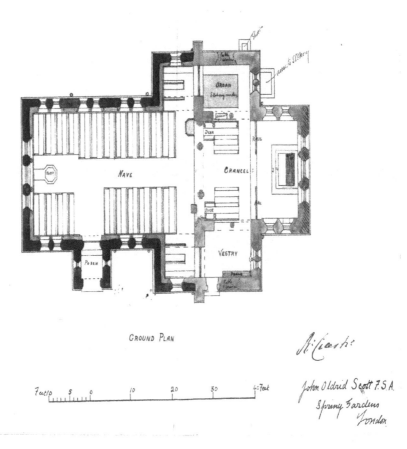

S. JOHN, COOLHURST.

⅛ SCALE

ORGAN

NAVE

CHANCEL

VESTRY

PORCH

PORCH

GROUND PLAN

John Oldrid Scott F.S.A.
Spring Gardens
London

69. Scott's plan for St John's church at Coolhurst, undated but approximately 1889 when refitting started. West Sussex Records Office, Ep/II/27/273.

to its building. Lewis described the church as a 'neat edifice' which contained 200 sittings, half of which were free. The free seating was in those pews that were available to anyone in the community, particularly the poor, whilst other, or appropriated, pews were those allocated to particular people or families either by money payment or custom.

The living was endowed with a rent charge on land of £135, and was at that point in the gift of the President and Fellows of Magdalen College, Oxford who built a parsonage on 20 acres. The land for the church was given by Robert Aldridge for this purpose. The architect was H. J. Underwood from Oxford who based the gothic design on the church of Saints Mary and Nicholas in Littlemore, Oxford, with large lancet windows and a stone belfry with a small spire, but no chancel. In 1861 the advowson, or living, and the rent charge was bought from Magdalen College by W. E. Hubbard of Leonardslee, who immediately set about improving the church.[40]

40. Lewis, 1848, pp. 148-199, and VCH, VI.3, p.27 and Elleray, 1981, pp. 71, 167.

70. Photo of Lower Beeding church.

According to the journal *The Builder* in their church building news in 1863, the greater part of the rebuilding was at the sole expense of W. E. Hubbard and executed by the London architect W. G. Habershon, and the builder Mr Patman. The stained glass was executed by a Mr. Wailes of Newcastle. Two side aisles were added and lengthened towards the west end to increase the number of sittings. Double pillars of Purbeck marble were introduced with capitals of Ancaster stone carved with fruit and flowers. The ends of the hammer beams in the roof were decorated with shields painted with a variety of 'ecclesiastical devices' by Mrs Hubbard herself. The triple stained-glass window in the chancel was donated by Ms Hubbard, the sister of W. E. Hubbard, most probably Louise Hubbard. Those on the north and south were given by the Boldero family in memory of Henry Boldero of South Lodge, the prior occupier to F. De Cane Godman.[41]

Goodliffe refers to Holy Trinity at the turn of the century as a modern church, noting that in 1884 a tower was added with a peal of eight bells as a memorial to Mr and Mrs W. E. Hubbard by their children, and four years later an automatic barrel organ was added, again by the Hubbard family. The parish church thus became very closely associated with the Hubbards. It was almost their own personal church, improved and maintained by them, for the family. Hurst was much impressed by the first incumbent, the Rev. John Montague Cholmeley, a fellow of Magdalen College, whom she described as an 'indefatigable worker in the parish', holding Sunday services and walking five miles through the forest from one church to another to hold weekday services. When Cholmeley moved on he was replaced by another Magdalen College fellow. It was normal practice that the livings of both Beeding (Rev. Dr J. R. Bloxham) and Lower Beeding

41. *The Builder*, 1863, Jan 3, pp. 14-15
42. Goodliffe, 1905, p. 66 and Hurst, 1889, pp. 161-2

went to fellows of Magdalen College Oxford while they held control of the advowson and rent charge.[42]

In 1871 it was proposed by the Ecclesiastical Commissioners that the contiguous portions of the parishes of Beeding or Sele, Lower Beeding and Horsham parishes be formed into a Consolidated Chapelry for all ecclesiastical purposes, and assigned to the Church of Saint Saviour at Colgate. This was agreed by The Queen in Council on 21 December 1871 and the Chapelry or Parish henceforth included the previously detached Broadwood portion of the parish of Beeding, which covered Bewbush, Kilnwood and Holmbush. The boundary of the new Chapelry was described in great detail in the *London Gazette* of December 22 1871. It ran from Faygate south through Colgate brickworks, south west to High Birch Gate and south down through Mick Mills Race towards Hawkins pond, past Great Grounds Farm and Tattleton Farm to Hammer Pond and then north again past Newstead Farm and across Shelley Plain to Pease Pottage, following the detached Beeding portion to arrive back at Faygate. Two boundary stones, inscribed 'CCC 1871', were set at certain points on the southern boundary, and the village of Colgate was encompassed in this new parish or Chapelry. A map on waxed paper of this new 1871 Colgate Chapelry is held in the Bloxham archives at Magdalen College, Oxford.[43]

In 1985 Mrs Elizabeth Calvert wrote in Baldwin's centenary memorial booklet for the church and village that when her grandfather, Col. J. Clifton Brown, moved to Holmbush after Thomas Broadwood, his 'earliest thoughts were to plan' for the building of a church in Colgate'. The cost of the building was £5,000 and this was gathered from subscriptions, although the bulk of the cost was borne by Clifton Brown, who consequently became the patron and had the gift of the living and rent charge which descended through the family. Hurst wrote that Clifton Brown re-built the church, enlarging and improving it and also built a vicarage at his own expense.[44]

The church of Saint Saviour at Colgate was consecrated by the Bishop of Chichester on Wednesday, November 22nd 1871 and newspaper reports of the time noted that 30 clergy from the local neighbourhood took part with a congregation of about 300, including the wealthy local families of the Clifton Browns, Aldridges, and Hursts. The Rev. G. T. Boddy of Horsham parish led the morning prayers and he later became the first incumbent in 1872. The Rev. Dr J. R. Bloxham of Beeding, who archived this information, read the first lesson. The church was described by newspaper reports as a 'neat and pretty little edifice' two thirds of which was new and included an enclosed burial ground.[45]

The Returns of the Diocese of Chichester Articles of Visitation and Enquiry of the Holy Trinity parish church at Lower Beeding made in September 1875 queried the condition of the parish, with the questions answered by the vicar Rev. J. H. Masters. From a population of Lower Beeding in 1871 of 820 he estimated his congregation was about

---

43. Magdalen College, Oxford, MS 741 papers including plan of proposed parochial district and cutting from *London Gazette*, December 22nd, 1871 pp. 5720-1.

44. Baldwin, 1985, pp 1-2.

45. Hurst, 1889, p. 163, and Magdalen College, Oxford, MS 741, newspaper cutting unreferenced.

150 but noted 'it very much depends on the weather as the parish is so scattered' and he hoped this number was increasing. Figures for communion were an average of 42, with 32 that Christmas Day. His answers appear quite positive although much seems to be wishful thinking; for example, he thought there had been an increase over the previous ten years in marriage and baptism and a decrease in illegitimacy, although he gave no figures. He estimated 111 had attended for confirmation classes but found it difficult to estimate how many of these were regular attenders as 'so many leave home for service it is impossible to say', indicating that much of the employment in the parish for young people was in domestic service outside the parish. Towards the end of the questionnaire he was asked whether certain conditions had improved since he became the incumbent of the parish. There followed a long list of conditions including matrimony, number of illegitimate children, drunkenness, education, morals in general and the physical condition of the working class, to which he answered 'yes' to all. One might think, perhaps unkindly, 'well he would, wouldn't he'.[46]

The results of the Religious Census of 1851 had alarmed the established church and state. Behind the facade of conventional religious attendance lay a crisis of faith that continued to grow. Vickers raised the point that the Victorians took religion seriously even if a growing percentage of the population were not particularly religious. An example of this was the growing movement for reform of the Church of England towards a higher church, particularly in rural areas. This was the Oxford movement, and the parishes of Lower Beeding and Beeding with their incumbents from Magdalen College, Oxford, such as the Rev. Dr Bloxham, friend of Cardinal Newman, must have been leading promoters of this Anglo-Catholic movement. At the same time there had been a slowly increasing popularity of Methodism and other nonconformist Christian religions, which in itself had political overtones. The High Anglican Church was associated with the Tories and the landowning classes in the country, while the dissenter chapels were associated with the Liberals and the working classes in the industrialised cities.

The 1851 Religious Census was designed to provide an overview of church provision, attendance and religious allegiance. There was opposition to this census from within the Anglican Church who felt threatened by possible inaccuracies and misinterpretations. However, the count went ahead and although there were statistical problems with ambiguities, gaps and double counting, the results were alarming to those who held the prevailing view that England was a religious, church-going, thoroughly Anglican country. What was discovered was that attenders at Anglican churches were under half the total of all attenders, and of the total population less than half were church-goers of any denomination, with urban areas having the lowest attendance of all.[47]

At the time of this census in 1851 St Saviours at Colgate had not been built and consecrated; the census thus only dealt with Holy Trinity at Lower Beeding and St John's at Coolhurst. The census recorded that the parish church of Holy Trinity had accommodation of 200 sittings with 135 attending morning service and 185 the afternoon, while at St John's, accommodating 200, had an attendance of 130 in the morning and 165

46. WSRO EPI/22A/2/562.
47. Elleray, 1981, pp. 1-7, and Vickers, 1989, pp. 118-124..

in the afternoon on alternate Sundays. It was recorded that there was a Bethel chapel at Crabtree, built in 1835 for Particular Baptists, the building also being used as a day school. Attendances at the chapel were quite respectable with 50 in the morning and 60 in the afternoon. In Lower Beeding nonconformist chapels appear to have been built more towards the end of the century, acccording to the Directories and Ordnance Survey maps. Kelly's Directory of Sussex 1899 states that the Mars Hill Baptist Chapel was built in 1890 of brick and had 100 sittings. It was built opposite St Saviour's church, but has since been demolished.[48] There was also a Methodist chapel nearby at Faygate in a terrace of cottages called The Carylls, which Baldwin wrote was built in 1893 on a site allocated by Capt. A. Fraser to T. A. Denny of Beedingwood, who appointed the ministers, until the chapel was sold to Wesleyan Methodists in 1903-4.[49]

Brian Short noted that the Sussex Weald interior had increased in population by 72% over the period from 1801 to 1851, although in certain central Weald communities such as Crawley, Lower Beeding and Slaugham, the population had more than doubled. As noted at the beginning of the chapter, it was this increase that had so alarmed the clergy. The area around Horsham remained reasonably prosperous during the first half of the 19th century but by the second half the town began to pull in the rural population, due to a number of factors including underemployment in agriculture and the impact of the railways, so that Horsham parish population increased by 118% in the 50 years from 1851 to 1901. Lower Beeding population increase, in contrast, was considerably slower at only 12%, and the fact that there was an increase at all was due to the loss of young people looking for work being balanced by an influx of wealthy London professionals and managers settling in family villas with gardens within easy travelling distance of railway stations.[50]

In the early 19th century the church had taken on much of the responsibility for educating both the poor and the middle classes. The Schools Inquiry Commission 1858-61 found that nine tenths of elementary schools in England were church schools, and three quarters of the children being educated in Anglican schools with a smaller proportion in Catholic and Nonconformist schools. Magdalen College, Oxford supported the education of middle-class boys, and with the energetic advocacy of the curate of St Mary de Haura, New Shoreham, Nathaniel Woodward, it made substantial grants for the establishment of Lancing College and two other schools at Hurstpierpoint and Ardingly, all with impressive chapels for high church Anglican worship.[51]

Horsfield wrote in 1835 that Thomas Broadwood of Holmbush had also established a school, built on the roadside near Crawley, which was sufficient to educate 80 boys and 46 girls under the direction of the Rev. J. S. Lewin of Ifield, the land having been given by a Col. Clithero. Most schools in the 18th century had been charity schools or independently founded, the church Sunday schools contributing much to the spread of reading and writing. The 19th century did however see some demands for a rate-supported system of

---

48. Mars Hill is an English translation of the Greek 'Areopagus' which was the rock where the Apostle Paul preached to the Athenians (Acts 17 v 19-27), also Kelly's Directory of Sussex 1899 accessible through: www.historicdirectores.org

49. Baldwin, 1985, p. 36.

50. Short, B., Population Change 1801-1851, pp. 88-9 and Sheppard, J., Population Change 1851-1901, pp.90-1, both in Leslie & Short, 1999, and VCH, II pp. 215-21.

51. Elleray, 1981, pp. 10-11.

71. St Saviour's Church, Colgate. With kind permission of Wendy Sloan.

secular education such as espoused by Richard Cobden (1804-1865) the radical and Liberal statesman born near Midhurst, Sussex, who railed against parliamentary grants going to the building of schools for the established church, the lack of transparency, and the poor and unequal quality of teaching. The British government did intervene eventually with the Education Act 1870 which brought into being elected school boards, with the power to build and manage schools, an inspectorate for standards and compulsory attendance up to the age of ten. Certificated teachers were not college-trained but had often been ex-pupil teachers who studied part-time for their certificate. Voluntary schools declined in the face of competition from Board Schools, however church schools were still running and represented a good portion of education provision. Universal secular education became a reality with the 1902 Education Act in which local authorities took on responsibilities for elementary, secondary and technical education.[52]

Comment on the provision of education in Lower Beeding was made in the meeting of representatives for Horsham sitting on Thursday, November 7th, 1867 for the Commission on the Employment of Children, Young Persons and Women in Agriculture. It was stated that there were two government schools in Lower Beeding parish, plus one infant school supported by Mrs Dickins. This was Mrs Anne Marie Scrase-Dickins, nee Aldridge, from Coolhurst.[53] The 'government schools' were stated to be both under certified masters, were liberally supported by the nearby landowners and took about 200 children. It was too early for these to be Board Schools and so they were probably parliamentary grant aided church schools, and this is confirmed by the later report of 1870. There were also two evening schools with a total attendance of 50 and it was noted that 'within the last six years much has been done to civilise and educate the people in this

52. Horsfield, 1835, p. 223, and Caffyn, J., Schools in the 18th Century, pp. 82-3, in Leslie & Short, 1999. Also William, E. A. (1908) Cobden and Secular Education, *Westminster Review,* January 1908, p. 13, and and Hey, D. (ed.) (1996) *The Oxford Companion to Local and Family History*, Oxford University Press, pp. 144-149 (hereafter Hey, 1996).

53. The identity of Mrs Dickins was confirmed by Maj. Mark Scrase-Dickins, who also noted that it was common for the family to be referred to by just the one surname, Dickins.

54. Royal Commission on the Employment of Children, Young Persons, and Women in Agriculture, 1867, First Report (P.P. 1867-8, XVII), pp. 81-2, (hereafter P.P. 1867-8, XVII) and Davey, R., Schools in the 19th century, pp. 84-5 in Leslie & Short, 1999, and TNA ED17/36 Report of the Committee of the Privy Council on Education, 1870-1.

wild district'. Three years later the Report of the Committee of the Privy Council on Education, 1870, noted that annual parliamentary grants had been given to two schools in the parish. The first was in Lower Beeding village, to the school of the Holy Trinity parish church. With an average attendance of 76 they received £37, whilst in Colgate the school with an average attendance of 54 received £23 5s per annum in 1869. [54]

Village Development in the 19th and 20th Centuries

Previous historical and geographical studies of Sussex communities, such as Ambrose's study of Ringmer and Short's study of Plumpton, have used the model of 'open' and 'close' communities as an analytical tool, and this still remains a useful way to look at communities. Dennis Mills began this approach in the 1950s looking at 'dispersed' and 'grouped' types of community near Lincoln. These communities, he suggested, were based on the poor law and its administration through parish vestries. He called estate villages 'closed' and freeholder villages 'open'. In reality there is a continuum between the two, plus additional anomalies such as where the estate landowner was absent, and where there was a separation between the landlord and authority, or power.[55]

It should also be noted that 'parish' and 'village' were not interchangeable terms. Many villages, hamlets, farms and estate buildings fell within a parish, and decisions on the poor of that parish would have been decided at the parish vestry meetings. This could be quite a financial burden on a single parish and so eventually The Union Chargeability Act 1865 moved the responsibility for setting the parish poor rate to larger Unions of parishes, thereby loosening a single landowner's control in the 'close' parishes where power struggles had been played out. Horsham parish, due to its market town and subsequent infrastructure, would also have had a major impact on the surrounding parishes, including Lower Beeding and the forest.[56]

Both Colgate and Lower Beeding appear to lie towards the closed end of the 'Open-Closed' settlement model as a result of the patronage and control exercised by the few landowners on the three Anglican churches, the schools, and their rented and tenanted properties. However, the power exercised through the parish vestry could not have been wielded by the landowners here, unlike in older established villages. This was because the Parish of Lower Beeding was created quite late in 1837-8. In 1840 the parish church of the Holy Trinity was consecrated, but until 1861 it remained under the control of Magdalen College, Oxford. Then the Union Chargeability Act 1865 removed any power of the vestries to set poor rates.

In other ways the two villages could be regarded as similar to many Wealden villages, towards the open end of the spectrum. There were small brickmaking industries, shops

55. Ambrose, P. (1974) *The Quiet Revolution, Social Change in a Sussex Village 1871-1971*, Sussex University Press, and Short, B. (ed.) (1981) *Scarpfoot Parish: Plumpton 1830-1880*. CCE Occasional Paper No. 16. University of Sussex, (hereafter Short, 1981) and Jackson A. J. H. (2012) The 'Open-Closed' Settlement Model and the Interdisciplinary Formulations of Dennis Mills: Conceptualising Local Rural Change, *Rural History*, Vol. 23.02, pp. 121-136 (hereafter Jackson, 2012).

56. Short, B. (ed.)(1992) The Evolution of Contrasting Communities within rural England, *The English Rural Community*, Cambridge University Press, pp. 19-43 (hereafter Short, 1992).

and public houses, a non-conformist chapel, and dispersal of property ownership as some of the estates came up for sale at the end of the 19ᵗʰ century. Other important geographic and economic factors in the development of these two villages were their close proximity to the open and prosperous market town of Horsham, and access to London and Brighton through the establishment of the railways in 1848. These growing towns and the metropolis of London provided opportunities for work, while the railways provided the means for people to travel more widely and take up those opportunities. Likewise, in the other direction people were able move out of London into quiet rural areas such as Horsham and the Forest. Thus, the proximity of the towns, and particularly London, was an important factor in the development of the villages.[57]

Another way of looking at why settlements developed where they did, is to consider three factors. These factors are the economics of farming, social value and the role of the church. For example, farms needed workers to live within walking distance, social value lay within the sharing of skills such as midwifery, dressmaking, or carpentry, and of course churches needed a population from which to pay for their vicar. However, the two villages here, Colgate and Lower Beeding, were rather different, being new Victorian villages in a rural setting created by minor middle-class landowners, and open to the impact of expanding towns and the capital city.[58]

Before looking at the populations for both villages of Colgate and Lower Beeding it should be noted that in comparing enumeration districts over time the geographic areas are not necessarily consistent. Enumeration districts had originally been set up in 1841 as sub-divisions of the Registrar's sub-districts for births, marriages and deaths. They were given numbers within the Registrar's district and were intended to be meaningful areas such as a village, or parish, or sensible divisions of such. They also had to be of a standard size of about 200 houses in a town, and in rural parts no more than 15 miles in area but containing fewer than 200 houses. However, with 19ᵗʰ Century changes in population and administrative areas, enumeration districts could be split or amalgamated to keep them a reasonable size. Detached parts of parishes, such as at Lower Beeding, caused anomalies that cannot easily be tracked, in fact Higgs wrote that it was difficult to know the extent by which enumeration districts changed over time as they varied not only according to changes in population and boundary complexities, but also the interpretation and conscientiousness of the local officials. The numbering system established in 1841 also went through changes, and Higgs thought it full of local idiosyncrasies, which should all be borne in mind when comparing population, such as the tables in illustrations 72 and 77 page 175.[59] Another point to note is that I have used a one-kilometre radius around the central village point, such as the church, in order to count what is in the village and what is not, since this is not always clear in the enumeration districts. Such imprecise comparisons obviously have their failings, but it is a guide only to growth and type of population in the two villages over time, and hopefully of some interest.

---

57. Short, 1992, p. 30.

58. Beckett, J. (2012) Rethinking the English village, *The Local Historian* Vol. 42 No. 2, pp. 301-311.

59. Higgs, 2005, pp. 37-42.

Colgate

Enumeration district ten in the census of 1841 stretched north of Hammerpond Road to Holmbush and included Colgate, but did not name it as a village. In this enumeration district there were 50 houses accommodating 282 people, including children, and only 48 of these in nine houses had the address of Colgate, illustration 72: below. It is difficult to know where these were, but it is reasonable to assume they were on the Forest Road, near the turn to the road to Faygate, and near the chapel which would later become St Saviour's church.

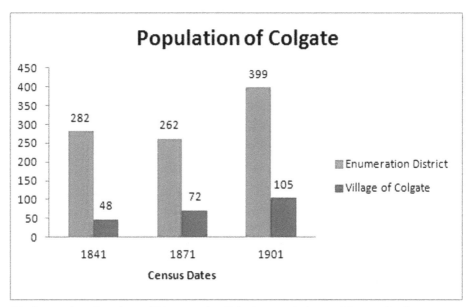

72. Comparison bar chart of Enumeration District population and figures for the approximate village population of Colgate.

On the 1876 OS map there were only 11 houses marked, apart from the vicarage, church and school, illustration 73: page 166. Of the nine households in 1841 the average age of the head of household was 33. With regard to the occupations of the men, seven were agricultural labourers, two were sawyers and one was a farmer. All were from Sussex apart from the two sawyers, Richard and Henry Chapman, who were probably brothers aged 29 and 26 respectively, and came with their wives and families from outside Sussex. In the 1841 census the county of birth outside Sussex was not noted, so it is not possible to know where they came from. Four families had four children, one had six, and those parents with fewer were in their early twenties, and there was one couple in their 50s with either no children, or at least no children living with them.[60]

The condition of these 'villagers' is illuminated by a newspaper report of July 1844, three years after the census, which told of a serious food poisoning occurrence. The report tells that the diseased carcass of a cow that had contracted murrain was sold for 10s to a poor man from Colgate, Mr Chapman, to feed his pigs and chickens.[61]. It seems that the

60. HO 107/1095/11 Horsham North/10 Census 1841

61. Murrain was a general non-specific label for an infectious disease in cattle and sheep such as foot and mouth or anthrax.

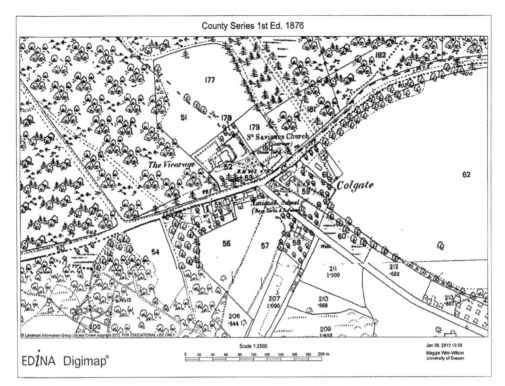

73. Colgate village showing increase of houses to approximately 11. OS County Series 1:2500, 1st Edition, 1876, reproduced with permission of Edina Historic Digimap.

Chapman family ate some of the meat and fed it to the chickens and pigs. The chickens died and the pig either died or was killed and they ate that as well. It was reported that after a short time, symptoms of an 'alarming nature' appeared and the medical officer from the Union was sent for. He found that the family were living in a hut 'which scarcely deserved the name of a house' and by consulting the neighbours discovered that the family had been eating putrid meat for some time. The medical officer, Mr Lovegrove was appalled by the conditions they were living in. The smell arising from the contents of the house was overwhelming as the pigs, chickens and family had been living in the same room. He moved them into a tent, but by this time Chapman and two of his children were sinking fast and died, and a third child of about seven was not expected to survive. Reference to the 1841 census would indicate that the Mr Chapman referred to was Richard Chapman, the sawyer from outside of Sussex, who on the 1841 census had a wife, Elizabeth and four children, Caroline aged seven, Edward aged five, William aged three and James aged three months. His wife was not mentioned in the newspaper report and it may be that she succumbed earlier to the poor food and conditions. The reporter was further astonished by the fact that the family were quickly buried with no notice sent to the coroner, only the medical officer's report given to Horsham Union. The report does indicate the dire living conditions of some of the residents of the Forest, the poor labourers who had no ties to the area and no security of work.[62]

---

62. *The Morning Post,* Tues 2 July 1844, Issue 22923.

63. Friswell N. C. (2000) The Indian Princess: Helena Bennett, *Asian Affairs,* 31:3, pp. 259-302, and Exhibition at Horsham Museum, 'The Black Lady of St Leonard's Forest – The Life and Times of Horsham's Persian Princess' 1.10.10-30.10.10.

Helena Bennett, a single woman living in the Forest with a servant, was said to be warmly remembered as being kind and generous by the ordinary people of Colgate. Friswell wrote that she was good to the impoverished and had bread brought from Horsham for distribution to the poor of Colgate. It is worth remembering here the story of Helena Bennett, who, having suffered hardship in her own life, at least attempted to alleviate some distress. Helena Bennett was born in Lucknow, India, of Persian descent, and when young was married to a French soldier, Benoît de Boigne. She and her two children were abandoned by him in London when he remarried a young French heiress. With the help and support of friends in London she moved to Rangers Lodge, St Leonard's Forest after the death of her 15-year-old daughter. Although she had a son, he was at boarding school in Hertfordshire, and spent little time with his mother, eventually joining his father in France. She lived quietly in the Forest and was known as the 'Black Princess' until her death in 1853. Her sad life story apparently inspired the locally born poet, Percy Bysshe Shelley, to begin writing a verse drama based on an Indian enchantress abandoned by her lover, although it was never finished. He wrote 'He came like a dream in the dawn of life, He fled like a shadow before its noon, He is gone, and my peace is turned to strife, And I wander and wane like the weary moon'.[63]

In 1867-8 a report gave an insight into the conditions of housing in Lower Beeding parish. *The First Report of the Commissioners on the Employment of Children, Young Persons and Women in Agriculture 1867-8* noted that whilst the conditions of cottages in the south of Lower Beeding parish were fair and not crowded, for those in the north, which would have included Colgate, the condition was said to be bad and often too crowded. It was noted in the report that a number of turf huts had been put up early in the 19th century and about a dozen were still remaining and occupied by Irish families, although there is little evidence for this in the 1841 or 1871 census for Colgate. However, it is very possible that they were not at home at the time of the census, or that they were itinerant and moving on, so one cannot assume they were never there.[64]

The 1871 census, together with the sales particulars for parts of the St Leonard's Forest estate, first offered for sale in 1878 and subsequently in 1881, give some indication of the growth of Colgate in the 30 years since the census in 1841 and a change in the ownership of land. Colgate village as a settlement at this time is difficult to define, but for this study it is determined to be those houses near the church, school and public house, on land owned by the Aldridges to the south west and Clifton Brown to the north east. An approximation of the extent of the village for this book will be taken as a kilometre radius from the centre, which is St Saviour's church, and excluding the mansions of Holmbush and New Lodge and their immediate estate cottages, apart from Blue Gate Lodge and Holmbush Tower which fall within the kilometre. Ivy Cottage on the west is excluded but New Barn farm immediately south of Colgate Hill is included, and to the south east Colgate Lodge is included. Black Hill farm to the east was only established after 1841 and does not appear in the census until 1901, see illustration 74: page 169.[65]

---

64. P.P. 1867-8, XVII, p. 82.

65. RG10/1099 Horsham North/13 Census 1871 and Horsham Museum (HM) MSS SP 203, SP 218.

The 1871 census, Enumeration District 13, surprisingly shows a decrease in the 30 years from 1841 in that same Enumeration District from 50 houses and 282 people to 48 houses and 262 people, but an increase in Colgate village from nine houses to 13 and from 48 people to 72, half of whom were children. It is noticeable that there was much more variety in the village profile, from occupations, and places of birth to female occupations. However, perhaps the most important developments in the building of the community were the establishment by 1871 of the church and vicarage, a school, a grocery shop and a beer shop. The idea of a beer shop was introduced by the 1830 Beer Act by which a householder could apply for a license to brew and sell beer from their domestic premises. The beer brewed this way was often unreliable and its quality dubious when up against the bigger brewing companies that were expanding, such as King & Barnes in Horsham.

Of the 13 households within the one-kilometre central village in 1871 the average age of the head of the household was 46, indicating that the community had aged due to the older shopkeepers and farmers and fewer agricultural labourers. There were two farmers, James Lee, 36, at Coombe Land farming 24 acres with his wife Emily and four children, and James Sheathen [sic] of Colgate Lodge, 40, farming 241 acres with his wife Susanna and one young son. In the village there were 11 labourers in total, although they were not specified as agricultural labourers as in the 1841 census, for example, George Payne, 35 was listed as a woodsman labourer. George Agate, 56, remained as an agricultural labourer, and his wife Sarah with their children are the only family that are recognisable in the 1871 census from the 1841 census. Their two older sons, James, 21 and William, 19 were labouring, and the three other children were at home, the middle one listed as scholar. Seven years later in the 1878 Aldridge sales details record George Agate as a yearly tenant of a cottage, garden, woodhouse and land at Barnsnap totalling three acres, mostly pasture and orchard lying to the south of Colgate village, and let to him as a yearly tenant for £3 a year. By the 1901 census the family was back again in the village, living at Langley cottages, and the head of household, 59-year-old John Agate born in Colgate, is labouring on a farm.

James Budgeon, 66, another labourer, had married Caroline Colin, 48, the personal maid to Helena Bennett. By 1871 they had twin boys, James and Henry, both 16 years old and both labourers, and two younger children. They had one of two cottages with three acres, all pasture apart from the garden, and there was a yearly tenancy for the two properties of £10 a year. There was one gardener in the village, Henry Funnell, 42, with his wife and six children, their eldest son, Benjamin, being an 18-year-old labourer. There was a charcoal burner, William Hughes, 29, with his wife and three lodgers, although it is difficult to place where they lived, in or near the village. One of their lodgers, Thomas Harlow, 45 years old and married, also gave charcoal burning as his business. The other two younger lodgers and Hughes' wife had the occupation of 'splitter' with 'lath', also connected with charcoal burning. To the west of the village was Colgate brickyard, five acres including cottage, garden, brickfield and brick kiln and yard. Although noted as 'in hand', or unoccupied, in 1878, the 1871 census shows a brick maker, Matthew Dearing, 32, living and working there, with his wife and three children.

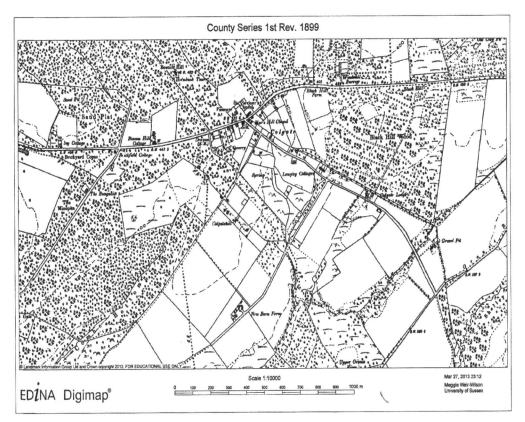

74. Colgate village, showing named properties such as Black Hill Farm, Beacon Hill Cottage and the appearance of Mars Hill Chapel. OS County Series, 1:10560, 1st Revision, 1899, reproduced with permission of Edina Historic Digimap.

The house, grocer's shop, offices and gardens were let on leases of 99 years from 1869 and 1874 to James Langley, 53, with his wife, two sons and the lodger, Solomon Waldrew, who was employed as a gamekeeper. Further along Forest Road to the west was the Dragon beer shop with house, offices and gardens, occupied in 1871 by Reuben Ashby, 66, his wife, two sons and three daughters. The eldest son, also Reuben, was a 21-year-old labourer and the eldest daughter an employed housekeeper, but the next daughter of 20 was noted as 'imbecile', that is having mental health problems, and her younger sister of 17 was noted as her helper. By 1878 it appears that the Ashbys had moved on and the beer shop was let on a 44-year lease to H. Mitchell for £4 a year. The attached cottage was let to Harriet Davy for the term of her life at a nominal rent of 1s per annum. The 1871 census, recorded seven years earlier, had a Mary Ann Davey, 65, a widow kept by the Parish, and it seems likely that this was the same person, or a relative.[66]

Finally, according to the 1871 census, there is the schoolmaster, Charles Reynolds, 31 and his wife Elizabeth, 31, their three children and - at the time of the census – a visiting cousin Alice Hammond, 17, from Chichester near Reynold's birthplace. The census notes that Elizabeth Reynolds was also a teacher, and Baldwin wrote that before marriage she was Elizabeth Venus, daughter of George Venus, bailiff to the Coolhurst estate, and had

66. HM MS SP203.

been married in St John's church with a Scrase-Dickins as witness. When George Venus died in 1877 the family moved to take up his now vacant position at Coolhurst. However, it was said that Reynolds had built four cottages in Colgate and that he sold these to finance an unsuccessful trip to prospect for gold in the Klondike, so gold fever reached as far as Colgate! It appears that in 1878 two houses with gardens in Colgate owned by the Aldridge estate were let on a 99-year lease to Reynolds, he may well have bought these and others that were up for sale twenty years before the gold rush in the United States. Reynolds was clearly a multi-talented and interesting man. Baldwin quotes his great grandson, Peter Reynolds, as saying that he was also a good gardener and developed a new potato variety which he called 'The Teacher'.[67]

Although Colgate village was becoming older, larger and more varied in its profile, with some female occupations noted, there were still not many incomers from outside of Sussex. Birth places for adults showed only one from Dorset, two from Surrey and the remainder from Sussex. However, surprisingly only one family, the Agates appear to have remained in Colgate for 30 years, so there was considerable movement of families to and from Colgate, perhaps due to the newness of the village and the close proximity of Horsham, the market town.

Looking at Colgate through the data of the 1901 census, again with a period of 30 years since the 1871 census, it can be seen that the numbers of houses and households in enumeration district 14 had grown considerably from 48 houses and 262 people to 201 houses and 399 people. It is interesting to note that the average density is down from five people per household to fewer than two per house. In Colgate village itself the overall growth was from 11 to 35 houses and from 72 to 105 people, a much greater growth than from 1841 to 1871, but again a drop in the average number of people in each house from six to fewer than three.

Somewhat surprisingly the age of the head of household had again increased to an average age of 50 years, and this is not necessarily due to older people in trade or professions but older workers as well. This may account for the reduced density of each household, perhaps fewer children at home. Examples of the older head of households were a 72-year-old charcoal burner, Thomas Harper, a 60-year-old gardener, Richard Gates and 76-year-old farmer, Caroline Budgeon, who clearly would have had help from her son Henry, a 46-year-old agricultural labourer living with her. Older people of note as head of households and part of the burgeoning middle classes were Jean Lebeque, a French wine merchant, 58, living at Colgate Lodge with his wife and a housemaid of 21, and Thomas Mansbridge, 55, with his wife, 57, both from Hampshire and living on their own means at Beacon Hill Cottage. Finally, there was James Langley, 66, with his wife Ruth at the Mars Chapel, stated to be living on his own means. By this time the chapel must have ceased to be used for worship and converted to a private house. Later, the Land Valuation Survey of 1910-15 clarified that the chapel was used as 'Colgate Recreation Rooms', still owned by the Langleys, but that they had moved away to New Street in Horsham.[68]

67. Baldwin, 1985, p.35 and RG10/1099 Horsham North/13 Census 1871 and Horsham Museum MSS SP 203 and SP 218.
68. RG13/949 Horsham North/14 Census 1901 and TNA Field Book IR58/94090.

Occupation	1841	1871	1901
Agric. Labourer	7	-	7
Brick Maker	-	1	-
Carter	-	-	1
Charcoal Burner	-	1	1
Charwoman	-	-	1
Clergy	-	-	1
Coachman	-	-	1
Coal Merchant	-	-	1
Farmer	1	2	5
Game Keeper	-	-	1
Gardener	-	1	3
Grocer	-	1	1
Inn Keeper	-	1	1
Labourer	-	3	1
Own Means	-	-	3
Parish Relief	-	1	-
Press Worker	-	-	1
Sawyer	2	-	-
School Master	-	1	1
Shepherd	-	-	1
Wine Merchant	-	-	1
Woodman	-	-	1

75. Statistics from Census returns of village of Colgate showing changing pattern of employment through head of household occupations for 1841, 1871 and 1901.

What strikes one about this older village population is that there are not as many children as one would anticipate in such a village which has an elementary school with school teachers in the centre of the village. There are only ten households out of the 35 who have children, and one of them, The Vicarage, has a working 15-year-old maid, Florence Ingram from London, and another 17-year-old, Emily Grimshaw from nearby Southwater, which illustrates the continuing employment of very young domestic servants away from their homes. The widow and charwoman, Elizabeth Reed had a 15-year-old son noted to have the occupation of 'houseboy' again in domestic service but able to live at home.

69. Kelly's Directory of Sussex, 1899, accessible through: www.historicaldirectories.org

Out of a total population in Colgate village alone of about 105 only 28 of these were children below the age of 18. Given that the elementary or primary education at that time took children from five to 14, there would only be a possible 15 eligible to attend the school built for 100 places. The catchment area would have been larger than just the village and would have included Holmbush, Bewbush, and south of the Forest but not Lower Beeding village which had its own school. Kelly's Directory of 1899 stated that attendance at the school was an average of 65, which was well below capacity.[69]

Discounting the young housemaids at the Vicarage who had been born in London and nearby Southwater, of the nine households with children, most had one or two children, the Ashby family had three small sons, the Langley family had two sons and two daughters. There were two larger families: the Pink family had five young children under eight. However, the largest family was that of the Nichols at Blue Gate Lodge on the Holmbush estate with eight children, six daughters and two sons aged from 14 to eight months. Reay explored fertility in English villages and wrote that family sizes reduced over the 19th century, particularly after 1835, and that there was a shift from natural fertility to family limitation after the 1880s, following changes in attitude to childbearing.[70]

It is clear with what has been noted about Colgate and the 1901 census so far, that the village had grown and become further varied with regard to occupation and place of birth. Considering the variety in occupation it appears that four were in trade (wine merchant, coal merchant, grocer and inn keeper), two were professional (teacher and clergy), 16 were still in agriculture, six in service and three were living on their own means plus another three reliant on family members for support. One head of household of the Nichols family was absent on census day and not noted, although since the family were living on the Holmbush estate it is likely he was working in service, or in agriculture on the estate, see illustration 75: page 171.

Looking at the places of birth it can be seen that families are being attracted in from nearby southern counties such as Surrey, Kent, Hampshire, Devon and Buckinghamshire, as well as the capital, London. From further afield came Jean Lebeque from France, wine merchant, with his wife Catherine from Reigate in Surrey and a very local housemaid, 21-year-old Catherine Ashby from Colgate. The Ashby family were inn keepers in the 1871 census and Catherine may have been a later daughter or even granddaughter. William Ashby was the youngest son of Reuben Ashby the inn keeper in 1871 and the 1901 census found him running the public house with his wife Emily and three small sons, and living with them was his sister-in-law, a 25-year-old housemaid. From the same family was George Ashby, 25-year-old gamekeeper from Colgate, who was living with his wife Emily from Kent.

Other families who had been recorded in the 1871 census still appeared 30 years later on the 1901 census. Caroline Budgeon was still living at Colgate but as a widow with her 48-year-old son Henry as small farmers. Henry Funnell, who had been a gardener with wife and four children in 1871 was now at 77 a widower living with two adult sons, Frank,

70. Reay, B. (1994) Before the transition: fertility in English villages, 1800-1880. *Continuity and Change*, Vol. 9, Issue 1, pp. 91-120.

39 and a brick maker, and Charles, 34 and a gardener like his father. Sophie Payne, now a widow at 59, was living with her adult son George, a carter. She had clearly married George Payne with whom she was living in 1871 as Sophie King with her two King children, Fred and George. Only one family record stretched back to 1841 and that was the Agate family. In 1901 John Agate and his wife Elizabeth, both 59, lived in one of the Langley cottages with a lodger, Percy Smith, 23. The Agates had been farm labourers in 1841 and remained so in 1901.

Of the 35 households, only five were established Colgate families over the previous 30 years, which again indicates migration in and out of the village. Clearly this is only a snapshot of the village within this study's defined boundaries and it may be that people moved within the parish, but Horsham town would have been a draw to the young for employment, as would Brighton and London, due to the higher wages. Malcolm Kitch, Emeritus Reader in History at the University of Sussex, has studied rural migration from numerous sources from the 16th to the 19th centuries in many English counties including Sussex. He suggested that in contrast to an idealised impression of static unchanging English villages, there were always both long-term movement and seasonal movement, even amongst freehold and tenant farmers. It was stability over several generations, such as with the Aldridges of St Leonard's Forest, that was unusual. Most people moved once in their lives, either for work or marriage, but this tended to be short distances. In Kitch's research he found that most moves in pre-industrial England were within ten-15 miles, or a day's walk, some moving many times but not much further than the neighbouring village, parish or town. He noted that geography did have an impact on migration and cited the Sussex Weald as notoriously hard to get around, particularly before the mid-19th century. [71]

Details from the Field Books of the Land Valuation Survey of 1910-15 confirmed that much property passed from the Aldridges to the Saillards of Buchan Hill. For example, with reference to the maps of the village produced for the land valuation, see illustration 76: page 174, numbers: 185, 149, 67, 68, 180, 184, and 177 which included the Public House and shop all have Saillard as the freeholder. In addition he owned Beacon Hill Cottage to the west of the village and Colgate Lodge to the south east. Clifton Brown from Holmbush continued to own property on the east of the village such as 264, 265, 266, 267, 268 and 269. However, individual property owners were beginning to appear, for example, Mrs A. M. E. Cot from Chapel Street, Liverpool, who owned the cottages 189 and 190. The Vicarage, shown on the map as 66, had an owner and occupier of W. Harsfall, who had fruit trees, tennis courts and a coach house in the grounds. Interestingly plot 428 in the centre of the village next to the school was cited as allotments, until a house was built on part of the land in 1909. The owner of this plot was N. S. Langley of 121 New Street Horsham. The Langley family, both Mrs Langley at 111 New Street and N. S. Langley, owned the leasehold of a number of cottages such as 215 and 216 which they subsequently rented out.

71. Kitch, M. (1992) Population movement and migration in pre-industrial rural England, Short, B. (ed.), *The English Rural Community,* Cambridge: Cambridge University Press, pp. 62-84.

72. HO 107/1095/11 Horsham North/9 Census 1841 and RG10/1058 Horsham North/11 Census 1871 and RG13/949 Horsham North/16 Census 1901, and P.P. 1867-8, XVII, p. 82.

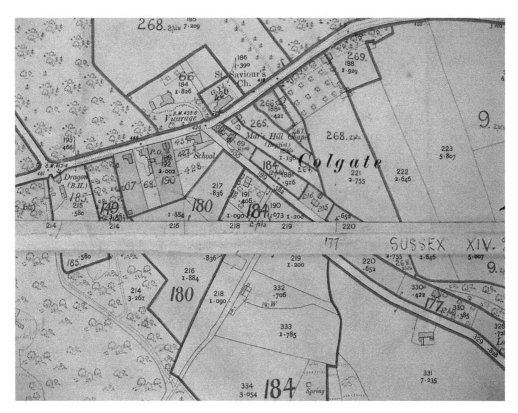

76. The 1910-15 Land Valuation Survey maps of Colgate village TNA IR124/9/113 and IR124/9/117.

Lower Beeding

Lower Beeding village had a similar development to that of Colgate in that a large part of it was owned by the Aldridge estate, so that properties and land became available for purchase in 1878 and again in 1881, thus giving more opportunities for the middle classes to settle in the area. *The First Report of the Commissioners on the Employment of Children, Young Persons and Women in Agriculture 1867-8* had noted that the south of the parish was more populous and the houses in better condition than the north. This is confirmed in the figures for the enumeration districts that dealt with Lower Beeding and Crabtree. For example, in the 1841 census enumeration district 9 there were 86 inhabited houses and 232 people, four of whom were living in a tent. In the 1871 enumeration district 11 these figures had grown to 124 houses and 612 people, and by 1901 enumeration district 16 showed 148 houses and 670 people. The strongest growth in this small area was from 1841 to 1871 when the population increased by 164%, and that was before the sale of the Aldridge estate, see illustration 77: page 175.[72] These figures are for the enumeration districts through time, rather than my one-kilometre estimation of the village.

It is clear from the 1841 census that the village of Lower Beeding was not a defined settlement, as it was not named as an address on the census; however, there was a 'St Leonard's village' which appeared to be Crabtree, a cluster of houses to the south of Leonardslee on Mill Lane and the Horsham-to-Cowfold road. Crabtree looked to have

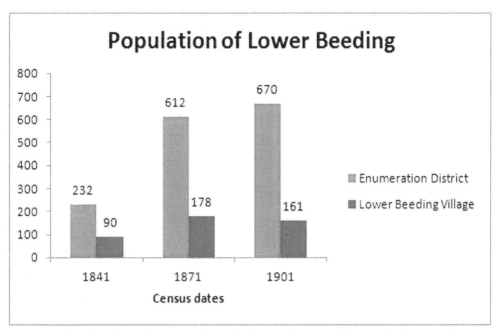

77. Comparison bar chart of Enumeration District population and figures for the approximate village population of Lower Beeding.

more houses at this time, with an old Inn and later a post office. It is therefore perhaps surprising that the parish church of Holy Trinity was built in Lower Beeding in the 1840s rather than at Crabtree, however this was probably due to that fact that Robert Aldridge donated the land for the church, 20 acres being a considerable gift. It is difficult to analyse the community at Lower Beeding in 1841 due to the lack of clarity of the addresses, however one can pick out Plummers Plain and Sandygate either side of the Plough Inn which could be considered to be Lower Beeding village. It is assumed that Cross Ways is otherwise known as Ashfold Crossways and therefore further east than the development of the actual village.

Of the ten houses noted as Plummers Plain, there were three farmers and one brick maker listed as head of households, four agricultural labourers and two ordinary labourers. The three houses on Sandygate contained as head of household one agricultural labourer, one labourer, and one 35-year-old cordwainer, or shoemaker, named as William Sherlock living with his wife, four children and two labourers, one in his 80s and the other in his 60s who may well have been assisting with the shoemaking business. The Plough Inn was being run by 40-year-old Thomas Barnes, his wife and their seven young children of whom the eldest boy, at 14, was an agricultural labourer. Also at the Inn were Barnes' 70-year-old father, and three lodgers, a 60-year-old agricultural labourer and a 60-year-old labourer, and, rather unusually, a 14-year-old girl, Frances Stoner, noted as an agricultural labourer.

There were moral concerns over girls working in the fields, and this is emphasised by *The First Report of the Commissioners on the Employment of Children, Young Persons and Women in Agriculture 1867-8*. Minutes from the local collective meeting of representatives from Horsham, Nuthurst and Lower Beeding meeting at Horsham in November 1867 reported

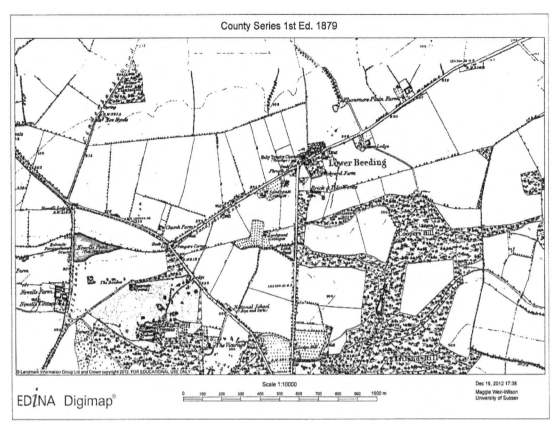

78. Lower Beeding, OS County Series 1:10560, 1st Edition, 1879, reproduced with permission of Edina Historic Digimap.

to the Commission that it would like to see the employment of girls of between 13 and 18 prohibited from working on the land unless under the supervision of their mothers or natural guardians. It is worth noting, as Howkins does, that the number of women working in agriculture was underestimated by successive censuses, and farmers' wives were often discounted as workers. As with Colgate at this date, there was a majority of agricultural labourers, and also like Colgate there were brick makers employed by the brick yard and kiln opposite the church. All inhabitants of Lower Beeding were given as coming from Sussex apart from the inn keeper and his father, one of the farmers' wives and the 60-year-old labourer living in the cordwainer's house. In the 1841 census the actual county of birth was not noted, just whether or not they were born in the same county, Sussex.[73]

By the 1871 census the boundaries of the actual village of Lower Beeding are no clearer, but for this study one can continue to look at Sandygate Lane to the west as far as Church Farm and to the east on Plummers Plain as far as Plummers Plain Farm and then south towards Leechpool cottages and Lodge Hill, not including Leonardslee, but to the east to include the national school, all approximately within one kilometre of Holy Trinity church, see illustrations 78 and 79. It is possible to identify 36 households in this area and of these the head of household average age was 46 with a total of 81 school aged children.

73. P.P. 1867-8, XVII, p. 82 and Howkins, A. (2003) *The Death of Rural England*, London, Routledge, pp. 8, 19, (hereafter Howkins, 2003).

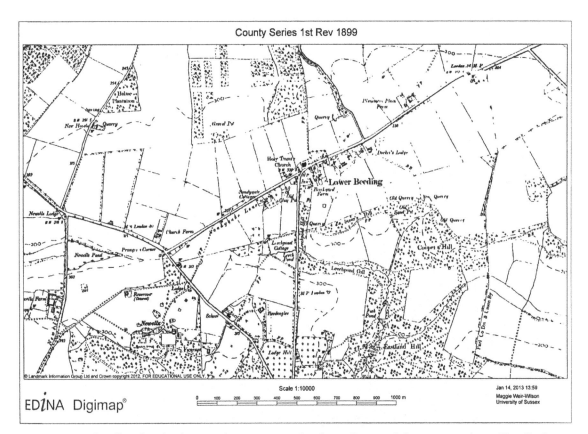

79. Lower Beeding showing increase in cottages on Sandygate Lane and the new mansion of Beedinglee. OS County Series 1:10560, 1st Revision, 1899, reproduced with permission of Edina Historic Digimap.

A number of young children were working. There were three female domestic servants aged 17, 16 and 15, one 15-year-old barmaid, and of the boys, the youngest was George Vials an 11-year-old under-gardener, and still very young were 13 and 14-year-old farm labourers and a 15-year-old brick maker. Apart from the schooling that the 11 and 13-year olds were missing, it does highlight the very long working life of a labourer, older labourers in the village being 75-year-old agricultural labourer, William Wheeler, and 76-year-old William Wales.

The profile of occupations of the 36 heads of household in Lower Beeding in 1871 were: seven in trade, which included carpenters and the cordwainer, two professionals, the vicar and schoolmaster, 19 agricultural workers which included ordinary labourers and carters,[74] and seven in service. There were none living on their own means although the head of household of the 'new mansion' was absent for the census. A number of households were living as extended families with elderly fathers or mothers, a niece, or next door to siblings. Two households were coping with the care of adults recorded as 'lunatic from birth'. For example, James Fiest, 58-year-old labourer, was living near to his adult son of the same name, and with his wife, 18-year-old son and 16-year-old daughter and his 56-year-old brother, William, noted as 'lunatic from birth'. Next door to them was 77-year-old widow Ann Standing, with her 45-year-old daughter, Harriet, also noted as

---

74. Higgs, 2005, pp. 159-163. Given the rural position of the village of Lower Beeding the author has included Carters and Labourers in the Agricultural group of occupations.

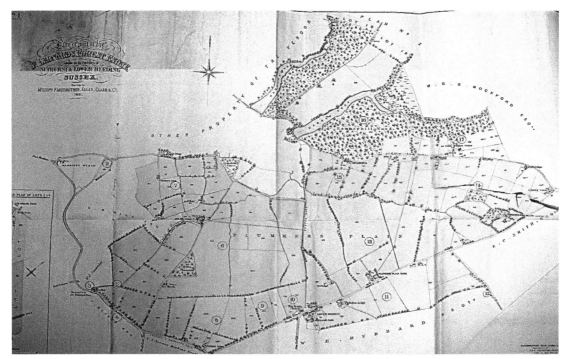

80. Map attached to sales particulars SP 218, sale of St Leonard's estate July 1881, showing southern portion Lots 10,11,12 and 13. Horsham Museum & Art Gallery (Horsham District Council)

'lunatic from birth'. It was probable that these neighbours were able to assist each other in the daily care of their relatives. Higgs notes that the category of 'lunatic from birth' was very loose and quotes from the 1881 census report that the term 'lunatic' was vague and would include 'some persons suffering from congenital idiocy, and many more suffering from dementia', however it seems as this mental incapacity was 'from birth' it was unlikely to be dementia.[75]

The first sale of the Aldridge estate in eight lots in 1878 produced few sales and the estate was offered again in 1881, this time in 56 lots. One can see from Lots 11 and 12 that a large part of Lower Beeding village had been owned by the Aldridge estate, although leased in large part to W.E. Hubbard, jnr., see illustrations 80 and 81. The later OS 1899 map, see illustration 79: page 177, shows some filling in of cottages between Dockers Lodge and the older ones opposite the church. However, the 1901 census, enumeration district 16 covering Lower Beeding and Crabtree, shows a slower growth from 1871 to 1901 from 124 house and 612 people to 148 houses and 670 people, a population increase of barely 10%. Looking at the 1901 census in the same kilometre area from the church, one can count 37 households, and one empty property on Sandygate Lane. This is virtually the same number as in 1871 and may reflect the difficulties of identifying properties from the census, even with reference to historic maps, rather than a lack of increase in housing.

The pattern of occupations had shifted over the previous 30 years from the majority being in agriculture to an almost similar number now being in service to the large houses, such as a porter, butler, maids, coachman, gamekeeper and gardeners, see illustration 82:

75. Higgs, 2005, pp. 92-3.

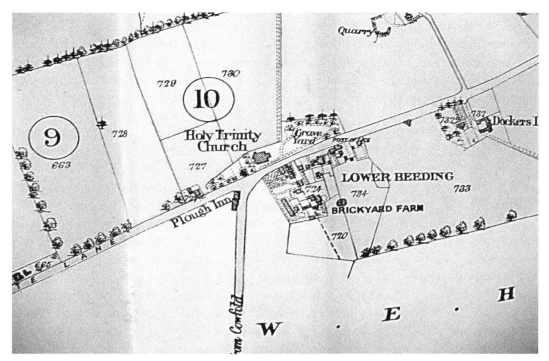

81. Detail of Lower Beeding village on map attached to sales particulars SP 218, sale of St Leonard's estate July 1881. Horsham Museum & Art Gallery (Horsham District Council)

page 181. Not surprisingly, with so many now in service, places of birth amounted to 14 different counties from as far away as Yorkshire and Devon, although the majority came from Sussex and the nearer counties of Surrey, Kent, Hampshire and parts of London. The population in the village had aged slightly from 1871, with the average age of the head of household now 50 years of age. This clearly had an impact on the number of children of school age, between five and 14 years of age, and these amounted to 47 from only 16 of the households, with 21 young children coming from four families. Again, one is struck by the age of some of the labourers; 81-year-old Spencer Palmer was a general farm labourer, 75-year-old George Baines was a gardener's labourer and Alexander Tyrall, was a 70-year-old labourer. Although evidence from a study from Plumpton, Sussex, suggests working into old age was not uncommon, it was not relieved until a state pension was introduced in January 1909 by the reforming Liberal Government for those over 70.[76]

One of the mansions within Lower Beeding, known as Beedinglee, was built for Louisa Hubbard in 1883 by her brother W. E. Hubbard, Jnr., on land owned by the family. On the 1901 census day it appeared that the mansion was missing the head of household. In 1899 Louisa Hubbard had been partially paralysed by a stroke while on holiday in the Tyrol, Austria, and so there she stayed until her death in 1906. Meanwhile, in Beedinglee there was a resident cook, parlour maid and housemaid and - rather oddly - an eight-year-old boy lodger from the Isle of Wight, in addition to a gardener and coachman in the cottage and stables.[77] The Land Valuation Survey 1910-15 shows Beedinglee was still in the freehold ownership of E. G. Loder (brother-in-law of Louisa Hubbard) but rented on a

76. Short, 1981, p. 26, and Hey, 1996, p. 331.

77. Kelly, S. (2004) Hubbard, Louisa Maria (1836-1906), *Oxford Dictionary of National Biography*, Oxford University Press. Accessible through: www.oxforddnb.com/view/article/34030.

three-year tenancy to a Mrs. Rutherford for a yearly rental of £50. It was described as a modern brick and tile house, with four bedrooms and a box room, two servants' rooms, a dressing room, hall, dining room, morning room, study, kitchen, scullery, larder butler's pantry, and two staircases. Outside there was a coach house, stable, grooms' room, electric light plant, and the modern addition of a garage, all valued at £4,200.[78]

With reference to the Land Valuation Survey, it shows that much of the core village of Lower Beeding in about 1911 was owned by E. G. Loder, who would have purchased these properties from the Aldridge estate. Thus, Sandygate cottages, The Plough Inn, the Post Office shop and three cottages, Fir Tree Villa, Dockers Lodge and Leechpond Cottage were all owned by E. G. Loder with tenancies which varied from one month to 21 years. Since the 1901 census, the Plough Inn had changed hands to a James Jenkins, who rented it with 15 acres of grassland and timber. Trinity School House was also owned by the Loders and rented from 1903 on a 21-year tenancy to the schoolmaster, E. J. Hill, for an annual rent of £27. Other substantial properties in the village that E. G. Loder owned freehold were Brickyard Farm with 61 acres, stables and hovel, in the centre of the village. He also owned the Plummers Plain Brickyard which was one acre of land with four sheds and two kilns. Both farm and brickyard had no other occupier, or tenant, at the time of the Land Valuation Survey. A Gazetteer noted that the Brickyard on the east side of Leechpond Hill went out of use shortly after 1882 when the tenant was John Dearing. Its successor, further along Sandygate Lane, called Plummers Plain Brickyard opened in early 1890s with Jason Brewer as the manager, and kept going until the 1930s.[79]

A property to the east of the village on the A281 called Newells was a part of the Coolhurst estate and the Land Valuation Survey confirms the freehold was owned by Charles R. Scrase-Dickins and occupied by W. S. Graves, who was not resident at the time of the 1901 census as his 21-year lease ran from 1903. Graves is noted in *Kelly's Directory of Sussex 1905* as a Justice of the Peace. Newells was a large mansion and park of 180 acres with a gross value estimated at £20,500. The mansion was described by the assessor as 'modern and in very good condition' and it appeared to be quite large with hall, drawing room, dining room, study, morning room, eight bedrooms and servants' accommodation. Outside there were loose boxes, stables, motor garage, coal house, electric light plant, pump engine for water, and three additional cottages. These large mansion properties such as Newells and Beedinglee, with electricity generators, motor garages and stables, appeared to have embraced the latest technology with electricity and the combustion engine, and yet they still had their coachmen, grooms and horses as a mode of transport, although this would not last beyond the coming Great War.[80] Beedinglee survived into the 21st century with associated properties, whilst Newells was enlarged and converted to a preparatory school in the 20th century, only to burn down in 1968. Only Newells Farm, Lodge house, Pond Cottage and woodland, plus some new houses, remain today.

78. TNA IR58/94086.

79. Beswick, M.(2001) *Brickmaking in Sussex, A History and Gazetteer,* Midhurst: Middleton Press, pp. 181-2, and TNA IR58/94086.

Lower Beeding, Occupations of Head of Household

Occupation	1841	1871	1901
Agric. Labourer	5	7	5
Bailiff	-	1	-
Baker	-	-	2
Brick Maker	1	1	-
Butler	-	-	1
Carrier	-	-	2
Carter	-	1	1
Clergy	-	1	1
Coachman	-	1	2
Cordwainer	1	1	-
Farmer	3	2	3
Game Keeper	-	1	1
Gardener	-	2	6
Grocer/Shopkeeper	-	1	1
Groom	-	1	-
Housekeeper/Porter	-	1	1
Inn Keeper	1	1	1
Labourer	3	8	2
Own Means	-	-	1
Painter	-	-	1
Parish Relief	-	-	1
Sawyer/Carpenter	-	3	1
School Master	-	1	1
Shepherd	-	-	1
Warehouseman	-	-	1

82. Statistics from Census returns of village of Lower Beeding showing changing pattern of employment through head of household occupations for 1841, 1871 and 1901.

Evidence points to the fact that the villages of Colgate and Lower Beeding were both dependent on their local wealthy landowners for their initial establishment. Churches and schools established by landowners in these communities became the focal point for growth rather than the response to growth. Landowners, clergy and state were all keen to make sure that an Anglican type of Christianity 'civilized' the 'wild' population of the Forest. In addition, for landowners the opportunity of church building brought status and a monumental legacy for their families. As can be seen from the census figures, population in the Forest did grow but tailed off after the 1870s, leaving the churches and schools of the villages half full.

Perhaps unsurprisingly the majority of the landholdings remained in the hands of the few, despite the large-scale sales of the St Leonard's Forest estate which, rather than enabling the tenant to buy his home, just transferred large portions of land from one wealthy landholder to another. Most of the local landowners had a Victorian philanthropic attitude towards the villages. For example, in 1875 the Hubbard's built Crabtree Hall, a workmen's club and library which by 1905 had over 500 books for the education of the workers. Louisa Hubbard herself had strongly promoted teaching as a suitable profession for women, and the local elementary school had been built on land donated by her family, next to her home, Beedinglee. The gift of land and funds for village benefit ran through the history of both villages, and was based on the ethics of paternalism, service, rights and responsibilities.

However, by the early 20th century these ethics were shifting as the larger landowners became more remote from their estates, and the smaller landowners felt the pinch of falling values of rents and fewer labourers. The old order of landowner, farmer and labourer was changing. The state was becoming more involved in welfare and education, and socialist ideas and trade unions were gaining ground. In addition to a new type of less deferential worker, came a different type of landowner, newly wealthy from London business and commerce and more concerned with individuality and private ownership than community.[81] These developments brought about an interesting clash between private and public interests, which was illuminated by the 1901 Forest Footpath Dispute as described in Chapter 4. Although not addressed in this book, it is clear that these shifts in society were accelerated by the First World War 1914-18.

80. Kelly's Directory of Sussex, 1905, accessed through www.historicaldirectories.org.
81. Howkins, 2003, pp. 7-26.

Holly, with berries, *Ilex aquifolium* by Dr Maggie Weir-Wilson.

Chapter 7

A Final Word

> The trees encountered on a country stroll
> reveal a lot about a country's soul
> A small grove massacred to the last ash,
> An oak with heart-rot, give away the show:
> … A culture is no better than its woods.

W.H. Auden, from *Bucolics II: Woods*, 1952.

In this book I have explored how St Leonard's Forest, Horsham, changed from a devalued heath and secondary woodland in the early 18th century to a highly valued area of private estates with gardens, forest and lakes two centuries later. It is a question that has ranged over a large area, both literally and metaphorically, with uncertain boundaries and different paths to explore. Due to the uncertainty of the actual historical boundaries of the Forest, it was necessary for me to define, and therefore limit, the area of Forest and the villages that I would review and include in this book. I have managed to pull together some of the disparate elements of a history of landscape settlement, ownership and use of resources in this specific Sussex Wealden forest, St Leonard's Forest, to give an interesting account of these changes over time.

This Forest has not been dealt with before as a coherent local history or landscape study, and there have, inevitably, been historical, social and environmental areas that could have been explored further. However, it is hoped that the information presented in this book might prompt further interest in the reader in the ways that other forests of the Sussex Weald Forest Ridge, or elsewhere, may also have changed over a similar period.

I have thrown some light on the kinds of social, economic and environmental influences which affected the particular character of this Forest landscape, and how it developed over several centuries. Researching the social, economic and cultural impacts of local human activity on a landscape has shown that the attitudes of the landowners, the social context of ownership, resource use, memory and meaning associated with living in a forest landscape have all proved to be of importance in shaping the changes to this specific Forest landscape.

Although the focus of this book was from the early 18th century, it was important to uncover what was the character of the Forest at this starting point in time, and it was therefore necessary to look back at the impact that the iron industry had wrought on the Forest in the 16th century, and the subsequent large-scale felling of timber trees through Royal warrants. But where does one begin with exploring the impact of human activity on a landscape? A forest, or woodland, is a palimpsest written by generation after generation responding to the forest as they find it following previous human activity. Daniels and Cosgrove suggest that landscape is less of a palimpsest whose authentic meanings can be 'read' through correct techniques and theories, and more of a computer screen whose meaning can be 'created, extended, altered, elaborated and finally obliterated by the merest touch of a button'. So, meaning and interpretation can change, but the facts remain that the rabbit warrens of the 17th and early 18th century Forest would not have come about without the iron industry moving north, and the subsequent over-felling, over -grazing, poor drainage, and profit in rabbit meat and fur. A modern, ecologically aware, interpretation might emphasise that the clear warning voices against destroying a sustainable well-timbered environment were ignored by those focussed on immediate returns from timber, with the inevitable consequence of a degraded landscape.[1]

Although archival evidence of rabbit warrens is limited, newer technology in the form of archaeological Lidar investigations carried out in 2009-12 confirmed that there were remains of pillow mounds and boundary banks in the Forest, and this information was particularly useful for this book. Today it is difficult to grasp the size and importance of the rabbit warrens of St Leonard's Forest, with mid-20th century plantings of Scots and Corsican pine obscuring their contours. However, the study has clearly shown that the centre of the Forest had degenerated into bare heathland useful for the production of rabbits, until the proliferation of wild rabbits and changes to the poaching laws made rabbit meat much cheaper, new drainage techniques improved the soil, and returns on agricultural production improved.

How did the French and Napoleonic wars of 1793-1815 and the enclosure of Horsham Common impact the Forest? It could be assumed that such major events as war and land enclosures would leave their mark on the Forest and its people. However, this did not appear to be the case. The Napoleonic Wars had little impact on the Forest, as it was the Common that had been used for camps and training. The agricultural boom of the Napoleonic war years did encourage two lessees to divide the 3,000 acres of Forest under their control into small tracts of land, allowing poor tenanted farms and hovels to be created, until the reality of the difficult and unsuitable soil contributed to their failure, as noted in the Employment in Agriculture Report of 1867-8 and oral evidence given in the footpath dispute of 1900.

It has been interesting to discover how far the cultural appreciation of the picturesque encouraged a new interest in the landscape of the Forest and led to the subsequent planting of gardens and parks in the Forest. An appreciation of British wild and wooded landscape known as the 'picturesque' became popular in the early to mid-18th century and this looked on landscape with a painterly eye, concerned with the composition of the scene. Later in the 19th century aspiring modern industrialists and traders were looking to

---

1.Daniels, S. & Cosgrove, D. (eds.) (1988) Introduction: Iconography and Landscape. *The Iconography of Landscape*, Cambridge University Press, pp. 1-10.

83. Leonardslee Mansion House

invest in capital and status by purchasing small 'picturesque' estates, and St Leonard's Forest was eminently suitable both topographically and geographically, with a touch of the wild or sublime. Thomas Broadwood designed his parkland with echoes of an earlier style of the Italianate, which included avenues, towers, statues and prospects although by the time he had completed it, the plain landscape parks of Capability Brown had come into vogue and out again, as those with estates were beginning to return to elements of the picturesque, followed by the gardenesque. Thus, there was variety and mixture of garden landscape style in St Leonard's Forest. There was the persistence of an older 18th century style at Holmbush, and an early appreciation of the picturesque, alongside the later 19th century American gardens, arboretum and wild woodland style of Coolhurst and Leonardslee.

It is difficult to assess how much an aesthetic appreciation of a garden style impacted landowners' choices, as lifestyle and personal interest appeared to weigh more. The Victorian appetite for nature, as a contrast to the smoke and grime of London less than 50 miles from the Weald, was a selling point emphasised by the 19th century sales particulars of the Forest estates. As roads and rail opened up the Weald, it began to be seen as a restorative natural environment in which to live. The fact that the acidic sandy soil was suitable for gardens, rather than agriculture, encouraged the sale of small estates to the middle classes with a view to building villas set in attractive gardens. The new exotic plants and trees being introduced in the early 19th century grew well in the Wealden conditions, and this was a further encouragement to naturalists and gardeners to create beautiful gardens, as well as pioneer knowledge in the growing, propagating and hybridising of the new plants

The study has shown there was a close neighbourhood of amateur naturalists and plantsmen with the money and free time to indulge their interests in hybridising and experimenting with conditions suitable for the varied garden plants arriving from different parts of the world. There were the Loder's at Leonardslee, High Beeches and Wakehurst, Frederick du Cane Godman at South Lodge, Millais at Compton's Brow, Stephenson Clarke at Borde Hill and the Messels at Nymans. Sometime later, and not so well documented or remembered, was Charles Robert Scrase-Dickins and the Coolhurst woodland. It is interesting to consider how far these keen gardeners and naturalists influenced each other in design, choice of plants, hybridisation and scientific enquiry, and whether the area around St Leonard's Forest and the western part of the Wealden Forest Ridge was particularly rich at this time with innovative gardeners and naturalists. It should be remembered that the influential gardener and writer, William Robinson (1838-1935), lived not far away at Gravetye Manor near East Grinstead.

I have also shed some light on who lived in the Forest; where and how they lived, and whether landowner, farmer or villager, through the centuries under consideration. A study of the five main private estates has emphasised the importance of the interests and attitudes of the individual owners, and the impact this had on the Forest landscape. Those that used their estate as an opportunity to indulge their interests in horticulture and naturalist enquiry contrasted with those that used it as a sporting estate or source of income by selling or leasing as pressed by their circumstance. The thread of paternalism runs strongly through this history, and one is struck by the almost medieval largesse of the Aldridge family in inviting most of Horsham to the celebrations of the coming of age of Robert Aldridge in 1822. It should be noted, however, that this was not that unusual, a similar celebration of coming of age by another Horsham family, the Eversfields of Denne Park, occurred in 1843. The Eversfield party, as described by Henry Burstow, included the whole parish of Horsham, with 3,000 people invited to games and fireworks, with dinners for the tradespeople and dances for the gentry.

Of increased significance for the landscape was the later Victorian paternalism, hand in glove with the established church, as demonstrated by gifts of money and land to set up churches, schools and a library for the working classes close to the estates. These actions effectively created two villages, Colgate and Lower Beeding, firstly by establishing, and secondly by continuing, the patronage of important elements of village life. When considering the impact of paternalism, one would be tempted to look at the 'closed' villages where the pattern had been set early by the power and control of landowners over their estate villages and parish vestry. It was therefore interesting to see such paternalism at work in the later Victorian and Edwardian villages.

Horn noted that common perceptions of Victorian villages were impressionistic and sentimental, so she set out to uncover the historical reality of villages in her comparative research of eight Victorian villages, using the 1871 decennial census. She wrote that there was scope for greater use of the census in this way, and in thinking about this, it would be very interesting to compare the two villages of Colgate and Lower Beeding with other villages in Sussex to find out how common or unusual their establishment and development was.[2]

Of particular value has been the building up of a picture of these two communities over the period from 1841 to 1901 through the census, and then to read the recollections of some of the people living in and around the Forest at the turn of the 20th century, recorded during a Court hearing of the Footpath Dispute. It has been interesting to discover, from so much historical data, a departure from the common assumptions about English forests and villages. It is sobering to note that only 175 years and the Welfare State separate the current generation from the appalling poverty that could be found in villages such as Colgate. From childhood into old age, with no state pension and no savings, the alternative to surviving the long working life of labourers in the villages was the dreaded workhouse in Horsham.

Young adults were not as present as one would imagine, possibly because they would be working away from home in domestic service, and also because families were smaller than the Victorian stereotype would suggest. Those living in the Forest and the two villages moved more frequently than one would assume. They moved house to gain employment, and local youngsters left Colgate and Lower Beeding while others moved into these villages for domestic service. From oral reports, it appears that villagers often walked through and into the Forest for both work and leisure.

Lower Beeding grew larger than Colgate, and from an examination of occupations it seems likely that the large and successful gardens and houses of the Loder's, Godman's and Scrase-Dickins provided both employment and leisure, in addition to developing village life around church, school and library. Colgate was originally more dependent on Holmbush and Buchan Hill for employment, but as New Lodge began to be sold, the number of independent farmers increased, together with those living on their own means. The railway and Horsham town were less than eight kilometres away from Colgate and would have provided services not available in the village, thus perhaps drawing people there to live, such as the Langley family. In Colgate the older skills of charcoal burning and brick making survived into the 20th century, alongside newer professions such as the wine merchant, and at Buchan Hill, Phillip F. R. Saillard, the ostrich feather importer catering to the Victorian fashion for feather boas and mourning plumes. However, growth in Colgate was slower than in Lower Beeding, until there were more incomers after the world wars.

One cannot look at the 1901 and 1911 censuses without being aware of the impending two world wars that would claim the lives of the many children and young men of the families recorded. However, reading the names on two memorials, one in St Saviours Church, Colgate, and the other in Holy Trinity at Lower Beeding, one is struck by how

2. Horn, P. (1982) Victorian villages from census returns, *The Local Historian* Vol. 15 No. 1, pp. 25-32.

84. WWI memorial in Holy Trinity Church, Lower Beeding.

few names do in fact concur with the 1901 census, perhaps suggesting a continuing movement of people in and out of the two villages. For example, a particularly detailed memorial to those who lost their lives in World War I stands in the parish church of the Holy Trinity at Lower Beeding, and from this only one name, John G. Feist, can be positively identified as coming from Lower Beeding village, as he was of the right age in the 1901 census.

John G. Feist from the 1st Battalion Royal Sussex Regiment was killed in action in Mesopotamia on 25th January, 1917, at the age of 25. The 1901 census shows that he had lived with his father, a warehouseman, his mother, six siblings and a 75-year-old lodger at Church Cottage, next to the Plough Inn in Lower Beeding. The memorial lists 23 deaths from World War I and the last honour is to Major General Spencer W. Scrase-Dickins CB, AM, younger brother of Charles Robert Scrase-Dickins of Coolhurst, who died from the effects of exhaustion due to active service on 23rd October 1919, aged 57.[3] Another striking memorial in Holy Trinity church is a plaque and two stained glass windows to the memory of Captain Robert Egerton Loder, only son of Sir Edmund and Lady Loder,

3. CB, Companion of the Order of the Bath for military meritorious service, AM Albert Medal which became the George Cross, the highest award for gallantry for action not in the face of the enemy (information from Major Mark Scrase Dickins, 26.3.13).

wounded in the battle of Gaza, who died on 29th March 1917, aged 30, and was buried at Khan Yunus in the Holy Land.

Similarly, in St Saviours church at Colgate on a much smaller wooden memorial to the dead of World War I, only one name - that of William John Ashby - can be found in the 1901 census when he was a small boy of five years old living at the Colgate public house, The Dragon. There are eight names altogether; two appear to be a father and son, Walter and Frederick Allingham, farmers from Hopper Farm on the Holmbush estate, north of Colgate village on the Crawley Road and not within the bounds of the village for this study.

Taking the longer view of the landscape of the Forest, it is clear that ownership of the Forest dictated its character, shape and use. At the start of the 18th century the Forest had been regarded as a source of quick money through timber and grazing, with no regard to the sustainability of the large timber trees. The woodland hence deteriorated into heathland, important in itself for biodiversity, but a changed landscape. Agricultural improvement was tried and failed and so the production of rabbits became a good economic option. When the price of rabbit meat and fur devalued due to wild rabbit being widely available, agriculture was attempted again with new techniques of drainage, enclosure and better access. The acres at the centre of the Forest were leased and sublet to small aspirational farmers, but the geology and topography were against them, and soon the economics were as well.

The near proximity of Horsham and the Forest to London was important, as the city's growth was unstoppable from the mid-18th century, swallowing towns and villages to form one great world metropolis. It pulled people in for work through the improving communications of rail and road, but also allowed the wealthier business managers and merchants to escape from the city to the rural landscapes of the Sussex Weald. The picturesque setting of St Leonard's Forest, along with the soil to cultivate trees, rhododendrons and other acid-loving exotics, gave the Forest a real value to this new class of landowner. They, and their friends and families, brought to the Forest typical Victorian interests of collecting and experimenting with exotic plants and animals. Their philanthropy and paternalist feelings provided churches and schools for their workers, which effectively created the 19th century Victorian villages of Colgate and Lower Beeding.

How different were these developments in comparison to the other Wealden ridge forests? Worth Forest, which included Tilgate Forest to the south and which later became known just as Tilgate Forest, was virtually coterminous with St Leonard's Forest, only the old boundaries between the rapes of Bramber and Lewes separating them, so there are undoubtedly more similarities with the development of St Leonard's Forest than with other Sussex forests such as Ashdown. Ashdown Forest was situated east of the Ouse in the next rape of Pevensey, and according to the *Victoria County History* it was the largest and most important of all the Sussex forests.

All three forests had a history of iron production, with Worth Forest furnace, at the time of ownership by Sir Thomas Seymour, making canon and ordnance in large quantities. In the north of Worth Forest was the wild heathland of Copthorne Common, known for its lawless smugglers and horse stealers, close as it was to the London-Brighton road which cut through the forest. Two other large areas of heathland are noted on the Old Series OS map of 1813 as Highbeech Warren to the south and Old House Warren to the east. The names clearly indicate rabbit husbandry, so it appears that as in St Leonard's Forest, rabbits followed iron. Budgen's earlier map of 1724 shows three mansions in the Tilgate Forest area: Crabbett Park, Rowfant House and Fen Place. Their owners were farming gentry and businessmen similar to those around St Leonard's Forest in the 18th century. The Bysshe family of Fen Place married into the Shelleys of Field Place, Horsham, producing the poet Percy Bysshe Shelley in 1792. Socialising amongst the families was not surprising, given that Horsham, rather than East Grinstead, was the market town for Worth, Ifield and Crawley.

Worth Forest was divided into estates by a private enclosure act in 1828 and therefore began to attract London incomers. Worth Park House on an estate of 2,000 acres and including 15 farms was bought by Sir Joseph Montefiore, a wealthy London banker, in about 1850, while Crabbett Park had been inherited by Wilfred Scawen Blunt in 1873 and became a well-known stud for Arabian horses. By examining an 1855 directory one can see that Worth had the greatest proportion of gentry and greatest population growth in comparison to Crawley and Ifield. Crawley developed an urban society on a major road and rail route while Ifield remained a rural farming community. There are similarities to St Leonard's Forest not only in the geology and early history, but in the later influence of London, improved communications and incoming gentry, although individual personalities and their interests make a difference, such as in St Leonard's Forest where the church and individual patronage created new Victorian villages in the heart of the forest.

The development of Ashdown Forest shows more of a departure from St Leonard's Forest and Worth, or Tilgate Forest. It was high open heathland further from London, with poorer communication routes, and a complex system of ownership and rights of ancient origin with different groups enjoying different rights. There were many abuses and disputes regarding rights in Ashdown Forest with cottagers, squatters and those with no rights at all, encroaching on and taking resources from the Forest. This escalated in the late 19th century, and climaxed in 1876 with the 7th Earl De La Warr of Buckhurst Park, Lord of the Manor of Duddleswell, informing the commoners, who included both gentry and cottagers, that the practice of cutting litter, that is taking forest resources such as leaves, branches, ferns and turf from the Forest, was forbidden. This was challenged, depositions taken, and the case won by the commoners on appeal. The depositions illustrate that for many their rural life was very dependent on the Forest for economic and social survival. As Short wrote, it made the difference between poverty and pauperism. Ashdown Forest therefore had a very different development in the 18th and 19th century

4. Short, B. (ed.) (1997) *The Ashdown Forest Dispute 1876-1882,* Lewes: Sussex Record Society, 80, pp. 26-8, 34-9, and Short, B. (2004) Environmental Politics, custom and personal testimony: memory and lifespace on the late Victorian Ashdown Forest, Sussex, *Journal of Historical Geography,* 30, pp. 470-495.

from both St Leonard's Forest and Worth, due to its commoners' rights, geographic position and lack of good rail and road links to London.[4]

Changes of the St Leonard's Forest landscape continued into the 20th century with large purchases of the Forest by the local authority and Forestry Commission (now Forestry England). World War II had more of an impact on the Forest than the Great War, with the setting up of camps for Canadian troops and prisoner of war camps, the bombing of Colgate, and the encroachment into the Forest of private houses, all altering the Forest landscape yet again. Changes to the Forest continue to this day, and so a study of the 20th and 21st century Forest landscape would make for further interesting reading.

In retrospect one is struck, possibly from a modern perspective, by how much has been taken from the Forest. It has been dug for iron, stone and clay, its ghylls dammed and its timber of oak and beech felled. Its heathland has been planted over with pine and consequently suppressed, its archaeological remains and lily beds have been torn up by logging machinery and its peace shattered by motocross in what was New Lodge's laurel walk. No wonder it can be an uncomfortable forest in which to walk, a concept picked up by a branch of psychology called terrapsychology. This is the study of how land, place, the elements and natural processes all affect human psychology and action, including recorded story, myth and legend. Therefore, terrapsychology rejects the concept that the earth is of use only as a source of resources for humanity, but rather looks at it as a living ecosystem which impinges on the human psyche in a positive or negative way. The ways it does this can be recognised as feelings, dreams and archetypes, such as the dragon and devil that appear so frequently in the myths of St Leonard's Forest.

Earlier writers from different disciplines laid the foundations for these concepts. Two such are the geographer Yi-Fu Tuan who explored the relationship of different types of human fear in varied landscapes, and the historian Simon Schama in part 1 of his book *Landscape and Memory* in which he explored historical attitudes and feelings to European woods and forests. A psychological approach adds another layer of depth to the two-way influence of landscape and human activity.[5]

Robert Macfarlane in his book *The Wild Places* describes forests as 'places of correspondence, of call and answer' echoing this psychological concept of a two-way influence. He suggested that if woods and forests disappear it is not only unique habitats that disappear but our unique memories and forms of thought. Woods, he wrote, 'kindle new ways of being and cognition in people' and this can urge their minds in different ways.[6] In his later book *The Old Ways* he gives the example of this in thoughts about the effects of nature and landscape on the poet Edward Thomas, of whom he wrote 'trees, birds, rocks and paths cease to be merely objects of contemplation, and instead become actively and convivially present, enabling understanding that would be possible nowhere else, under no other circumstances', thus emphasising the psychological importance of place and of particular landscapes to individuals.

---

5. Chalquist, C. (2007) *Terrapsychology: Reengaging the Soul of Place.* New Orleans, USA: Spring Journal Books, pp.53-89, and Tuan, Y-F. (1979,2013) *Landscapes of Fear,* Minneapolis, MN (USA): University of Minnesota Press, and Schama, S. (1995,2004) *Landscape and Memory,* Hammersmith: HarperCollins Publishers.

6. Macfarlane, R. (2007) *The Wild Places,* London: Granta Books, pp. 85-111.

There are two aspects of forest landscapes that I would like to highlight before finishing this book. The first is to call for a gentler management of forests, as advocated by forester Peter Wohlleben in his fascinating book *The Hidden Life of Trees*. He suggests that understanding the complex networks that sustain a woodland, and the importance of native trees to this woodland web, is essential for maintaining a thriving forest. Again, Robert Macfarlane has something to say about this in his latest book *Underland*, suggesting that myth, stories and literature got there before science in recognising the animate life force in all of nature, and that greater respect and care are now long overdue.[7]

The other interesting, and not dissimilar, development with regard to forests is the understanding of their impact on both physical and mental human health and wellbeing. This was perhaps brought into sharp focus during the Covid-19 pandemic when people were under lockdown in their homes but encouraged to get outside into nature for their daily exercise. In 2013 a study from the University of Michigan found that walking in woodland improved mood and memory amongst sufferers of depression. In 2015 the Mersey Forest team, near Liverpool in the UK, pioneered a project called the 'Natural Health Service' helping vulnerable people get active in woodlands.

More recently, in 2018, the University of East Anglia gathered evidence from 140 studies worldwide and confirmed that walking in green space not only engendered feelings of immediate wellbeing, but there were long term impacts for the better on Type II diabetes, heart disease, preterm births, stress and high blood pressure. Currently, the Woodland Trust is contributing to a Bangor University PhD looking at the long-term health benefits of woodland exposure. Results so far look as if the benefits are transformative.[8]

Much of this book has focused on how human activity in the 18th and 19th century impacted the landscape of St Leonard's Forest; how individual and community attitudes and ambitions, social and economic, changed the Forest. It is of course more difficult to ascertain how the Forest impacted those same people. However, the author hopes that this book will encourage everyone who reads it to consider the value of the landscape, and forests in particular, not purely in terms of the financial value of their land, mineral and plant content, but also in terms of their undoubted value for the mental health and well-being of our society.

---

7. Wohlleben, P. (2015, 2017) *The Hidden Life of Trees,* London: William Collins, and Macfarlane, R. (2019) *Underland,* UK: Hamish Hamilton, imprint of Penguin Books.

8. www.sciencedaily.com/releases/2018/07/180706102842, and Buchan, K. & Collins, F. "Natural Health Service' *Broadleaf,* Woodland Trust, No. 101, Summer 2020, p.18.

85. The dragon bench, carved by O'Neill, situated on the northern end of Mick Mills Race in St Leonard's Forest.

'You have said; but whether wisely or no, let the forest judge'

From Shakespeare, *As You Like It,* Act 3, ii.

Appendix

St Leonard's Forest Timeline

1075	Sele Priory founded by William de Braose, Lord of Bramber. The Priory was endowed with pannage, wood and timber, tithes from underwood, assarts and colts born in the Forest.
1208	Free chapel (chantry) of St Leonard established in the Forest by the de Braoses who supplied chaplains.
1232	John de Braose died and was succeeded by William de Braose, 5th Lord of Bramber.
1235	Confirmation of grant of tithes of pannage and herbage of the Forest of St Leonard and Crochurst to Sele Priory as they had previously received them.
1290	William de Braose dies at Findon and is succeeded by his daughter, Mary de Braose.
1329	Evidence that Sir John de Ifield is in possession of Shelley, Bewbush, Knepp and parts of St Leonard's Forest.
1369	William de Braose, 6th Lord of Bramber dies, and is succeeded through his daughter, Aline by her husband John de Mowbray, Earl of Nottingham.
1398	Thomas de Mowbray created Duke of Norfolk.
1440	Accession of Henry VI and Rape of Bramber granted to Thomas Lord La Warr.
1459	John, Duke of Norfolk made over Sele Priory to Bishop of Winchester and his College of Magdalen at Oxford.
1494	Lordship of Bramber sold to Thomas Howard, Earl of Surrey.
1530	Duke of Norfolk suppresses the Free chapel or chantry of St Leonard's.
1547	Edward VI dissolved all Chantries. Thomas, 3rd Duke of Norfolk is attainted and St Leonard's Forest granted to Thomas Seymour, Lord High Admiral. Later also attainted.

1561	On Mary's succession back in the hands of Thomas Howard, 4th Duke of Norfolk.
1562	Mortgage conveyed by Thomas Howard to the Crown, Queen Elizabeth I.
1570	To convey from the Crown back to Thomas Howard, 21 Year Lease drawn up.
1572	Thomas Howard, 4th Duke of Norfolk, executed for treason. Ownership taken by Crown and the Forest is opened up to a variety of leases, including two ironmasters, John Blennehasset and William Dix.
1577	Part Sublet to Roger Gratwick.
1578	Leases given by Crown to take large quantities of wood from the Forest.
1586	Edward Caryll of Shipley was working the Gosden Furnace, while Roger Gratwick was working at Hawkins Pond.
1588	Lease disputes, Gratwick's title contested by Walter Covert.
1602	To Sir John Caryll of Warnham, 60 Year Lease from the Crown. Caryll now has control of the Forest including Sedgwick and Chesworth.
1613	Succeeded by his son, also Sir John Caryll. Parts of the Forest further sublet to Sir William Ford who sublets again to John Gratwick.
1614	In August a serpent or dragon is reported to be living in the Forest and causing fear and destruction.
1617	Walter Covert holds southern part of the Forest.
1631	Crown granted Reversion in Trust for Sir William Russell, Bt.
1634	Sir William Russell, Bt. Conveyed interest to Sir Richard Weston of Sutton Place, Guildford.
1660	The Restoration - King Charles II grants the Forest to his physician, Sir Edward Greaves, Bt. The Caryll's recover Knepp and Sedgewick. Edward, Earl of Sandwich obtains Bewbush and Shelley.
1681	Sir Edward Greaves is succeeded by his daughter, Mary Calfe and her husband Peter.
1684	Depositions taken against Peter and Mary Calfe for poor management and destruction of wood. Area of St Leonard's Forest suggested to be 8,000 acres.

1689	Peter and Mary Calfe are succeeded by her nephew, Capt. William Powlett
1746	Forest willed to Abel Aldridge of Uxbridge.
1782	Succeeded by his son, John Aldridge, MP for New Shoreham.
1795	Succeeded by his son, also called John Aldridge.
1801	John Aldridge grants a 100-year lease to George Railton and William Hulls those parts of the Forest known as Great Warren and Plummers Plain Warren, 3,000 acres in all.
1803	Succeeded by his son, Robert Aldridge.
1803-15	Napoleonic Wars.
1830	Arthur Chichester sells his Coolhurst estate of 55 acres to Mary Compton, Dowager Marchioness of Northhampton.
1836	29th November great storm damages trees in the Forest, in particular the trees along Mick Mills Race.
1838	Lower Beeding Parish formed by Act of Parliament, Bewbush excluded.
1839	St John's, the Forest Church at Coolhurst, consecrated.
1840	Holy Trinity, the Parish Church of Lower Beeding was built in the south of the Forest, in the village of Lower Beeding.
1843	Coolhurst inherited by Mary Compton's daughter, Lady Frances Elizabeth who married Charles Scrase-Dickins.
1852	Sale of part of St Leonard's Forest estate of total 1,919 acres in the south of the Forest. The largest portion of 955 acres included the residence of St Leonard's Lodge (later known as Leonardslee) and Stonewick farm. This was bought by Charles George Beauclerk. The three other lots plus cottages were Park Farm, Eastlands Farm, and Free Chase Farm.
1855-7	106-foot Holmbush Tower erected by T. Broadwood, owner of Holmbush estate, and opened to the public.
1871	Col. John Aldridge, MP for Horsham, inherited the north part of the Forest, St Leornard's Forest Estate.
	Creation of Colgate Consolidated Chapelry from parts of lower and upper Beeding, and Horsham. The church of St Saviour in Colgate was consecrated on 22nd November.

1878	Sale of part of St Leonard's Forest estate, 3,400 acres in the north and east, including parts of Plummers Plain and Colgate village, approximately 30 farms.
1888	Succeeded by his son, Robert Beauclerk Aldridge, who died unmarried in 1892.
1896	Sale of main residence and rest of St Leonard's Forest estate, 1,731 acres in the west. New Lodge (later known as St Leonard's House) and The Grange forming 1,422 acres in one lot. This was bought by Edward Molyneux. The other three lots being a building site, The Goldings, and Hammer Pond Farm .
1900-1	The Forest Footpath dispute Molyneux versus Horsham Rural District Council.
1906	Brother and heir Maj. Charles Powlett Aldridge inherited the rest of the Aldridge lands and sold them.
1910	St Leonard's Park (previously known as St Leonard's House) owned and occupied by H. E. Dennis, pioneer of motoring.
1913	St Leonard's estate bought by Jack McGaw, sheep farmer in Australia, and his wife, Pauline Blanche Tate, heiress of the sugar fortune.
1914-18	First World War.
1919	Forestry Commission (now Forestry England) was founded in order to restore national forests after the First World War.
1939-45	Second World War.
1943	Holmbush Tower dismantled after bomb damage.

[i] VCH Sussex Vol II 1907 Legge

[ii] Salzman,L.F. (1923) *The Chartulary of Sele Priory*, Cambridge p7-10

[iii] VCH Sussex Vol II 1907 Legge 307

[iv] Ibid

[v] Salzman,L. F. (1923) *The Chartulary of Sele Priory*, Cambridge p7-10

[vii] VCH Sussex Vol II 1907 Legge 308, SAC 135 (1997) Jack S p242

[viii] PRO E134/36Chas2/East22

[ix] HM MS 3142

[x] Hurst, D.E. (1889) *The History and Antiquities of Horsham 2nd Ed* Lewes

[xi] ESRO SAY 2831

[xii] Hurst, D.E. (1889) *The History and Antiquities of Horsham 2nd Ed* Lewes p162-3

[xiii] HM SP 230

Bibliography

Albery, W. (1927) A Parliamentary History of Horsham 1295-1885, London: Longmans, Green and Co. Ltd.

Albery, W. (1947) A Millennium of Facts in the History of Horsham and Sussex 947-1947, Brighton: Southern Publishing.

Albery, W. (ed.) (1975) Reminiscences of Horsham being Recollections of Henry Burstow, The Celebrated Bellringer and Songsinger, Norwood, Pa: Norwood Editions.

Ambrose, P. (1974) The Quiet Revolution, Social Change in a Sussex Village 1871-1971, Sussex University Press.

Andrews, M. (1999) Landscape and Western Art, Oxford: Oxford University Press.

Anon., (1895) South Park, The Gardeners' Chronicle, XVII Third Series Jan-June 1895, April 20 1895 p. 485 and (1906) 39, Third Series Jan-June 1906, pp. 98-9.

Anon., (1906) Leonardslee, The Gardener's Chronicle, October 13 1906, pp. 253-4 and continued October 20 1906, pp. 272-3.

Baldwin, M. (ed.)(1985) The Story of the Forest, Colgate: Parish of Colgate.

Banks, S. (1988) Nineteenth Century Scandal or Twentieth Century Model? A New Look at 'Open' and 'Close' Parishes, The Economic History Review, Vol. 41.1, pp. 51-73.

Barnard, J. (ed.) (1973) John Keats, The Complete Poems, London: Penguin Books Ltd.

Beckensall, S.G. (1967) The Excavation of Money Mound, Sussex Archaeological Collections, 105, pp. 13-30.

Beckett, J. (2012) Rethinking the English village, The Local Historian, 42 No. 2, pp. 301-311.

Beswick, M. (1993,2001) Brickmaking in Sussex, A History and Gazetteer, Midhurst: Middleton Press.

Birch, R. (2006) Sussex Stones, the story of Horsham stone and Sussex marble, Horsham: R. Birch, rdb@collyers.ac.uk

Bird, P. (2014) 'Open' and 'Closed' Villages: A new methodology for assessing landownership concentration, The Local Historian, Vol. 44.1, pp. 35-50.

Blaauw, W. H. (1856) Extracts from the 'Iter Sussexiense' of Dr John Burton, Sussex Archaeological Collections, VIII, pp. 250-265.

Black, J. (2009) London, a History, Lancaster: Carnegie Publishing Ltd.

Blunden, J. & Curry, N. (eds) (1985) The Changing Countryside, Milton Keynes: Open University with Croom Helm Ltd.

Blunt, W. S. (1909) Extracts from Mr John Baker's Horsham Diary, Sussex Archaeological

Collections, 52, pp. 38-82.

Boorman, D. & Djabri, S. C. (2009) Country House Cricket at St Leonard's Forest, Horsham Heritage, 18, Autumn, pp. 46-59.

Bovill, E. W. (1962) English Country Life 1780-1830, Oxford: Oxford University Press.

Bowen, E. J. (2007) The Enclosure of Horsham Common, Horsham: Horsham Museum Society (Friends of Horsham Museum).

Brandon, P. (1974) The Sussex Landscape, London: Hodder and Stoughton. Brandon, P. (1984) Wealden Nature and the Role of London in the Nineteenth Century Artistic Imagination, Journal of Historical Geography, 10.1. pp. 75-104. Brandon, P. (1998, 1999) The South Downs, Chichester: Phillimore and Co. Ltd. Brandon, P (2003) The Kent and Sussex Weald, Chichester: Phillimore and Co. Ltd. Brandon, P. (2010) The Discovery of Sussex, Andover: Phillimore & Co Ltd. Burchall, M. (2010) A Lost Parish, Sussex Family Historian, 19 No 4, pp. 190-195.

Bright J. S. (1884) A History of Dorking and Neighbouring Parishes, London: Simpkin, Marshall & Co.

Burke, B. (1852) A Visitation of the Seats and Arms of the Noblemen and Gentlemen of Great Britain and Ireland, Vol. 1, London: Colburn.

Burstow, H. (1911) Reminiscences of Horsham being Recollections of Henry Burstow, The Celebrated Bellringer and Songsinger, Horsham: The Free Christian Church Book Society.

Byrne, H. (2005) The Broadwood Family and their Local Connections, Horsham Heritage, 13, Autumn, pp. 29-39

Caffyn, J. (1999) Schools in the 18th Century, Leslie, K. and Short, B. (eds) An Historical Atlas of Sussex, Chichester: Phillimore & Co. Ltd., pp. 82-3.

Campbell, S. (1999) Walled Kitchen Gardens, Princes Risborough: Shire Publications Ltd.

Cartwright, E. (1830) The Parochial Topography in the Western Division of the County of Sussex, London: J.B. Nichols and Son.

Chalquist, C. (2007) Terrapsychology: Reengaging the Soul of Place, New Orleans: Spring Journal Books.

Chatwin, D. & Gardiner, M. (2005) Rethinking the Early Medieval Settlement of Woodlands: Evidence from the Western Sussex Weald, Landscape History, 27, pp. 31-49.

Christian, G. (1968) Ashdown Forest, Forest Row: The Society of Friends of Ashdown Forest.

Church leaflet (1999) The Parish and Priory Church of St. Peter (Sele Priory) in the Parish of Beeding and Bramber with Botolphs, Published by the Parish and available at the Church of St. Peter, Upper Beeding.

Cleere, H. & Crossley, D. (1985,1995) The Iron Industry of the Weald. Cardiff: Merton Priory Press.

Cobbett, W. (1830, 1979) Rural Rides, Harmondsworth: Penguin Books Ltd.

Comber, J. (1931) Sussex Genealogies, Horsham Centre, Cambridge: W. Heffer & Sons Ltd.

Cook, W. A. (1907) Liriodendron Tulipifera, and A Large Camellia Tree Out of Doors, Gardeners' Chronicle, March 30 1907, pp. 208-9.

Cook, W. A. (1907) Magnolias at Leonardslee, Gardeners' Chronicle, April 6 1907, p. 223.

Cox, E. H. M. (1924) Leonardslee, Country Life, July 19 1924, p. 98.

Crook, D. (2006) Defying the Demon, Smallpox in Sussex, Lewes: Dale House Press.

Crookshank, A. C. (undated) Saint Leonard of Sussex, London: Arthur H. Stockwell, Daniels, S. & Cosgrove, D. (eds) (1988) The Iconography of Landscape, Cambridge: Cambridge University Press.

Daniel-Tyssen J. R. (1872) Parliamentary Surveys of the County of Sussex 1649-1653, Sussex Archaeological Collections XXIV, pp. 238-241.

Darby, H. C. & Campbell, E. M. J., (eds) (1962) The Domesday Geography of South-East England, Cambridge: Cambridge University Press.

Dasgupta, S. (2010) Drayton's 'Silent Spring': Poly-Olbion and the Politics of Landscape, The Cambridge Quarterly 39(2) pp. 152-171.

Davey, R. (1999) Schools in the 19th Century, Leslie, K. and Short, B. (eds) An Historical Atlas of Sussex, Chichester: Phillimore & Co. Ltd., pp. 84-5.

Defoe, D. (1731, 1962) Tour Thro' the Whole Island of Great Britain, divided into circuits or journies, Vol. I, London: J.M. Dent.

Desmond, R. (1994) Dictionary of British and Irish Botanists and Horticulturists, London: Taylor and Francis.

Dixon Hunt, J. and Willis, P. (eds) (1988) The Genius of Place, the English Landscape Garden 1620-1820, Cambridge, MA: MIT Press.

Djabri, S. C. (ed.) (2002) A Little News from Horsham, Some 18th century letters from Hills, Horsham: Horsham Museum Society.

Djabri, S. C. (2005) Charles Beauclerk of St Leonard's Lodge, Horsham Heritage, 12 Spring, pp. 31-45.

Djabri, S. C. (2006) The 'Dragon' of St Leonard's Forest. Horsham Heritage, 14, Spring, pp. 3-16.

Djabri, S. C. (2008) The Eversfields of Denne House, Part 1, Horsham Heritage, 17, Autumn, pp. 11-33.

Djabri, S. C. (ed.) (2009) The Diaries of Sarah Hurst 1759-1762, Stroud: Amberley Publishing.

Dudley, H. (1836, 1973) History and Antiquities of Horsham and its Vicinity, Horsham: Jury Cramp Ltd.

Dymond, D. (2011) Does local history have a split personality? Dyer, C., Hopper, A., Lord, E., & Tringham, N. (eds) New Directions in Local History since Hoskins, Hatfield: University of Hertfordshire Press. pp. 13-28.

Elleray, D. R. (1981) The Victorian Churches of Sussex, Chichester: Phillimore & Co. Ltd.

Elliott, B. (1986) Victorian Gardens, London: B.T. Batsford Ltd.

Elliott, P., Watkins, C. Daniels, S. (2007) 'Combining Science with Recreation and Pleasure': Cultural Geographies of Nineteenth-Century Arboretums, Garden History, 35, Supplement 2, pp. 6-27.

Ellis, H. (1861) Inventories of Goods etc., in the Manor of Chesworth, Sedgwick, and Other Parks, the Manor Place of Sheffield, and in the Forest of Worth, with the iron-works belonging to the Lord Admiral Seymour, at the time of his attainder, taken 1549, Sussex Archaeological Collections, XIII, pp. 118-131.

Ellis, W. S. (1885) The Parks and Forests of Sussex, Ancient and Modern, Lewes: H. Wolff.

Elwes, D. G. C. and Robinson C. J. (1879) A History of the Castles, Mansions and Manors of Western Sussex, London: Longman.

Evans, J. E. and Crosby, A. G. (1978, 1997) Tithes, Maps, Apportionment and the 1836 Act: a guide for local historians, Salisbury: British Association for Local History.

Everson, P. and Williamson, T. (1998) Gardens and designed landscapes, Everson, P. and Williamson, T. (eds) The Archaeology of Landscape, Manchester: Manchester University Press, pp. 139-165.

Friswell, N. C. (2000) The Indian Princess: Helena Bennett, Asian Affairs, 31:3, pp. 259-302.

Frost, R. (2011) The Road Not Taken, The Robert Frost Collection, Blacksburg, VA: Wilder Publications.

Fryer, N. (ed.) (1983) Natural History of St. Leonard's Forest, Horsham: Horsham Natural History Society.

Fuller, G.J. (1953) The Development of Roads in the Surrey-Sussex Weald and Coastlines between 1700 and 1900, Transactions of the Institute of British Geographers, 19, pp. 37-49.

Gallois, R.W. & Worssam, B.C. (1993) Geology of the country around Horsham; memoir for 1:50,000 geological sheet 302 (England and Wales), British Geological Survey, H.M.S.O.

Garraway Rice, R. (ed.) (1915) The Parish Register of Horsham in the County of Sussex, 1541 -1635, Burials, Sussex Record Society, Vol. XXI pp. 291-408.

Gelling, M. (1984) Place-Names in the Landscape, London: J.M. Dent & Sons.

Girouard, M. (1978) Life in the English Country House, New Haven & London: Yale University Press.

Glover, J. (1997) Sussex Place-Names, their Origins and Meanings, Newbury: Countryside Books.

Goldring, W. (1887) Coolhurst, Sussex, The Garden, 31, pp. 21-2, 25.

Goodliffe, W. (1905) Horsham and St. Leonard's Forest with their Surroundings, London: The Homeland Association.

Griffin, C. J. (2012) The Rural War: Captain Swing and the Politics of Protest, Manchester: Manchester University Press.

Groombridge, G. (2010) A Short History of Brooms, Broom-making and Broom-makers, Horsham Heritage, 19, Autumn, pp. 44-55.

Gwynne, P. (1990) A History of Crawley, Chichester: Phillimore and Co. Ltd.

Hadfield, A. (2012) News of the Sussex Dragon, Reformation, 17.1, pp. 99-113.

Hadfield, M. (1967) Landscape with Trees, London: Country Life Ltd.

Heller, C. (1999) Ecology of Everyday Life, Rethinking the Desire for Nature, London: Black Rose Books.

Hey, D. (ed.) (1996) The Oxford Companion to Local and Family History, Oxford: Oxford University Press.

Hicks, C. (2001) Improper Pursuit, The Scandalous Life of Lady Di Beauclerk, London: Macmillan Publishers Ltd.

Higgs, E. (2005) Making Sense of the Census Revisited, London: University of London with The National Archives of the UK.

Hill, J. & James, M. (2005) Swing Riots in Surrey, Holland, M. (ed.) Swing Unmasked, the Agricultural Riots of 1830 to 1832 and their wider implications, Milton Keynes: FACHRS Publications, pp. 26-61.

Hindle, P. (2002) Medieval Roads and Tracks, Princes Risborough: Shire Publications.

Hobsbawm, E.J. (1968) Industry and Empire, The Pelican Economic History of Britain, Vol 3, Harmondsworth: Penguin Books Ltd.

Hobsbawm, E. & Rudé, G. (1969, 2001) Captain Swing, London: Phoenix Press.

Hodgkinson, J. (2008) The Wealden Iron Industry, Stroud: Tempus Publishing.

Holderness, B. A. (1972) 'Open' and 'Close' Parishes in England in the Eighteenth and Nineteenth Centuries, The Agricultural History Review, 20.2 pp. 126-139.

Honywood, T. (1877) Discovery of Flint implements near Horsham, in St. Leonard's Forest, Sussex Archaeological Collections, XXVII, pp. 177-183.

Horn, P. (1980) The Rural World 1780-1850, London: Hutchinson & Co. Ltd.

Horn, P. (1982) Victorian villages from census returns, The Local Historian, 15, No. 1, pp. 25-32.

Horsfield, T. W. (1835) The History, Antiquities and Topography of the County of Sussex, Vol. 2, Lewes: Sussex Press.

Hoskins, W. G. (1955, 1985) The Making of the English Landscape, Harmondsworth: Penguin Books Ltd.

Hoskins, W. H. (1959) Local History in England, London: Longmans.

Howkins, A. (2003) The Death of Rural England, London: Routledge.

Hudson T. P. (ed.) (1986) The Victoria History of the County of Sussex, VI Pt. 2, Oxford: The Institute of Historical Research by Oxford University Press.

Hudson T. P. (ed.) (1987) Bramber Rape: Burbeach Hundred, Lower Beeding, The Victoria History of the County of Sussex, VI Pt. 3, Oxford: The Institute of Historical Research by Oxford University Press.

Hughes, A. (2005) St. Leonard's Forest, Horsham Heritage, 12, Spring, pp. 21-9.

Hurd, D. (2007) Robert Peel, a Biography, London: Weidenfeld and Nicolson.

Hurst, D. (1868) Horsham: its History and Antiquities, London: William Macintosh.

Jack, S. M. (1997) Ecological destruction in the 16th century, the case of St. Leonard's Forest, Sussex Archaeological Collections, 135, pp. 241-7.

Jackson A. J. H. (2012) The 'Open-Closed' Settlement Model and the Interdisciplinary Formulations of Dennis Mills: Conceptualising Local Rural Change, Rural History, 23.02, pp. 121-136.

James, N. D. G. (1981) A History of English Forestry, Oxford: Basil Blackwell.

Johnson, M. (2007) Ideas of Landscape, Oxford: Blackwell Publishing.

Jones, E. J. (2000) An Instinct for Dragons, London: Routledge.

Jones. G (2010) A 'Common of Hunting', J. Langton and G. Jones, (eds) Forests and Chases of Medieval England and Wales c 1000 to 1500, Oxford: St. John's College Research Centre, pp. 36-67.

Kain, R. J. P. and Prince, H. C. (1985) The Tithe Surveys of England and Wales. Cambridge: Cambridge University Press.

Kain, R. J. P. (1986) An Atlas and Index of the Tithe Files of Mid-Nineteenth Century England and Wales, Cambridge: Cambridge University Press.

Kain, R. J. P. and Oliver, R. R. (1995) The Tithe Maps of England and Wales, Cambridge: Cambridge University Press.

Keating, P. (ed.) (2000) Rudyard Kipling: Selected Poems, London: Penguin Books Ltd.

Kelly, J. (ed.) (1995) The Hillier Gardener's Guide to Trees and Shrubs, Newton Abbot: David and Charles.

Kitch, M. (1992) Population movement and migration in pre-industrial rural England, Short B. (ed.) The English Rural Community, Cambridge: Cambridge University Press, pp. 62-84.

Knight, J. (2006a) Horsham's History, Vol. 1, Prehistory to 1790 AD, Horsham: Horsham

District Council.

Knight, J. (2006b) Horsham's History, Vol. 2 1790-1880, Horsham: Horsham District Council.

Knight, J. (2008) Horsham's History Vol. 3 1880 to 1913, Horsham: Horsham District Council.

Laird, M. (1991) Approaches to planting in the late eighteenth century: some imperfect ideas on the origins of the American garden, Journal of Garden History, 11, No. 3, pp. 154-172.

Langton, J. & Jones, G. (2005). Forests and Chases of England and Wales circa 1500-1850, Oxford: St. John's College Research Centre.

Legge, W.H. (1907,1973) Forestry. Page, W. (ed.) The Victoria History of the Counties of England: A History of Sussex, II, London: The Institute of Historical Research by University of London.

Leslie, K. and Short, B. (eds)(1999) An Historical Atlas of Sussex, Chichester: Phillimore & Co. Ltd.

Lewis, C.P.(2011) The great awakening of English local history, 1918-1939, Dyer, C., Hopper, A., Lord, E., & Tringham, N. (eds) New Directions in Local History since Hoskins, Hatfield: University of Hertfordshire Press, pp. 29-53.

Linfield, M (2002) The Linfields of Coolhurst, Horsham Heritage, 7, Autumn, pp. 41-57.

Loder, R. (undated) Leonardslee, Lakes & Gardens, Guidebook published by Leonardslee Gardens.

Lower, M. A. (1849) Historical and Archaeological Notices of the Iron Works of the County of Sussex, Sussex Archaeological Collection, 2, pp. 169-220.

Lower, M. A. (1861) Old Speech and Manners in Sussex, Sussex Archaeological Collections, XIII, pp. 209-23.

Lowerson, J. (1980) A Short History of Sussex, Folkestone: Wm Dawson & Sons Ltd.

Lucas, E. V. (1904) Highways and Byways in Sussex, London: Macmillan and Co. Ltd.

Mabey, R. (1998) Flora Britannica, The Concise Edition, London: Chatto & Windus.

Macfarlane, R. (2007) The Wild Places, London: Granta Books.

Macfarlane, R. (2013) The Old Ways, London: Penguin Books Ltd.

Macfarlane, R. (2019) Underland, London: Hamish Hamilton, imprint of Penguin Books.

Margary, H. and Skelton, R. A. (ed.) (1970) Two Hundred and Fifty Years of Maps in the County of Sussex: a collection of reproductions of printed maps published between the years 1575 and 1825, Lympne: Margary, H.

Margary, I. (1950) The Development of Turnpike Roads in Sussex, Sussex Notes and Queries, XIII, pp. 49-53.

Margary, I. D. (1965) Roman Ways in the Weald, London: Phoenix House.

Margary, I. D. (1971) Traffic Routes in Sussex, 1724, Sussex Archaeological Collections, CIX, pp. 20-3.

Matthews, M. (2006) Captain Swing in Sussex and Kent, Rural Rebellion in 1830, Hastings: The Hastings Press.

Mawer, A. and Stenton F.M. with Glover, J.E.B. (1969) The Place-Names of Sussex, Part I The Rapes of Chichester, Arundel and Bramber, Cambridge: Cambridge University Press.

Mendelson, E. (ed.) (1979) W. H. Auden, Selected Poems, London: Faber and Faber Ltd.

Mingay, G. E. (1968) The Agricultural Revolution in English History: A Reconsideration, Minchinton, W.E. (ed.) Essays in Agrarian History, Vol. II, Newton Abbot: David and Charles, pp. 10-22.

Morris, C. (ed.) (1947) The Journeys of Celia Fiennes, London: The Cresset Press.

Mowl, T. (2000) Gentlemen and Players, Gardeners of the English Landscape, Stroud: Sutton Publishing.

Noble, A., Pennington, J., and Sleight, J. (eds)(2007) Beeding and Bramber Two Sussex Villages, A Study of the Probate Inventories, Wills and Accounts 1613-1775, Beeding: Beeding and Bramber Local History Society.

O'Leary, M. (2013) Sussex Folk Tales, Stroud: The History Press.

Page, W. (ed.) (1973) The Victoria History of the County of Sussex, II, London: The Institute of Historical Research by University of London.

Pawson, E. (1975) The Turnpike Trusts of the Eighteenth Century: A Study in Innovation and Diffusion, Research Paper 14, Oxford: School of Geography, University of Oxford.

Pease, A. E. (1923) Edmund Loder, Naturalist, Horticulturist, Traveller and Sportsman, A Memoir, London: John Murray.

Perry, S. (2017) The Essex Serpent, London: Serpent's Tail an imprint of Profile Books Ltd.

Pike, W. T. (ed.) (1910) Sussex in the Twentieth Century, Contemporary Biographies, Brighton: W. T. Pike.

Quest-Ritson, C. (2003) The English Garden, a Social History, London: Penguin Books Ltd.

Rackham, O. (1986) The History of the Countryside, London: J. M. Dent and Sons.

Rackham, O. (2006) Woodlands, London: Harper Collins.

Readman, A., Falconer, L., Ritchie, R. and Wilkinson, P. (2000) Lower and Upper Beeding, West Sussex Land Tax 1785, Lewes: Sussex Record Society, 82, pp. 49-51.

Reay, B. (1994) Before the transition: fertility in English villages, 1800-1880. Continuity and Change, 9, Issue 1, pp. 91-120.

Redwood, B. C. (ed.) Petworth Michaelmas 1647, Quarter Sessions Order Book 1642-1649,

Lewes: Sussex Record Society, 54, pp. 131-136.

Robinson, E. and Powell, D. (eds) (1984) John Clare, Major Works, Oxford: Oxford University Press.

Robinson, W. (1883, 1903) The English Flower Garden and Home Grounds, London: John Murray.

Salzman, L. F. (ed.) (1923) The Chartulary of Sele Priory, Cambridge: W. Heffer and Sons.

Salzman, L. F. (ed.) (1950) Record of Deputations of Gamekeepers, Lewes: Sussex Record Society, Vol. LI, pp. xv-xix.

Schama, S. (1995, 2004) Landscape and Memory, Hammersmith: HarperCollins Publishers.

Scrase-Dickins C. R. (1885) Garden Flora, Plate 506, Single Camellias, The Garden, 28, pp. 202 -3.

Seymour, M. (2000) Mary Shelley, London: John Murray Ltd.

Sheail, J. (1971) Rabbits and their History, London, David & Charles Ltd.

Sheail, J. (1978) Rabbits and agriculture in post-medieval England, Journal of Historical Geography, 4.4, pp. 343-55.

Sheppard, J. (1999) Population Change 1851-1901, Leslie, K. and Short, B. (eds) An Historical Atlas of Sussex, Chichester: Phillimore & Co. Ltd., pp.90-1.

Short, B. (ed.) (1981 and 2nd edtn 2013) Scarpfoot Parish: Plumpton 1830-1880, CCE Occasional Paper No. 16. University of Sussex.

Short, B. (ed.)(1992) The Evolution of Contrasting Communities within Rural England, The English Rural Community, Cambridge: Cambridge University Press, pp. 19-43.

Short, B. (1997) Land and Society in Edwardian Britain, Cambridge: Cambridge University Press.

Short, B. (ed.) (1997) The Ashdown Forest Dispute 1876-1882, Lewes: Sussex Record Society, 80.

Short, B.(1999) Population Change 1801-1851, Leslie, K. and Short, B. (eds) An Historical Atlas of Sussex, Chichester: Phillimore & Co. Ltd., pp. 88-9.

Short, B. (1999) Conservation, Class and Custom: Lifespace and Conflict in a Nineteenth-Century Forest Environment, Rural History, Vol. 10.2, pp. 127-154.

Short, B. (2000) Forests and Wood-Pasture in Lowland England, J. Thirsk (ed.) The English Rural Landscape, Oxford: Oxford University Press, pp. 122-149.

Short, B. (2004) Environmental politics, custom and personal testimony: memory and lifespace on the late Victorian Ashdown Forest, Sussex, Journal of Historical Geography, 30, pp. 470-495.

Short, B. (2006) England's Landscape, The South East, London: Harper Collins.

Short, B., Reed, M., Caudwell, W. (1987) The County of Sussex in 1910: Sources for a New Analysis, Sussex Archaeological Collections, 125, pp. 199-224.

Short, B. with May, P., Vines, G., Bur, A-M., (2012) Apples & Orchards in Sussex, Lewes: Action in rural Sussex & Brighton Permaculture Trust.

Simo, M. L. (1988) Loudon and the landscape, from country seat to metropolis 1783-1843, New Haven and London: Yale University Press.

Simpson, J. (2009) Folklore of Sussex, Stroud: The History Press.

Skeel, C. (1926) The Cattle Trade between Wales and England from the Fifteenth to the Nineteenth Centuries, Transactions of the Royal Historical Society, Fourth Series, 9, pp. 135-158.

Snell, K. D. M. (2006) Parish and Belonging: Community, Identity and Welfare in England and Wales 1700-1950, Cambridge: Cambridge University Press.

Solnit, R. (2001) Wanderlust, A History of Walking, London: Verso.

Straker, E. (1931, 1969) Wealden Iron, Newton Abbot: David & Charles Ltd.

Stuart, D. (1988) The Garden Triumphant, A Victorian Legacy, London: Viking.

Taylor, G. C. (1936) Lilies for Garden and Woodland, Country Life, Nov 14 1936, pp. 507-9.

Tebbutt, C. F. (1968) Rabbit Warrens on Ashdown Forest, Sussex Notes and Queries, 17, pp 52-4.

Thacker, C. (1994) The Genius of Gardening, The History of Gardens in Britain and Ireland, London: Weidenfeld and Nicolson.

Thirsk, J. (1984) The Rural Economy of England: collected essays, London: The Hambledon Press.

Thomas, E. (2009) One Green Field, London: Penguin Books Ltd.

Thompson, F. M. L. (1968) The Land Market in the Nineteenth Century, Essays in Agrarian History, Vol. II, Newton Abbot: David & Charles, pp. 50-4.

Thwaite, A. (ed.) (2003) Philip Larkin Collected Poems, London: Faber and Faber Ltd.,

Tiller, K. (1992, 2002) English Local History, An Introduction, Stroud: Alan Sutton Publishing Ltd.

Timbs, J. (1822) A Picturesque Promenade Round Dorking in Surrey, London: John Warren.

Tuan, Y-F. (1979) Landscapes of Fear, Minneapolis, MN: University of Minnesota Press.

Turner, E. Revd. (1858) Sele Priory, and some Notice of the Carmelite Friars at New Shoreham, and the Secular Canons at Steyning, Sussex Archaeological Collections, X, pp. 100-128.

Vickers, J. A. (ed.) (1989) Horsham District, 87, The Religious Census of Sussex 1851, Lewes: Sussex Record Society, 75, pp. 118-124.

Watson, J. N. P. (1988) Millais: Three Generations in Nature, Art and Sport, London: The Sportsman's Press.

Webb, N. (1986) Heathlands, London: Collins.

Weir-Wilson, M. (2008) Horsham Union Workhouse 1838-9, The Decision to Build and its Early Establishment, Horsham Heritage, 17, Autumn, pp. 35-51.

Wickens, C. (2001) The Terror of the County – A History of the Shipley Gang, Horsham Heritage, 3, Spring, pp. 3-23.

William, E. A. (1908) Cobden and Secular Education, Westminster Review, Jan 1908, p. 13.

Williamson, T (1995) Polite Landscapes, Gardens and Society in Eighteenth Century England, Stroud: Alan Sutton Publishing Ltd.

Williamson, T. (2007) Rabbits, Warrens and Archaeology, Stroud: Tempus Publishing Ltd.

Wilson, A. N. (2003) The Victorians, London: Arrow Books.

Windrum, A. (1978) Horsham, An Historical Survey, Chichester: Phillimore & Co. Ltd.

Winslow, C. (1975) Sussex Smugglers, Hay, D., Linebaugh, P., Thompson, E.P.(eds) Albion's Fatal Tree, Crime and Society in Eighteenth-century England, New York: Pantheon Books.

Witney, K. P. (1976) The Jutish Forest, A Study of the Weald of Kent from 450 to 1380 AD, London: The Athlone Press.

Wohlleben, P. (2015, 2017) The Hidden Life of Trees, London: William Collins.

Wojtczak, H. (2008) Notable Sussex Women, Hastings: The Hastings Press.

Wooldridge, S. W. & Goldring, F. (1960) The Weald, London: Collins.

Young, Revd. A. (1813, 1970) General View of the Agriculture of the County of Sussex, Newton Abbot: David & Charles Reprints.

Zell, M. (1994, 2004) Industry in the Countryside, Wealden Society in the Sixteenth Century, Cambridge: Cambridge University Press.

List of Illustrations

Glossary

List of Terms

Advowson	(in ecclesiastical law) The right to recommend a member of the Anglican clergy for a vacant benefice, or to make such an appointment.
Arboretum	A botanical garden devoted to trees.
Assarts	A piece of land converted from forest to arable use.
Attainted	To pass judgement of death or outlawry upon (a person); condemn by bill of attainder.
Baron of Beef	A joint of beef consisting of the two sirloins joined at the backbone; double sirloin.
Beech Mast	Beech mast may refer to: the nuts of the beech tree (Fagus).
Burgage	Historical: (in England and Scotland) tenure by which land or property in a town was held in return for service or annual rent.
Chapelry	A district served by an Anglican chapel.
Dower House	On an English, Scottish or Welsh estate, a dower house is usually a moderately large house available for use by the widow of the previous owner of the estate.
Drove Road	An ancient roadway along which cattle were driven to market.
Ha	Hectares.
Ha-Ha	A ditch with a wall on its inner side below ground level, forming a boundary to a park or garden without interrupting the view.
Harpy	In Greek and Roman myth, a half-woman half-bird monster, used colloquially for an argumentative woman.
Herbage	The succulent part of herbaceous vegetation, used as pasture. Historical: The right of pasture on another person's land.
Hinterland	The remote areas of a country away from the coast or the banks of major rivers. Or an area lying beyond what is visible or known.
Hundred Boundaries	The name of the hundred (called "wapentake" in the Danelaw) was normally that of its meeting-place. ... Hundred boundaries were independent of both parish and county boundaries, although often aligned, meaning that a hundred could be split between counties, or a parish could be split between hundreds.

List of Terms

Living — Ecclesiastical: a position as a vicar or rector with an income or property.

Pannage — The practice of releasing livestock-pigs in a forest, so that they can feed on fallen acorns, beechmast, chestnuts or other nuts.

Pauperism — The state or condition of utter poverty.

Postilion — A person who rides the leading nearside (left-hand side) horse of a team or pair drawing a coach or carriage, especially when there is no coachman.

Quarter Sessions — Historical: (in England, Wales, and Northern Ireland) a court of limited criminal and civil jurisdiction and of appeal, usually held quarterly in counties or boroughs, and replaced in 1972 by crown courts.

Reversion in Trust — In trust law terms, a reversionary interest is an interest that reverts back to the settlor of a trust once a beneficiary's interest has come to an end.

Rotten Borough — A borough that was able to elect an MP despite having very few voters, the choice of MP typically being in the hands of one person or family.

Sawyer — A person who saws timber for a living.

Sylvan — The adjective sylvan refers to a shady, wooded area. The word suggests a peaceful, pleasant feeling, as though you were far away from the noise of modern life.

Stipend — A fixed regular sum paid as a salary or as expenses to a clergyman, teacher, or public official.

Tithes — One tenth of annual produce or earnings, formerly taken as a tax for the support of the Church and clergy.

Turnpike Trusts — Were private organisations that built and operated toll roads in Britain and the United States during the 18th and 19th centuries. They emerged in 17th century Britain because local governments were unwilling to invest in roads. They issued bonds to finance investment and imposed tolls on road users.

Underwood — Small trees and shrubs growing beneath taller timber trees.

Weald of Anderida — In early medieval Britain, the area had the name Andredes weald, meaning 'the forest of Andred', the latter derived from Anderida, the Roman name of present-day Pevensey.

Index

Page numbers in **bold** refer to illustrations

Lightning Source UK Ltd.
Milton Keynes UK
UKHW051255100221
378546UK00002B/5